ANTISOCIAL MEDIA

SIVA VAIDHYANATHAN

ANTISOCIAL MEDIA

How Facebook Disconnects Us and Undermines Democracy

OXFORD
UNIVERSITY PRESS

OXFORD
UNIVERSITY PRESS

Oxford University Press is a department of the University of Oxford.
It furthers the University's objective of excellence in research, scholarship,
and education by publishing worldwide. Oxford is a registered trade mark of
Oxford University Press in the UK and in certain other countries

Published in the United States of America by Oxford University Press
198 Madison Avenue, New York, NY 10016, United States of America

A copy of this book's Cataloging-in-Publication
Data is on file with the Library of Congress.

ISBN 9780190841164

3 5 7 9 8 6 4 2
Printed by Sheridan Books, Inc., United States of America

To my parents

Some claim the world is gradually becoming united, that it will grow into a brotherly community as distances shrink and ideas are transmitted through the air. Alas, you must not believe that men can be united in this way. To consider freedom as directly dependent on the number of man's requirements and the extent of their immediate satisfaction shows a twisted understanding of human nature, for such an interpretation only breeds in men a multitude of senseless, stupid desires and habits and endless preposterous inventions. People are more and more moved by envy now, by the desire to satisfy their material greed, and by vanity.

—Fyodor Dostoevsky, *The Brothers Karamazov* (1880)

CONTENTS

ANTISOCIAL MEDIA

The Problem with Facebook Is Facebook

On the afternoon of June 27, 2017, Mark Zuckerberg posted a brief message on his Facebook page. "As of this morning, the Facebook community is now officially 2 billion people!" the company founder and chief executive officer wrote. "We're making progress connecting the world, and now let's bring the world closer together. It's an honor to be on this journey with you."[1]

The idea of bringing the world closer together has animated and driven Zuckerberg from the beginning. His speeches, his letters to investors, his essays on Facebook, his interviews with journalists, and the quiet tour he took of the United States in early 2017 all resonate with that theme. He believes that his company can and should unite people from across the globe. He also believes that the consequences of that process of connecting people are predictable and largely beneficial.[2]

"For the past decade, Facebook has focused on connecting friends and families," Zuckerberg wrote in a wide-ranging manifesto he published on his Facebook page in early 2017. "With that foundation, our next focus will be developing the social infrastructure for community—for supporting us, for keeping us safe, for informing us, for civic engagement, and for inclusion of all." This marked something of a shift for Zuckerberg and for Facebook. Zuckerberg was coming to terms with the fact that through 2016 Facebook had hosted and promoted propaganda that influenced the referendum to move the United Kingdom out of the European Union and the election of Donald Trump in the United States. Beyond that, Facebook had received significant criticism for its Facebook Live video streaming service after multiple people used it to publicize suicides and homicides they were committing. The company was being called irresponsible. So Zuckerberg took to his own platform to promise to do better, to explain the problems in the most general terms, and to shift blame where he could.[3]

"Beyond voting, the greatest opportunity is helping people stay engaged with the issues that matter to them every day, not just every few years at the ballot box," Zuckerberg wrote in that 2017 manifesto. "We can help establish direct dialogue and accountability between people and our elected leaders." Then Zuckerberg chose to mention some of the most astounding examples of how he believed Facebook helps democratic processes. "In India, Prime Minister Modi has asked his ministers to share their meetings and information on Facebook so they can hear direct feedback from citizens," Zuckerberg wrote. "In Kenya, whole villages are in WhatsApp (a messaging platform that Facebook owns) groups together, including their representatives. In recent campaigns around the world—from India and Indonesia across Europe to the United States—we've seen the candidate with the largest and most engaged following on Facebook usually wins. Just as TV became the primary medium for civic communication in the 1960s, social media is becoming this in the 21st century."[4]

Those who study or follow the rise of authoritarianism and the alarming erosion of democracy around the world would by 2017 list India, Indonesia, Kenya, Poland, Hungary, and the United States as sites of Facebook's direct contribution to violent ethnic and religious nationalism, the rise of authoritarian leaders, and a sort of mediated cacophony that would hinder public deliberation about important issues, thus undermining trust in institutions and experts. Somehow, Zuckerberg missed all of that. By November 2017, as Facebook officials were compelled to investigate and reveal the extent of Russian interference with the U.S. election through advertisements purchased on Facebook and Instagram and targeted precisely to reach at least 126 million Americans, Zuckerberg would be silent. He no longer crowed about Facebook becoming the most powerful political platform in the world. Still, the company offered a proposal to improve political culture: more services from and trust in Facebook. The company would just promise to do better.[5]

In the manifesto Zuckerberg did describe a central problem with Facebook that led to so many unwelcome developments. "These mistakes are almost never because we hold ideological positions at odds with the community, but instead are operational scaling issues," he wrote. Facebook is just too big to govern. We are victims of its success.[6]

The story of Facebook has been told well and often. But it deserves a deep and critical analysis at this crucial moment. Somehow Facebook devolved from an innocent social site hacked together by Harvard students into a force that, while it may make personal life just a little more pleasurable, makes democracy a lot more challenging. It's a story of the hubris of good intentions, a missionary spirit, and an ideology that sees computer code as the universal solvent for all human problems. And it's an indictment of how social media has fostered the deterioration of democratic and intellectual culture around the world.

Silicon Valley grew out of a widespread cultural commitment to data-driven decision-making and logical thinking. Its culture is explicitly cosmopolitan and tolerant of difference and dissent. Both its market orientation and its labor force are global. Silicon Valley also indulges a strong missionary bent, one that preaches the power of connectivity and the spread of knowledge to empower people to change their lives for the better. So how did the greatest Silicon Valley success story end up hosting radical, nationalist, anti-Enlightenment movements that revolt against civic institutions and cosmopolitans? How did such an enlightened firm become complicit in the rise of nationalists such as Donald Trump, Marine Le Pen, Narendra Modi, Rodrigo Duterte, and ISIS? How did the mission go so wrong? Facebook is the paradigmatic distillation of the Silicon Valley ideology. No company better represents the dream of a fully connected planet "sharing" words, ideas, images, and plans. No company has better leveraged those ideas into wealth and influence. No company has contributed more to the paradoxical collapse of basic tenets of deliberation and democracy.

POLLUTION

On February 2, 2012, about a year before President Barack Obama would take his second oath of office and a year after the abdication of Egyptian president Hosni Mubarak, Zuckerberg released a remarkable letter to his shareholders. "People sharing more—even if just with their close friends or families—creates a more open culture and leads to a better understanding of the lives and perspectives of others," Zuckerberg wrote in the letter. "We believe that this creates a greater number of stronger relationships between people, and that it helps people get exposed to a greater number of diverse perspectives. By helping people form these connections, we hope to rewire the way people spread and consume information." The letter, issued just weeks before the company's $16 billion initial public offering of stock, was the strongest and clearest articulation of the goals that Zuckerberg held for his company, then merely eight years old. Facebook, Zuckerberg promised, would not grow into a company obsessed with revenue and profits. It had a global social mission "to make the world more open and connected," he declared in the letter.[7]

But in fact, the opposite has happened. Just four years later it's clear that Facebook divides people as much as it connects them. And the idealistic vision of people sharing more information with ever more people has not improved nations or global culture, enhanced mutual understanding, or strengthened democratic movements.

The situation is paradoxical. Facebook has contributed to so many maladies because its leaders are so deeply committed to making the world a better place. If Zuckerberg were more committed to naked growth and profit, and less blinded by hubris, he might have thought differently about building out an ungovernable global system that is so easily hijacked.

Facebook's leaders, and Silicon Valley leaders in general, have invited this untenable condition by believing too firmly in their own omnipotence and benevolence. These leaders' absolute belief in their sincerity and capabilities, combined with blind faith in the power of people to share and discuss the best and most useful information about the world, has driven some terrible design decisions. We cannot expect these leaders to address the problems within their own product designs until they abandon such faith and confidence in their own competence and rectitude.

The dominance of Facebook on our screens, in our lives, and over our minds has many dangerous aspects. The first is the way in which false or misleading information can so easily spread through Facebook. We've seen this in post-election stories about the flurry of "fake news," which is actually just one form of information "pollution." Types of content in the Facebook News Feed are often visually indistinguishable, especially as we rush through our feed on a small screen. Items from YouTube to the *Washington Post* to Target stores all come across with the same frames, using the same fonts, in the same format. It's not easy for users to distinguish among sources or forms of content. It's also impossible to tell an opinion piece written for one of the dozens of blogs the *Washington Post* hosts from a serious investigative news story that might have run on the front page of that daily newspaper. The aftermath of the 2016 election was consumed by analyses and reports about how easily images and text carrying absurd lies about the major candidates echoed around Facebook. And that's largely because Facebook has none of the cues that ordinarily allow us to identify and assess the source of a story. It's not just a demand-side problem, though. Those who wish to propel propaganda to echo through Facebook long ago cracked the code.

A second structural problem is that Facebook amplifies content that hits strong emotional registers, whether joy or indignation. Among the things that move fast and far on Facebook: cute puppies, cute babies, clever listicles, lifestyle quizzes, and hate speech. Facebook is explicitly engineered to promote items that generate strong reactions. If you want to pollute Facebook with nonsense to distract or propaganda to motivate, it's far too easy. The first step is to choose the most extreme, polarizing message and image.

Extremism will generate both positive and negative reactions, or "engagements." Facebook measures engagement by the number of clicks, "likes," shares, and comments. This design feature—or flaw, if you care about the quality of knowledge and debate—ensures that the most inflammatory material will travel the farthest and the fastest. Sober, measured accounts of the world have no chance on Facebook. And when Facebook dominates our sense of the world and our social circles, we all potentially become carriers of extremist nonsense.[8]

The third, better understood phenomenon is the "filter bubble"—a term coined by author and entrepreneur Eli Pariser to describe the ways that Google and Facebook reward users with more of what they tell the companies they want, thus narrowing fields of vision and potentially creating echo chambers of reinforced belief. That does not mean that Facebook looks for liberal or conservative points of view within the text of items. It means that if you habitually reward certain sites, friends, or web pages with likes or heart emojis, frequently share that content on your Facebook page, or comment on certain pages, Facebook knows you are highly engaged with them. So it gives you more of the stuff with which you would engage and less of the stuff with which you would not. Facebook does this with predictive scoring of each item, whether posted by a friend or purchased as an advertisement. Your preferences become clear to Facebook over time. Facebook does not want to bother you with much that you have not expressed an interest in. Over time your feed becomes narrower in perspective by virtue of the fact that friends and sites tend to be politically consistent in what they post. Because reading the News Feeds of our friends is increasingly the way we learn about the world and its issues, we are less likely to encounter information that comes from outside our group, and thus are unaware of countervailing arguments and claims. It's important to note that no filter bubble is sealed, and no News Feed is exclusively limited to interests expressed by the Facebook user. Sometimes surprises puncture the bubble. Also, filter bubbles are not just about politics, and they don't only form along left-right axes that might seem familiar to North Americans or Western Europeans. They can form about anything a user expresses habitual interest in. So filter bubbles affect different people differently. This makes them very hard to study and measure. Many people actively work to prevent the formation of such bubbles, so they seek out new influences or diverse Friends.* But Facebook tends toward comfort and rewards the common habits that push us to convene with those who think like we do.[9]

When we combine the phenomena of propaganda with filter bubbles, we can see the toxic mixture that emerges: Facebook users are incapable of engaging with each other upon a shared body of accepted truths. That post from Snopes.com debunking the claim that Pope Francis endorsed Donald Trump never reaches the users who most need to see it. Many of us are more likely to find the debunking claim before we see the story it is debunking. Arguments among differently minded users often devolve into disputes over what is or isn't true. It's usually impossible within the Facebook platform to drive a conversation beyond sputtering contradictions. So filter bubbles distance us from those who differ from us or generally disagree with us, while the bias toward sensationalism and propagandistic content undermines trust. In these ways Facebook makes it harder for diverse groups of people to gather to conduct calm, informed, productive conversations.

MOTIVATION AND DELIBERATION

The structure and function of Facebook work powerfully in the service of motivation. If you want to summon people to a cause, solicit donations, urge people to vote for a candidate, or sell a product, few media technologies would serve you better than Facebook does. Facebook is great for motivation. It is terrible for deliberation.

Democratic republics need both motivation and deliberation. They need engaged citizens to coordinate their knowledge, messages, and action. They need countervailing forces to be able to compete for attention and support within the public sphere. But when conflict emerges, a healthy democratic republic needs forums through which those who differ can argue, negotiate,

---

* I will capitalize "Friend" throughout this book to distinguish the Facebook-mediated relationship from actual friendship.

and persuade with a base of common facts, agreed-upon conditions, clearly defined problems, and an array of responses or solutions from which to choose. A republic needs norms through which those who differ can maintain mutual respect for the process, if not for each other. Those who lose a debate or conflict retreat to rally their facts, ideas, and supporters for the next deliberation, without resorting to undermining basic trust in institutions and traditions.

Nothing about Facebook, the most important and pervasive element of the global media ecosystem in the first few decades of this millennium, enhances the practice of deliberation. The very structure of a Facebook post and the threads of comments that run beneath it resist full and calm consideration. Posts and comments are designed to respond to just the comment directly above. They are nested to inhibit any member of a discussion from considering the full range of responses. Participants are encouraged to respond rashly, so they often respond rudely.

The problem is much bigger and broader than what happens on Facebook. Through its destructive influence on other media firms, industries, and institutions, Facebook undermines their ability to support healthy public deliberation as well. Facebook distorts the very sources of news and information on which a democratic republic relies. On the one hand, Facebook is rapidly draining away advertising revenue from responsible and reputable news sources. If a firm has a small advertising budget, it is likely to shift spending toward targeted, accountable advertising systems such as Google and Facebook and away from display ads that offer no way to measure user engagement. Facebook has grown so adept at targeting ads and generating attention that advertising companies design entire campaigns around the "viral" potential of their messages. As reputable news organizations lay off reporters and pay less for freelance work, they have altered their editorial decisions and strategies to pander to the biases inherent in Facebook's algorithms. Editors and publishers spend much of their working days trying to design their content to take flight on Facebook. They have to pander to the very source of their demise just to hold on to the audiences and the potential for a sliver of the revenue they used to make.

Facebook has invited publications to join into partnerships in which Facebook's servers deliver the content and Facebook splits the revenue with the publications. But this has only marginally slowed the decline of revenues for those publications while encouraging them to design their content to echo among Facebook users. Facebook is feeding our worst appetites while starving the institutions that could strengthen us.

Beginning in late 2016 desperate Facebook officials proposed various experiments and interventions to limit the proliferation of propaganda, misinformation, and general garbage. They also proposed ways to certify the truthfulness of news sources and stories. They tried to limit who could purchase campaign advertisements in the United States and Germany. They scrambled to improve and enhance the systems Facebook uses to moderate and filter offensive content. Later they resorted to repressing news and amplifying Friends' posts, hoping to improve the mood of the service and engender goodwill among users.

"Our job at Facebook is to help people make the greatest positive impact while mitigating areas where technology and social media can contribute to divisiveness and isolation," Zuckerberg wrote in his 2017 manifesto. "Facebook is a work in progress, and we are dedicated to learning and improving." In addition to internal reform efforts, legislators and regulators in the United States moved to require political ads on social media to conform to the same standards of transparency as television ads do. All of these efforts were cosmetic. None struck at the root of the problem. None of them addressed the simple yet powerful truth: the problem with Facebook is Facebook.[10]

A global system that links 2.2 billion people across hundreds of countries, allows every user to post content indiscriminately, develops algorithms that favor highly charged content, and is dependent on a self-service advertising system that precisely targets ads using massive surveillance and elaborate personal dossiers cannot be reformed at the edges. A company that has no serious competitors in most of the world for a growing array of important and addictive services cannot be expected to fall from its dominant perch on its own. Facebook is too big, too powerful, and too intrusive—and it works too well—for shallow reform to make a difference. All of the problems that Facebook has amplified were intensified because Facebook worked exactly how it was supposed to work.[11]

Through all the turmoil, Zuckerberg ignored the fact that no reform or repair around the edges of Facebook was going to fix the problems. A service that has invited more than 2.2 billion people to use it habitually and promiscuously for all sorts of purposes cannot expect all those people to behave well. Facebook is too big and the people who use it are too diverse. And those who profit from the most powerful, efficient, and inexpensive advertising service ever invented cannot expect those who purchase ads to resist precisely targeting hateful and destructive propaganda where it can do the most harm.

This book explains why and how that happened. Basically, there are two things wrong with Facebook: how it works and how people use it. The company has no incentive to change how it works, even if it did cop to that level of responsibility. And Facebook users, as individuals, have little incentive to restrict their use to the good things in life. Facebook undermines our ability to think collectively about our problems—especially if one of those problems is Facebook. The painful paradox of Facebook is that the company's sincere devotion to making the world better invited nefarious parties to hijack it to spread hatred and confusion. Zuckerberg's firm belief in his own expertise, authority, and ethical core blinded him and his company to the damage it was facilitating and causing. If Facebook had been less obsessed with making the world better, it might have avoided contributing to forces that have made the world worse.

To make its case, this book starts with an account of why so many of us decide to spend so much time and live so many important parts of our life on Facebook and the other major services it owns, Instagram and WhatsApp. Then the book explains how and why Facebook watches and records our every move and what it means for our social, economic, and political fortunes. To do this, we must consider how Facebook harnesses and monetizes our attention and the high cost the "attention economy" imposes on us. Facebook's commitment to social responsibility takes the form of social engineering. This ideology allows Facebook to celebrate when people use it to push for political change that cosmopolitan elites might cheer, like the 2011 revolution in Tunisia. But it also prevents those who make decisions at Facebook from interrogating the effect they have on politics around the world. The last third of the book works its way from street protests in North Africa through the Brexit vote and the election of Donald Trump, and finally to the ways that Facebook amplifies distracting and destructive words and images, empowering ethnic nationalists and violent autocrats around the world. The book concludes with some modest policy proposals, but ends with a plea for a reinvestment in institutions that promote deep thought conducted at analog speed.

THE AGE OF SOPHISTRY

Whether one called the phenomenon "fake news," "propaganda," "garbage," or "disinformation," the result was the same: a constant and alarming undermining of public trust in expertise and the possibility of rational deliberation and debate. This struggle to reinforce standards and methods of asserting truth and establishing trust hit the United States in 2016, after Americans woke to the realization that Donald Trump had masterfully exploited Facebook during his campaign and that forces aligned with Russia had spread misinformation widely across various Facebook groups in hopes of undermining faith and trust in democracy. But the storm had been building for some time and had already raged through Ukraine, India, Myanmar, the Philippines, Cambodia, and other parts of the world. The storm fed on the connective power of social media—mostly Facebook.

Just days after the inauguration of the forty-fifth president of the United States, reports rose that sales had suddenly spiked for copies of George Orwell's novel *1984*. What had precipitated this sudden interest in a sixty-nine-year-old British novel? Spokesperson Sean Spicer had stood behind the seal of the presidency and told a spectacular lie about the size of the crowd that had cheered on Donald Trump as he took his oath of office on January 20, 2017. Under incredulous and somewhat dumbfounded questioning by the veteran reporters of the White House press corps, Spicer dismissed all official accounts of the size of the crowd, images and video taken by journalists, and the eyewitness accounts of not only the thousands who attended but the millions who saw on television the gaping patches of bare ground on the National Mall in Washington, D.C. The reporters, cynical people accustomed to cutting through lies told guilefully and for some purpose, were floored. They could not understand why the person who had a duty to maintain the credibility of the presidency when speaking directly to the American people felt the need to lie so boldly about something that mattered so little. A few days later one of Trump's top aides, Kellyanne Conway, appeared on an NBC News program where she defended Spicer. When veteran journalist Chuck Todd, clearly exasperated by the gumption of the White House, asserted that the facts were clear in this matter and that the crowd was significantly smaller than those for the two previous inaugurations, Conway declared that Spicer was not spewing lies but merely giving "alternative facts," a phrase she seemed to conjure in the moment but which she instantly grew comfortable defending. "Alternative facts are not facts," Todd retorted. "They are falsehoods."[12]

Many Americans were instantly reminded at that moment that Orwell had conceived of a totalitarian state in which the dictator and his associates insisted that absurdities were logical and falsehoods true. Citizens capitulated to the message that the state was so powerful it could successfully assert that the only test for truth was force. The reaction of the reading public was understandable. People were reaching for stable, familiar parables like *1984* to ground their understanding of a time of great turbulence and anxiety.

Thus the White House staff, and by extension the president, set forth the method by which Trump would assert his dominance over the public sphere. Trump would flatly deny provable or proven facts. He would flood the media systems of the world with nonsense. He would demand that everyone respond to him, either by acclamation or by appalled rejection. He would create torrents of noise and spark even more echoes and responses. All noise, all responses, would serve his ego. This project of flooding our minds and fields of vision with absurd, untrue, unexpected, and unwarranted statements would take advantage of a media ecosystem designed for rapid response. The president's words and countenance would spend the day rocketing around various news channels and social media services. News services would feed social media. Social media would feed news services. And whatever everyone had been discussing yesterday would be swept away from collective consciousness.[13]

The problem is much more dangerous than Donald Trump, much larger than the United States. The autocrat, the de-territorialized terrorist organization, the insurgent group, the prankster, and the internet troll share a relationship to the truth: they see it as beside the point. If they can get the rest of us scrambling to find our balance, they have achieved their goals. Those who oppose or dismiss democracy and the deliberation and debate that make democracy possible do not care whether claims are true or false, or even how widely they are accepted as true. What matters is that a loud voice disrupts the flow of discourse, and that all further argument will be centered on the truth of the claim itself rather than on a substantive engagement with facts. Power is all that matters when trust and truth crumble.[14]

Much of the world is suddenly engaged in a reignited battle over truth and trust. "Credibility" and "authority" seem to be quaint, weak concepts. Experts are derided for their elitism, their choice to reside in comfortable social and intellectual bubbles. Scientific methods are dismissed for reflecting the class interests of the scientists and institutions that produce and certify knowledge. Vast bodies of knowledge are doubted repeatedly by elected officials through powerful media outlets to the point where substantial portions of Americans have ceased to believe basic facts about the oceans that are rising around them. Across the globe communities of doubters invite renewed outbreaks of deadly measles among children because publicity-seeking, soft-minded doubters have fooled just enough parents into believing that the risks of vaccines outweigh the benefits. Journalism has collapsed as both a practice and an industry as advertisement revenue fled to online platforms and a cacophony of new voices asserted their newfound potency, certified by high Google search ranks or millions of Twitter followers.[15]

The erosion of truth and trust is more acute in the United States than it is in Canada, the United Kingdom, France, or Germany. But much of the rest of the world is shaking as well, as authoritarian governments have assumed control of Turkey, Hungary, and Poland and economic and political chaos has tested institutions in Spain, Portugal, Italy, and Greece in recent years. Pluralistic, liberal democracy finds too little favor these days in Russia, India, the Philippines, or Venezuela. Democracy has seen better days in Brazil and Mexico, both of which danced for a while with competitive elections and peaceful transitions of power, only to see traditions of grift and graft creep back again. Egypt flashed an interest in democracy, then quickly reverted to brutal military rule. Tunisia and Myanmar offer some hope for the sort of transitions to democracy and the rule of law we so recently celebrated as the emerging norm, but ethnic and sectarian strife threaten to bludgeon any hopes in both of those countries.

For those of us who wish for the world the comforts of calm, liberal, pluralistic, gradual, peaceful, deliberate change, these are trying times. The connection between recent turbulence and the erosion of truth and trust is hard to ignore. In the United States in 2016, confidence in essential institutions such as journalism, organized religion, organized labor, government, industry, banks, schools, and even the medical community was at an all-time low, with fewer than 20 percent of those polled expressing a great deal of confidence in any of these.[16] By 2017 Americans reported very little confidence in basic civility, the set of norms a nation needs to convene and compromise across differences.[17]

Sophistry is the dominant cultural practice of the moment. We can't agree. We can't agree to disagree. We can't agree on what distinguishes a coherent argument from a rhetorical stunt. We have flipped the very notion of a classic logical fallacy like "slippery slope" such that we take it seriously as a form of argument ("It's a slippery slope. If we let the government take away our semiautomatic weapons, what's next?"). How can a democratic republic succeed if so many citizens refuse to settle on a common set of facts, to subscribe to rules of intellectual engagement, or to trust the institutions we have long depended on to generate and certify processes and the facts they create? The battle is not over this claim or that claim, over whether, as Orwell described, two plus two equals four or five. It is over the power to dictate truth itself. Or, rather, the power to declare the pursuit of truth futile and beside the point.

Despite the erosion of trust in long-established institutions, there are two sources of trust that are growing in their power to claim truth. Americans trust Google search results and links much more than they trust traditional news outlets. And Facebook users judge the trustworthiness of information that comes across their News Feed based on who posted it rather than the source of the original post itself. Many people judge whether a claim is true or false based on how much prominence Google gives it or which of their Facebook Friends choose to push it forward to others.[18]

This should trouble us. Two of the wealthiest global corporations in the world have earned vast reserves of public trust as well as wealth and influence. They serve as models for success. They are the lenses through which we view the world. Their leaders are called upon to ponder and pontificate on education, politics, public health, and world affairs. They don't just channel our prejudices and predilections. Google and Facebook concentrate and amplify them.

Meanwhile, the very institutions we have carefully constructed and maintained to filter out nonsense and noise and to forge consensus of thought and action are withering. This has occurred over just a few decades, from that moment in the late twentieth century when it seemed the Enlightenment had finally prevailed and democracy, freedom, pluralism, and universal dignity just might have a chance to flower.[19]

THE GREAT SCRAMBLE

What I have just described is the information and political climate of the first two decades of the twenty-first century. It is the background that must inform our examination of Facebook and of our relationship with Facebook. Facebook is a stage on which people and movements perform. A stage, after all, is both an ecosystem and a medium itself. Facebook is a significant and growing factor in all of this cacophony. If Facebook were designed differently, it might be able to mitigate the worst excesses of our current global state. If most people used Facebook differently, limiting engagement to personal matters and entertainment, it could be a powerful tool that enhanced well-being. Instead, Facebook has hosted and amplified some of the most damaging trends that have afflicted us, including bullying and bigotry. These trends do not have their roots in Facebook. Clearly, they predate Facebook by years if not decades or centuries. But Facebook has been a factor in their acceleration and growth.

Let's not fall for the temptation to be lazy or simplistic. A shallow tirade against a big, rich company would do no one any good. Google and Facebook did not generate this vertigo of trust and truth. Many of the essential institutions that have suffered a reputational downgrade of late earned distrust through long-term malfeasance, incompetence, or unresponsiveness. It's certainly true that political forces had reasons to seed and cultivate distrust, much the way the tobacco industry actively undermined years of scientific research on the harms of its product.[20]

This book does not argue that Facebook is the source of these troubles. Facebook is, however, the most pervasive and powerful catalyst of information pollution and destructive nonsense. Facebook has no competition as a connector of motivated people and a distributor of propaganda. Its only serious rival for advertising revenue is the equally powerful search engine Google. Facebook has acquired several of its potential competitors for social media use, including Instagram, ConnectU, and WhatsApp. It dominates our mobile phone data usage around the world. Twitter, which has cultural power in some quarters, lacks both the revenue and the audience to influence lives and minds like Facebook does. Simply put, in 2018 Facebook is among the two or three most powerful companies in the world.

Because his campaign figured out how best to exploit the features of Facebook, we can safely say that Facebook helped to put Donald Trump into office. But so did many other things. Facebook did not divide the world and make it hateful and violent. Facebook did not create the xenophobia, racism, Islamophobia, misogyny, and economic anxiety that gave Trump a fervent constituency. That's a longer, more complicated, and more troubling story.

Nor is Facebook bad for everyone all the time. In fact, it's benefited millions individually. Facebook has also allowed people to find support and community despite being shunned by friends and family or being geographically isolated. Facebook is still our chief source of cute baby and puppy photos. Babies and puppies are among the things that make life worth living. We could all use more images of cuteness and sweetness to get us through our days. On Facebook babies and puppies run in the same column as serious personal appeals for financial help with medical care, advertisements for and against political candidates, bogus claims against science, and appeals to racism and violence.

There is little hope for repair or redemption in the short term. Calls for "media literacy" assume that we could even agree on what that term means and that there would be some way to train nearly two billion people to distinguish good from bad content. There are few regulatory interventions beyond better privacy protections that would make a significant difference to how Facebook operates. Facebook itself has no incentives to reform. And efforts to launch a mass boycott of Facebook would be trivial and counterproductive.

Over the long term, however, there is hope. Reviving a healthy social and political life would require a concerted recognition of the damage Facebook has done and a campaign to get beyond its spell. If millions were urged to put Facebook in its proper place, perhaps merely as a source of social and familial contact rather than political knowledge or activism, we could train ourselves out of the habit. Norm-building is so much harder than technology development. But it's the only effective response we have to the problems we have invited. Ultimately, those of us who wish for a healthier public culture will have to strengthen other institutions such as libraries, schools, universities, and civil society organizations that might offer richer engagement with knowledge and community. That effort will take decades to come to fruition.

In the meantime, let's consider the synergistic effects of the rise of two useful and brilliantly executed suites of digital technologies offered at no or marginal cost to billions of users at the exact moment when much of the world had cause to lose trust in the promises of established institutions and ideologies. Facebook fulfills needs and desires. It gives us something to do when everything around us seems dull. It serves us thoughts and feelings that affirm our prejudices and satisfy our desires for attention. It satiates our hunger for status and connection, and it satisfies our curiosity while making navigating the world more convenient. More important, Facebook amplifies and energizes many of the irrational and antidemocratic forces that were boiling beneath the surface just as this century began.[21]

Facebook likely has been—on balance—good for individuals. But Facebook has been—on balance—bad for all of us collectively. If you use Facebook regularly, it almost certainly has enhanced your life. It has helped you keep up with friends and family members with regularity and at great distance. It has hosted groups that appeal to your hobbies, your interests, your vocations, and your inclinations. Perhaps you have discovered and enjoyed otherwise obscure books and music through a post from a trusted friend. Some image or video on Facebook has made you laugh. Some long post has made you think. Perhaps Facebook kept you abreast of cultural and political events in the place of your birth, even though you live time zones away from it now. Perhaps you met a romantic partner through it (it happens). Perhaps you rekindled a friendship dormant since grade school. You might have renewed valuable friendships once lost to moves and phone number changes. You could have been able to maintain family relationships over oceans and continents with minimal effort, like a click on a smiley face when a cousin's child appears in your Facebook News Feed. Social media allow you to encounter the occasional story from *Haaretz* or the *Guardian*, thus expanding your vision of the globe and the number of voices informing your base of knowledge. Perhaps you have led or participated in issue campaigns or political movements partially organized via Facebook or promoted over Twitter. You might have severed a few relationships after political arguments or revealed bigotries. You might have found yourself exhausted and distracted by the constant call for attention that Facebook imposes. Your office productivity might have declined since you enrolled with Facebook. Maybe Facebook was the medium through which you were threatened or harassed by a former romantic partner or someone who just resented how you think and what you represent. If, on balance, the positive effects of Facebook did not outweigh the negative effects, you likely would have quit it by now. For more than two billion people across the world, Facebook seems like an enhancement to their individual lives.

Life is better, that is, unless you have been the target of harassment, hatred, or threats. Many who have suffered terrible experiences through social media maintain their presence there. It's that important to us. We refine our public presentations and risk our reputations through these limited, highly structured commercial services. In less than a decade most of us have learned to depend on Facebook to such a degree that it's difficult to imagine living without it. What would we miss? The value to individuals has little to do with the computer code that drives Facebook. The value is in the other people. We find it hard to imagine living in a Facebook-free world because we mostly enjoy our frequent, easy, cost-free contact with our friends and family.

Yet we are collectively worse off because of Facebook. If you wanted to build a machine that would distribute propaganda to millions of people, distract them from important issues, energize hatred and bigotry, erode social trust, undermine journalism, foster doubts about science, and engage in massive surveillance all at once, you would make something a lot like Facebook.

Step back from your own experiences for a moment. Would the world be better today if Facebook had never been invented? If Facebook disappeared tomorrow, as Twitter could at any time unless it figures out how to make money, would the world improve? There is a strong case for the affirmative. While the *Guardian* story you encountered yesterday might have led you to a new novel or an interesting thinker, millions of others came across a story from Breitbart.com that drove up the barometer of bigotry in our society. Someone else decided not to vaccinate a baby because of something she read on Facebook. Someone else now believes climate change is a conspiracy constructed by Big Science.

Facebook scrambles our social worlds, our commercial worlds, and our political worlds. As we grow we teach ourselves that we should not reveal some information about ourselves to our friends that we could comfortably share with our parents. We can trust our coaches and clergy with some things, but not our siblings. We forge social contexts. Sometimes these contexts intersect, as when a friendship blossoms in the workplace. But in general we exercise autonomy over how we present ourselves among these spheres. Facebook puts everyone in one big room and calls them "Friends." While Facebook offers us ways to segregate these Friends, we rarely do. It's difficult to maintain distinct groups among a large collection of Friends, many of whom you have not seen for years and might not even like that much. This scrambling of our social lives causes anxiety and sometimes fractures relationships. Generally, it reminds us to be vigilant, imagining how the most hostile person might interpret what we are posting. Facebook also scrambles the commercial world by dominating the advertising economy and pulling revenue away from other sources of news and information. Facebook scrambles the political world by proliferating misinformation and disinformation meant to distract and divide a community. Facebook is disorienting. We are a long time from figuring out how to live well with it.

So one could comfortably conclude that a world without Facebook is one in which responsible media might have a better chance of influencing and enlightening an electorate. A world without Facebook might dampen bigotry and extremism rather than amplifying both. Without Facebook, at least, we might have a better chance of convincing a few more parents to vaccinate their children. Facebook is not going away. Even Mark Zuckerberg lacks the power to turn off the switch. We can only imagine what life in 2018 and beyond might be like without Facebook. To harness Facebook so it serves us better and harms us less, we must turn to regulation around the world. To learn to live better with Facebook, we must understand the ideologies and histories of technology. We must sharpen our critical tools so that we have better conversations about Facebook and other inventions that seem to offer us so much for so little, but ultimately take much more than they give. We must stop and think.

HOW TO THINK ABOUT MEDIA AND TECHNOLOGY

Exiting an elevator on the seventh floor of a former factory on Greene Street in lower Manhattan, I asked the receptionist where I might find the office of Professor Neil Postman. She pointed to the back corner office, past a maze of cubicles. I walked slowly, breathing deeply, unsure of what sort of interrogation I would face.

It was late spring in 1999, just weeks after I had defended my doctoral dissertation, a cultural history of American copyright law. I had been teaching for a year in the history department at Wesleyan University in Connecticut. Although I had been a professional journalist, dabbled in music criticism, installed Windows 95 on dozens of computers, and built web pages (in the earliest days of that medium), I had long thought of myself as a budding historian. The future, as a scholarly project, did not interest me much. So I was not convinced that this new department would be interested in what I had to offer. And I was fairly sure that Postman and I would not get along.

I was still riding the optimistic waves of the post–Cold War 1990s. My country was ascendant in the world, leading with its values of freedom, ingenuity, and grit. Crime was ebbing. Employment was booming. Real wages in the United States were creeping up for the first time in twenty-five years. And I was a fellow traveler in a movement that seemed to promise the full democratization of the Enlightenment. Digital technology seemed to offer a solution to the scarcity of knowledge and the barriers to entry for expression that had held so much of the world under tarps of tyranny and ignorance. My dissertation, still warm from the laser printer, had concluded that recent efforts to ratchet up the restrictions of copyright law would stifle creativity. Its argument was quickly being embraced by technologically optimistic communities around the world. These groups of hackers, librarians, and civil libertarians would champion my ideas and lift my profile, I hoped. I shared their disposition.

So there I was on a hot day, wearing a baggy black suit, a cultural historian with no serious record, about to interview for a job in a high-profile academic department devoted to the future. Its students and faculty spent their lives making holistic, ecological accounts of the influences of media on the world. I had spent weeks devouring the books that the department's faculty had produced.

I was to meet Postman, a legendary public intellectual who had emerged as the earliest and most vocal scold of all that I considered positive and revolutionary. He had written the 1985 bestseller *Amusing Ourselves to Death*, about the ways that television had deadened our public discourse by sucking all modes of deliberation into a form defined by the limitations of entertainment. He had gone on a decade later to raise concerns about our rush to wire every computer in the world together without concern for the side effects. What would I have in common with this famous man who was about to decide if my academic career would surge in the most exciting city in the world or start somewhere a bit less interesting?

He greeted me with a wide smile and a warm handshake. He wore a comfortable gray flannel suit—a uniform of sorts, I would later observe. I noticed he had a computer in his office, but he did not face it. His broad desk held piles of yellow legal pads and a date book. The computer sat on a separate desk a few feet to the left of his. His assistant was seated at it, and she politely introduced herself to me as she left us to talk. I would soon learn that Neil never read his own email. His assistant would read it to him and he would dictate responses.

The interview was unlike any I had ever had for any position. It lasted more than an hour. He did not ask me standard interview questions about my research agenda, my teaching style, or my publication plans. Neil asked me about Texas, where I had lived for fourteen years and earned my degrees. He asked about Mark Twain, a particular passion of his and the subject of much of my dissertation. We discussed baseball (he was a Mets fan; I am a Yankees fan). And he asked me a question that has stuck with me and in no small way directed my vocation ever since.

"Siva, around here we spend a lot of time teaching and writing about problems in media. We talk about how media limit us, how everything is shallow, how corporate interests dictate the nature of our democracy. Yet we expect and encourage our students to get jobs in these very industries we criticize. How can we justify this?"

I'm not sure why I didn't pause to gather my thoughts. But Neil had disarmed my defenses with his friendly rapport and easy manner. So I answered immediately.

"Well, we are in many ways like clergy," I said. "Sometimes all that clergy can expect from their work is to make their congregations feel just a little bit guilty about the damage they are about to do."

Neil grinned and leaned back. "Yes. Yes," he said.

This glib statement has served me throughout my career. I've never written a book or article about technology in realistic hopes that it will achieve legislation, renunciation, adoption, or any other action in the world. Instead, the most I hope for is that it makes a few people look at the phenomenon differently—perhaps ecologically—and ask different questions going forward. If my readers and students feel a little bit guilty or, better, become a little more circumspect, I have done my job.

During my interview, other questions from Neil followed. "What is your definition of 'postmodernism'?" "Do you think India will be more dominant than the United States in the twenty-first century?" "Is the United States too secular or too religious?" None of these questions had correct answers. I'm not sure he even had a stake in the questions or the answers. He wanted to see if I was interesting and interested. And, I now realize, he was teaching me how to teach.

Neil Postman was a teacher, first and foremost. All his writing was meant to prompt and provoke discussion and debate. He never lost his sense of humor or seemed personally invested in his subjects. And every conversation with him was Socratic. He would ask question after question after question. After many pinot grigio–enhanced lunches with Neil over the next few years I would realize that either the job interview had never ended or it had never begun. I had just joined a long conversation he had been having with hundreds of people for decades. He was always asking others to teach him something because that was the best way for him to teach others. Teaching, I soon learned, was a deliberate dance, a constant running conversation, a pleasure. And the teacher taught best when asking questions, as a student would.

Much of our conversation over those years, before Neil passed away in 2003, was—unsurprisingly—about the rise and influence of the internet and digital technology. Neil also taught me that like all those people who rushed out to buy Orwell's *1984* after Trump's inauguration, I had been paying attention to the wrong book.

A week after Trump's inauguration, Neil's son, Andrew Postman, published an essay in the *Guardian* called "My Dad Predicted Trump in 1985— It's Not Orwell, He Warned, It's Brave New World." In his 1985 bestseller,

Amusing Ourselves to Death, Neil had argued that Americans should not have been paying so much attention to the foreboding picture of totalitarianism in Orwell's novel. The prospect of that sort of social control—by centralized brute force and fear—was unlikely to spread or find purchase in societies so committed to consumerism, expression, and choice. Instead, Neil argued, we should be heeding the warnings issued by Aldous Huxley in his 1932 futuristic novel *Brave New World*. "What Orwell feared were those who would ban books," Neil wrote in 1985. "What Huxley feared was that there would be no reason to ban a book, for there would be no one who wanted to read one." Huxley, Neil explained, described a culture deadened by feelings, bored by stimulation, distracted by empty pleasures. What threatens those of us who live rather comfortably is not so much brutality as entertainment. I would only add a coda to Neil's invocation of *Brave New World*: our collective inability to think through our problems and our ability to ignore our problems invite brutality—or at least make it that much harder to confront brutality when it arrives and is aimed at the least visible or vocal among us.

Andrew Postman argued in that essay that his father's concerns were that citizens of the United States have been conditioned for decades to expect shallow engagement with ideas delivered faster and more conveniently. And this conditioning has rendered us unable to think and argue clearly about the challenges we face and the choices we make. Andrew wrote: "Who can be appalled when the coin of the realm in public discourse is not experience, thoughtfulness or diplomacy but the ability to amuse—no matter how maddening or revolting the amusement? So, yes, my dad nailed it."[22]

Amusing Ourselves to Death holds up well after all these years. References to television shows and celebrities of the 1990s sometimes demand a quick search on Wikipedia (Neil might have loved Wikipedia, or at least been amused by its pretensions). But the book's central argument, that the forms of entertainment media—and the delivery systems themselves—have slowly distorted our habits of mind and steadily atrophied our ability and willingness to engage with each other as responsible citizens, cannot easily be dismissed. The rise and dominance of television in the daily lives of billions of people in the last half of the twentieth century, Neil wrote, had rendered it a "meta-medium," a technology that contained, structured, altered, and delivered many if not all previous media forms. Television had become by 1985, as Facebook is on the verge of becoming in 2018, "an instrument that directs not only our knowledge of the world, but our knowledge of ways of knowing as well."[23]

Neil warned us to pay close attention to the television because it not only dominated any room in which it sat but had been absorbed into it. Television had become almost ubiquitous, expected, and unremarkable. By the late twentieth century television had become what Roland Barthes called a "myth," Neil wrote. "[Barthes] means by myth a way of understanding the world that is not problematic, that are not fully conscious of, that seems, in a word, natural. A myth is a way of thinking so deeply embedded in our consciousness that it is invisible." Once we were no longer fascinated by the presence of the television or surprised by its arrival, and it no longer had its special place in our homes, we were no longer able to remember life without it and thus deeply examine its effects on us.[24]

One of my motivations for writing this book, it should not surprise you, is to spark just such a conversation before Facebook becomes a myth and we can't imagine life without it. I fear I may be too late.

Neil inspired my lines of questioning and broadened my vision. But he did not convert me to the faith. Neil was an "orthodox" media ecologist. I am a "reform" media ecologist. Orthodox media ecologists believe that powerful new technologies such as writing and radio fundamentally change human beings. Neil, like his intellectual yogi, Marshall McLuhan, was a technological determinist. He believed that as a powerful or dominant technology enters a culture or society, it not only restructures daily life but deeply alters the cognitive capacities of the members of that society. That change happens gradually, orthodox media ecologists argue. But it happens profoundly, such that we can mark or classify the members of those societies by the technologies that structure their thought and communication. The technologies come first; the mental and social features come from the technologies. It's a strong, simple line of causation.[25]

McLuhan's technological determinism has influenced many recent writers and thinkers, from techno-optimist Clay Shirky to techno-pessimist

Nicholas Carr. Among the many problems with adopting this form of strong determinism is that it leads one to believe that when a new technology becomes so deeply embedded, it shifts society in such a way as to allow for few surprises, let alone corrections or reversions to old habits of mind. And by focusing on a technology at the exclusion of (and distinct from) economic and political factors one can generate a monocausal explanation for a complex series of changes. Another problem with technological determinists is their willingness to promote new technologies to correct for the problems created by the last technologies, as if that strategy could have profound influences on the human condition. I call this concept "techno-fundamentalism." It's rampant. Mark Zuckerberg, among many other wealthy and powerful people, articulates techno-fundamentalism with regularity.[26]

The relationships among culture, politics, economics, and technology are dynamic, synergistic, and unpredictable. You will not read in the pages that follow that Facebook's algorithms caused some calamity, some revolution, or some social change. Facebook is made up of people (those who develop and maintain Facebook as well as those who use it) and computer code. Its code is shaped by people, and people are shaped by code. I view technologies as indistinct from the people who design them, maintain them, and use them and the cultures, societies, economic, and political spheres in which they operate. There are, however, specific actors who are worthy of critical examination. These include institutions that invent and wield technologies, like some of our best-known global companies.[27]

The habit of mind that I shared with Neil is one committed to looking at media as an ecosystem—embedded within human relations and influencing human relations. Neil and I always differed on how much to consider factors beyond the medium in question. As you will see throughout this book, I trace how media systems are shaped by human relations, prejudices, ideologies, and political power as much as how media shape those phenomena. Neil saw the biases of technologies as fairly fixed, clearly identifiable, and powerful. I find such biases contingent on many factors, including how people choose to deploy and alter technologies once they have them in their hands. In my view, there is no distance between "technology" and "culture." Technology is an essential element of and force within culture. Culture forges technologies. And so on.

Despite following my curiosity and the academic market from American intellectual and cultural history into the study of digital media and communication, from Twain to Twitter, I am still a historian by method and temperament. I'm just a historian of the last ten minutes. This book, like my previous works, is a narrative argument compiled on the foundation of primary testimony and secondary documents of the moment. I have spent years among the finest scholars of social and digital media. I have interviewed, debated, and conversed with hundreds of engineers, lawyers, activists, and business leaders. Unlike more journalistic accounts or some recent caustic extended essays on Silicon Valley and social media, this work relies on my measured judgment of the social science, cultural assumptions, and public rhetoric that we use to assess Facebook and its environment. And unlike many of the notable titles that have been published in recent years about Facebook, social media, and Silicon Valley, this book takes a global and multinational view. While Neil focused his analyses on the mainstream culture of the United States and its dominant Western intellectual tradition, often deploying a universalizing tone, I prefer to view media ecosystems with an awareness of specific conditions around the world. Facebook has universalizing tendencies and embodies a globalist ambition. But it does not work the same way in Phnom Penh as it does in Philadelphia. Despite my differences with Neil on our visions of the ecological study of media, I've come to realize over the past two decades that he was more right than wrong. His habits of mind, his powers of observation, and his commitment to constant inquiry led him and his friends and students into some enlightened places.[28]

THE MISEDUCATION OF MARK ZUCKERBERG

Just two weeks after Neil passed away, a young man in Cambridge, Massachusetts, named Mark Zuckerberg hacked together a simple service using the Harvard network. He called it Facemash. It was Zuckerberg's first effort to mine the collective power of collective expression on a website.

Facemash would get Zuckerberg some early notoriety at Harvard for asking students to judge each other based on their relative attractiveness.[29] Its simultaneous popularity and notoriety over just a few days online would lead to his ability to conceive of the phenomenon that someday would remind everyone that Neil Postman really had been on to something back in the 1980s, before most people had even heard of the internet. Just thirteen weeks after Facemash debuted, in early February 2004, Facebook launched as a Harvard-only social network.[30]

I've never met Mark Zuckerberg. Nor do I expect to. But through immersion in transcripts of hundreds of his speeches and interviews and dozens of essays, articles, and Facebook posts issued under his name, I must concur with many writers who have spent time with him: Zuckerberg is a deeply thoughtful, sincere, idealistic, and concerned person. Zuckerberg's character could not be further from the manipulative, aggressive, inarticulate, and single-minded portrayal he received in the 2011 David Fincher film *The Social Network*.[31]

Reading transcripts of Zuckerberg's interviews and speeches left me with another, less generous conclusion. Mark Zuckerberg is profoundly uneducated. He lacks an appreciation for nuance, complexity, contingency, or even difficulty. Zuckerberg has a vibrant moral passion. But he lacks a historical sense of the horrible things that humans are capable of doing to each other and the planet. He is a brilliant builder. But when someone gets that rich that fast, powerful people start taking him seriously about matters on which he lacks any understanding.

Zuckerberg has long fancied himself a hacker among hackers. He embraces the old hacker tenets of constant iteration—no product is ever finished, and with more data and better code we can improve anything. His most famous order to his staff was "move fast and break things." This was a call to think and act rashly and boldly, and fix the mistakes later. This adage has guided everything Facebook has done since its inception. Now that it finally faces massive global public scrutiny for promiscuously exporting user data to unseemly companies, for undermining the news industry, and for—among other things—fostering genocide, it seems that Zuckerberg has indeed broken things. Despite spending his life building the most pervasive media technology phenomenon in the world, Zuckerberg seems to understand nothing about media or technology. Perhaps this book can help him.

CONFESSIONS

For a man older than fifty, I could be considered a social media power user. I have accounts with WhatsApp, LinkedIn, and Snapchat. I run an Instagram feed for my dog. I used to have an Orkut account before Google shut it down. I'm an early adopter. I explored Friendster back in 2002. I had a MySpace profile by 2003. And when Facebook became available to those with an @nyu.edu email address in 2004 I signed up immediately. I didn't think deeply about social networking in those days. But its importance in my life and the lives of more than two billion others has forced me to master it. I have way too many Facebook Friends and rely too much on Twitter for publicity and public affirmation. I'm deft at working the settings and features of Facebook. I can launch a successful publicity campaign on Facebook in no time at all. You might have discovered this book through advertisements for it on Facebook or Twitter. Or someone you trust might have shared a review or excerpt of it.

I have discovered many fascinating works of thought and culture via Facebook. Through Facebook I have befriended people I have not spoken to since we were small children. I have followed friends' (and Friends') children as they have grown up and left home. I have mourned the passing of more than a few friends and dear relatives. Through Facebook I reveled in the collective appreciation of the genius of David Bowie and Prince when they passed away too soon. And I have faced down threats and harassment by those who took offense at my family's presence in the United States of America. I have learned a lot through Facebook. I might have even taught a few people a few things through Facebook. I have certainly engaged in enough arguments on Facebook to have bored or annoyed most of my Friends. They have stuck with me anyway. As much as anyone in the world

I have lived my life through Facebook. Facebook has been the operating system of my life.

What does it mean for a person to live through Facebook? What are the consequences for a family, a community, most of a nation, and about 30 percent of the population of the world to live through Facebook? What if Facebook becomes the operating system of all of our lives?

1

The Pleasure Machine

strolled to the rear of the coach cabin on a flight from Frankfurt, Germany, to Charlotte, North Carolina. It was October 2016. I needed to stretch my legs and shake myself out of the drowsy effects of staring at a video screen for four straight hours. I enjoy long, international flights more than I should. They are bad for my body and my mind. But I get to indulge myself with foods I rarely stoop to eating, like chips and cookies. And I take the opportunity to watch films I would rarely spend the time or money to see in a theater, such as Marvel or DC Comics superhero stories. Still, I felt a bit guilty and a lot groggy, and my body sagged from underuse and abuse. I walked, stretched a bit, and then turned back toward my seat in row eight. I most often sit in the front of the coach section, close enough to business class to resent my cramped discomfort but far from most of the foot traffic that can annoy those farther back. I am that guy who bumps your shoulder as I stumble past you in light turbulence.

The stroll forward in the darkened cabin revealed a curious popular obsession. In a cabin of about 250 passengers I saw the very same glow coming from the raised hands of about fifty of them. I counted them because the scene was so odd. On mobile devices—phones and tablets—these fifty passengers were all playing Candy Crush Saga, the most popular game ever launched on the Facebook platform. The game, which also lives outside of Facebook on the Apple OS or Google Android mobile operating system, asks players to move different styles and colors of candy across a grid to line up three of a kind. As candy gets crushed, the player earns points. As players clear boards of candy, they move up levels. The more advanced levels, as with almost every mobile game, offer less frequent victories and thus sporadic positive feedback to the player. People who play Candy Crush Saga tend to stare at their screens, mouths agape, disconnected from their immediate environments. It's an image that does not seem far from narcotic.

I was tempted to sneer at, or at least feel sorry for, my fellow passengers. But I suspended my grumpy judgment just long enough to watch them. They were focused, not numb. They weren't exactly happy, but they were not uncomfortable. In fact, the Candy Crush Saga players seemed to have adjusted to the indignities of coach air travel better than those of us who chose books or movies. What most strongly struck me was the fact that they all played the same game. I didn't see anyone playing Subway Surfers or Clash of the Clans. Perhaps those games are more the domain of children and teens, while people of all ages seem to enjoy Candy Crush Saga. "Enjoy" might be the wrong word. Players immerse themselves in the game experience. But no one jumps up for joy. No one offers high-fives to a friend for candy well crushed. Their facial expressions remained calm and their body positions steady. They had delved into something that could help them cope with the long flight.

Does this game make them happy? Does this game bring them pleasure? Is this game fun? I have to concede that I don't get any reward out of Candy Crush Saga, Clash of Clans, Words with Friends, or—despite my love of sports—Top Eleven Football Manager. That's just me, though. My inability to generate pleasure from Facebook-based or mobile games only drives me to try to understand them better.

After lurking behind passengers for a bit too long, I sheepishly returned to my seat. I opened a small bag of potato chips. I inhaled all the chips within two minutes while watching one of the Captain America films (I forget which one). As soon as the Airbus A330 touched down in Charlotte I turned on my phone and logged into Facebook. I posted my observations about the proliferation of Candy Crush Saga among my fellow passengers. Within five minutes, just before I had to turn off my phone to go through customs, I checked Facebook to see if anyone had liked or commented on my post. I was in no position to judge anyone's transatlantic distractions.

Despite all the problems it facilitates and all the hatred it amplifies, Facebook is valuable. People derive value from reconnecting with old acquaintances, interacting with new Friends, finding causes to join, watching funny videos, and playing games. We should not slight these pleasures and services. These, and the puppy and baby pictures, are why many if not most Facebook users subscribed in the first place. Facebook lowers the transaction costs of maintaining relationships across great distances. Notices of life changes come to us, driven by Facebook's algorithm that structures these interactions. Facebook wants us to remain engaged with Facebook as deeply and for as much time as possible. It captures our attention as the price of the service. But we gladly pay attention—a lot of attention. We don't do that for frivolous reasons.

Nonetheless, Facebook manipulates us. Every aspect of its design is meant to draw us back to the flow of images and emotions that constitute the News Feed on our Facebook pages. Facebook has developed techniques that it hopes measure our relative happiness or satisfaction with aspects of the service. Facebook researchers have been trying to identify and thus maximize exposure to the things that push us to be happier and minimize exposure to things that cause us anxiety or unhappiness. Much of what we encounter, including many of our responses and interactions, leads us to be sad, frustrated, angry, and exhausted. Yet we keep coming back. And we can't seem to quit.

In December 2017 the leaders of Facebook finally conceded what mental health experts and social media scholars had been speculating for some time: spending too much time barraged by a constant flow of human misery and news of the world could make people anxious and unhappy. "We want Facebook to be a place for meaningful interactions with your friends and family—enhancing your relationships offline, not detracting from them," said the post on the Facebook Newsroom site. "After all, that's what Facebook has always been about. This is important as we know that a person's health and happiness relies heavily on the strength of their relationships." Facebook researchers surveyed some of the scholarly literature on social media use and well-being and concluded that the key to staying deeply engaged with Facebook is to interact more with other people rather than letting a depressing News Feed flow past.

Toward that end Facebook reduced the frequency of news content in the News Feed and promoted posts that generate significant comments. In January 2018 Facebook announced it would begin surveying a sample of users to rate news sources in terms of credibility, thus absolving itself of that duty. Facebook officials were never comfortable conceding that their algorithms effectively edit the human experience for more than two billion people. They have yet to concede that Facebook, like the human beings who built it and use it, is political. They made a firm move to try to make Facebook a pleasurable experience filled with both friends and Friends, as well as family, puppies, and babies. Still, the response to this problem of too much Facebook seems to be for people to engage more with Facebook.[1]

The thing is, studying "happiness" is futile. No one really knows what makes people happy in general or even if the concept of happiness is measurable and useful. Psychologists and economists who study happiness, or, as they often call it, affective well-being, recognize that the components of and influences on "happiness" are subjective and often culturally determined. So rather than come up with some universal standard or method, they rely on self-reported scores of happiness. We don't all have easy-to-read happiness meters in our heads. And there are not other objective measurements of our bodies that correlate to our affective states. So research subjects are asked to rate their states on some scale, often 1 to 3 or maybe 1 to 10. This, as economist Deirdre McCloskey points out, is unscientific. Those who gather such data deploy "non-interval scales" to measure happiness—not happy, happy, very happy. But that's like asking people how tall they feel—short, average, or tall—rather than measuring them with an "interval scale," like a number of centimeters, allowing one person to be compared to another or one time to be compared to another. This obsession with measuring and maximizing "happiness" goes back at least as far as Jeremy Bentham's early justifications for utilitarianism: maximizing happiness (he considered pleasure to equate to happiness) for the greatest number of people should be the core function of state policy. We can't maximize something we can't count. So for more than two centuries social scientists have been making up ways to count it. Facebook, under the sway of the ideology of quantification and utilitarianism, is constantly trying to gather data and quantify our moods. It's even sponsored academic studies to show it can slightly manipulate our moods via choices in what shows up in our News Feed.[2]

SNACK FOOD

If I offered you a choice between four cupcakes and a bag of potato chips, you would most likely choose to eat a cupcake. You would also most likely stop eating after one cupcake. A hungry person might consume two. If it was an exceptionally good cupcake, you might make a remark to that effect. If it was one of the finest cupcakes you had ever eaten, you might even tell your friends about it.

No one has ever said, "I ate the most amazing potato chip yesterday. I waited in a line for it." More significant is that, despite the fact that no single chip makes much of an impression, few if any human beings can stop eating at just one. Had I only offered you a bag of chips, there is a greater-than-zero chance you would have finished the entire bag. Cupcakes can be enriching, edifying, memorable experiences. Thin, fried, salted potatoes cannot. Yet we find value in both, derive pleasure from both, and gladly pay for and consume both.

Facebook engages us like a bag of chips. It offers frequent, low-level pleasures. It rarely engages our critical faculties with the sort of depth that demands conscious articulation of the experience. We might turn to Facebook in a moment of boredom and look up an hour later, wondering where that hour went and why we spent it on an experience so unremarkable yet not unpleasant. And even if we feel ashamed at the time spent on Facebook, we all too willingly click back to it at the next moment of stagnation or distraction in our day. If we post a photograph or message to our friends, perhaps crack a joke or render a comment that we hope others will find interesting, we engage with Facebook at a more immersive level than merely perusing others' posts. We then offer Facebook feedback. We change Facebook just a little bit with each interaction. It responds to us in subtle ways, offering us the possibility that our next interaction with Facebook will be slightly more pleasurable than the last. Now we are drawn back in. How many likes did my joke get? How many insightful replies did my political post generate? Did my GoFundMe appeal for help with my medical condition echo and generate donations? Did anyone I tagged take me up on the Ice Bucket Challenge? Does anyone get my jokes or care what I think? Do I matter?

It's easy to blame ourselves for this habitual return to the vortex of photos, jokes, news stories, appeals, and advertisements. I've certainly scolded myself for an hour or more blown on a flow of dog videos, family updates, shallow political expressions, and pleas for funds. Every one of those items has some value to me, just as each potato chip delivers some pleasure, some flavor. I savor them. But I lose count. And upon reflection I feel just horrible. But the thing is, snack foods are explicitly designed to make us behave this way. Food producers have studied, mastered, and tinkered with the ratios of salt, sugar, and fat to keep us coming back, even when the taste of much of the food is unremarkable. Facebook is designed to be habit-forming in just the same way.[3]

A SKINNER BOX

Facebook, as novelist and internet freedom advocate Cory Doctorow has explained, is like a Skinner box. It conditions us by intermittent reinforcement. "You give a rat a lever that dispenses a food pellet every time and he'll just get one when he's hungry," Doctorow told an audience in 2011. "But you give him a lever that only sometimes dispenses a food pellet, he'll just hit it until he runs out of steam because he's not sure what the trick is and he thinks he's going to get it if he just keeps on banging on that lever." Doctorow argues that Facebook's feedback mechanism is designed to work like such a system. "The more you embroider the account of your life, the more you disclose about your personal life, the more reinforcement—intermittent reinforcement—you get about your life," Doctorow said. "Every now and again you will post something that you think will be quite a bombshell, like 'I'm thinking of dropping out of Maths,' and no one cares. But then you say something like 'Bought some lovely new shoes' and you put up a picture of them and you'll get a million of your mates turning up to tell you how awful they are." Doctorow argues that Facebook conditions us through instant, constant, low-level feedback.[4]

The psychologist B. F. Skinner achieved great notoriety in the 1930s and 1940s by proposing that animals, and thus humans, could be conditioned to engage in repetitive behavior through the delivery of stimuli—positive or negative. This concept, "operant conditioning," could be demonstrated by placing rats into what Skinner called an "operant conditioning chamber" and just about everybody else called a "Skinner box."[5]

Skinner and his followers demonstrated how operant conditioning could alter behaviors with some resilience, generating widespread concerns about potential political and commercial manipulation. Despite those concerns, Skinner's observations had great impact among designers who hoped to create machines and systems that captured attention. We see operant conditioning at work in casinos, especially in the design of electronic gambling machines. But we've not seen any operant-conditioning technology in widespread use among human beings work quite as well as Facebook.[6]

Like casinos, slot machines, and potato chips, Facebook is designed to keep you immersed, to disorient you just enough so you lose track of the duration and depth of your immersion in the experience, and to reward you just enough that you often return, even when you have more edifying, rewarding, or pleasurable options for your time and effort within your reach. This is not an accident.

Skinner's work has affected many areas of our lives, and it seems to be growing in influence. Technology scholar Natasha Dow Schüll describes both the design of casino floors and the video poker machines that now dominate the gambling industry as embodiments of Skinner's observations about operant conditioning. They are, she explains, immensely profitable

Skinner boxes. Like Skinner's rats, those who play electronic gambling machines receive cues: they sometimes win, and they often almost win. This triggers a feeling of "cognitive regret," as though the player herself failed instead of the machine tricking or failing the player. So the player immediately pumps more money and time into the system. "It makes you want to press the button and continue," one gambler told Schüll. "You live in hope because you got close and you want to keep trying. You get to learn the pattern and just get it right."[7]

In her book *Addiction by Design: Machine Gambling in Las Vegas,* Schüll describes how patrons of casinos find themselves enthralled, attached, entranced, and ultimately drained of time, money, energy, and ambition by gambling machines and the carefully designed rooms in which they sit. "In the beginning there was excitement about winning," one patron told Schüll. "But the more I gambled the wiser I got about my chances. Wiser, but also weaker, less able to stop. Today when I win—and I do win, from time to time—I just put it back in the machines. The thing people never understand is that I'm not playing to win."[8]

It's not completely fair to equate the coercive tactics and pernicious effects of casinos and gambling machines to those of mobile phones and Facebook. Facebook has never emptied anyone's retirement account or— to my knowledge—broken up families and rendered people homeless the way that casinos have. For individuals using Facebook, the stakes are lower in terms of potential harms, temptations, and rewards. In fact, the personal rewards of Facebook use are often significant and the harms to individuals slight at most. And despite the collective harms of Facebook usage that I assert throughout this book, gambling has done more damage to economies and politics this decade than Facebook would in a hundred years. Casinos contributed directly to the rise of Donald Trump, despite the fact that he seems to be the only casino owner in history unable to run one profitably. Casinos made him famous, and several wealthy casino owners funded his campaign. Facebook's influence on our current political dilemmas is, as we will see later, complex, subtle, and significant. Facebook, in contrast to casinos, is not directly responsible for much, even as it contributes to and amplifies many unfortunate phenomena.[9]

Nevertheless, the invocations of casinos and gambling machines here are still apt. We have seen a proliferation of casinos across the world along with video and algorithmically driven gambling machines at the very moment that other algorithmically driven machines have come to occupy our hands, our minds, our time, our work, our family obligations, and our money. Schüll posits that our comfort with the tactile omnipresence of electronic devices has contributed to the "cultural normalization" of video gambling machines. The interfaces are so familiar that our bodies seem to melt into them, making users more comfortable when using them than when they step away.[10]

Another comparison is in order. Facebook, like snack foods, cigarettes, and gambling machines, is designed for "stickiness." Unlike these other things, Facebook is designed for "social stickiness." Every acquisition that Facebook has made has been in the interest of keeping more people interacting with Facebook services in different ways to generate more data. Not long ago there were two interesting photography-based social media applications that were competing for users and investment, Hipstamatic and Instagram. Instagram ultimately overtook Hipstamatic as the dominant mobile-based photography sharing application, despite Hipstamatic's early entry into the market. Both applications offered similar filters and features, but Instagram had a social function. Friends and followers could tag each other and signal approval to each other. Mark Zuckerberg understood that this social feature would make Instagram irresistible to people. He had already seen photography and the social potential of images spike interest in Facebook. So he bought Instagram for $1 billion in cash and stock.[11]

The experience of posting images to Facebook and Instagram is habit-forming. People often desire approval, or at least acknowledgment, from their peers. Clicking "like" on a photo says, "I'm thinking about you." A comment could indicate even deeper attention. The commerce in attention—a sort of "gift economy" of time and energy—is powerful and valuable. Like a gambling machine, rewards (likes and comments) are intermittent and unpredictable. A photo posted to Instagram could garner dozens of responses, while the same one posted on Facebook could generate none. The algorithms that determine which photos pop up on whose feeds in both services are opaque and unpredictable—just like the algorithms that fix the cards in video poker or fruit on a fruit machine.[12]

The same insight that sparked Zuckerberg's interest in Instagram launched Facebook in the first place. From the beginning he seemed to intuit the power of the drive for quantified and repeatable social affirmation. Four years before Zuckerberg started Facebook a couple of Silicon Valley friends set up a simple web page that allowed social feedback. It was called HotOrNot.com. It launched in late 2000 and became a raging hit by early 2001. HotOrNot.com followed a couple of earlier but similar services, RateMyFace.com and AmIHot.com. So the idea of rating others' attractiveness—in fact, voluntarily seeking such judgment from others—was in the air among those who followed web culture in the late 1990s. The success of HotOrNot.com showed Zuckerberg and many others that there was a significant number of people willing to subject their images to judgment and possible humiliation for the slight and sporadic reward of a signal of approval. This simple insight was strange but profound. It meant that many people were all too willing to put themselves through this risky and seemingly irrational social process and that even more people would get pleasure out of judging other people—often cruelly.[13]

In November 2003 Zuckerberg delved deeper into what would become a lifelong obsession with social engineering. He went beyond HotOrNot.com by posting photos of Harvard students without their permission on a service that he created just for the Harvard network. It was called Facemash. Zuckerberg had broken into the servers of various Harvard student houses to lift official university identification photos and download them to his laptop. His computer code would position two photos next to each other and ask users to choose the more attractive of them. It was a facial—and superficial—version of a standard computer science process of algorithmically sorting values. In this case, a human instead of an algorithm executed the judgment in real time and the computer merely tallied and displayed the results. Within hours after Zuckerberg sent a link to the service to just a few friends, more than 450 Harvard students had clicked on the link and voted on their peers' photos twenty-two thousand times. Zuckerberg claimed at the time he did not intend his experiment to reach a general audience or to generate so much attention. He quickly apologized to the Harvard community for violating the security of the house servers and the privacy and dignity of his fellow students. "I don't see how it can go back online," Zuckerberg told the *Harvard Crimson* in the aftermath. "Issues about violating people's privacy don't seem to be surmountable. The primary concern is hurting people's feelings. I'm not willing to risk insulting anyone." This process of pushing the boundaries of propriety and of others' expectations would repeat itself for many years as Zuckerberg moved from his failed Facemash experiment to the Harvard-only social network TheFacebook to Facebook.com.[14]

The impressive thing about Facemash, despite its unoriginality in the shadow of the better-known HotOrNot.com, was its rapid proliferation. Its "socialness" made the service go beyond Zuckerberg's control and put him under scrutiny from the Harvard administration. But it taught him the tricks of social stickiness. Facemash was Zuckerberg's first experiment in social engineering. And it demonstrated to him how habit-forming such designs could be. None of these lessons were unique to Zuckerberg. At the same time that Zuckerberg was enraging and enthralling Harvard students, designers of games and other web-based platforms were trying their best to hook users by hooking other users—exponentially increasing the attractiveness of their systems. The principles of habit generation through algorithmically driven social interaction have informed some of the most influential inventions and industries of the twenty-first century, including mobile games such as Candy Crush Saga, the very mobile devices on which people play Candy Crush Saga, and the Facebook platform itself.[15]

A SERIES OF PHOTOGRAPHS

I just logged into my Facebook account for the first time in a month. I had to deactivate it to make progress on this book. Like many people, I can't resist the siren call of attention, affection, and occasional derision that greets me through that series of boxes. Here is what I saw there, in descending order. I first saw a six-year-old "memory"—a photograph of my daughter (then five years old) walking our dog Ellie (now, sad to say, deceased) around the rotunda at the University of Virginia (Facebook presented this photo with an odd introduction: "Siva, we care about you and the memories you share here"). Then came a photograph of a graduate school colleague (and friend) proudly displaying the book that she worked for years to write. Next flowed an image of a train station posted by a colleague (and friend) commenting on the relatively pathetic state of passenger trains in the United States. Next was a solicitation for a donation to the University of Virginia School of Law. Then I saw a clip from the 1972 film *Midnight Cowboy* to advertise a festival about New York in the 1970s playing at the Film Forum. That was followed by a series of photographs of one of my co-workers and his son as they drove across the United States. Then came another set of photographs of a friend's fiftieth-birthday celebration. Next, unwelcomed, was a propaganda video from the National Rifle Association urging members to aggressively confront people like me because we are undermining the United States. Much more welcomed was a series of photos of fruits and cheeses from a Paris market, taken by a writer I have never met but admire (a paradigmatic Facebook Friend relationship). That was followed by a story from the *Dallas Morning News* about a woman—the aunt of an old friend—who has worked for fifty years in the same restaurant in Junction, Texas. Next came a photograph of a friend's child who is smiling because he just received a lovely New York Yankees jersey as a gift. That was followed by an advertisement from the *New York Times* using a large image of a crossword puzzle to urge me to subscribe (I have subscribed to the print edition without a break since about 1995). Next I saw a big photo of singer Dolly Parton smiling, part of a story in the *Guardian* by another writer whom I admire about how important Parton is to everyday feminism. By the time I glanced away at something beyond my screen I took in a collection of photos of my nieces as they toured New York City with their grandmother.

If you were to take the time to examine the nature of the material in my News Feed, it would seem like a diverse collection. Some of it is political. Some of it is purely commercial. Much of it is of some professional interest to me because it was posted by employees, former colleagues, or professional associates. My favorites among this material are from people I love dearly, like my nieces. And, of course, Facebook itself reposted and thus reminded me of my dear departed dog and a sunny day when my daughter was much smaller and had yet to discover Instagram. Some of the material, such as that old photo of my daughter and dog, tugged at my heart. The National Rifle Association video angered me. The three-year-old in a Yankees jersey made me smile. Nothing prompted me to think deeply. Everything made me feel something.

Most of these posts have substantial strings of comments beneath them. And Facebook reveals a slice of that commentary on the main page that greets me. Much of the comment strings are composed of GIFs, short moving images that repeat every second or so. Other comments are just images, often with text superimposed on them. But if you were to scroll through my News Feed the way I do most of the time, paying scant attention to details, flashing on the big words and images, liking, sharing, and commenting without reading the article to which the post links, you would experience Facebook as an endless strand of disconnected and decontextualized images.

The overall experience of the Facebook News Feed is—regardless of the type of content rendered—of a series of photographs. Even the video clips that begin playing without sound seem more like still images as the viewer scrolls past them. Large photographs anchor the newspaper articles (in this case, a lovely portrait of Dolly Parton) such that the headline of the article serves more as a caption for the photo than an introduction to a long collection of sentences. Links to text either fail to grab one's attention or serve only as a photograph of text, more like a billboard than an article.[16]

That the Facebook News Feed acts like a scroll of framed photographs means that we are limited in our ability to generate deep understanding of the content as it sits on our feed. If we clicked on a story because the image and caption intrigue us, we could gain insight, knowledge, appreciation, and understanding. But how often do we click? And on which items? If we click on none of the items that our News Feed offers (a common occurrence), then we only experience this flow of images. The images spark feelings, both positive and negative. They spark comments and reactions. They even spark actions such as sharing the content on one's own page and thus broadcasting it to some subset (selected by Facebook) of our Facebook

Friends. The experience of scrolling through these images guards against deep interaction with the content outside of the Facebook walled garden. Facebook invites us to comment within Facebook, rather than on the original source pages of the content. The News Feed also promises more—and perhaps more significant—emotional stimuli just a bit lower on the feed. Clicking, reading, and engaging with text outside of Facebook carry a cost. We suspend our pleasure flow by stopping to read something. When we return to the News Feed, it might have moved on. We might have missed the cutest puppy, the most alarming crime story, or the latest family news.

Neil Postman reminded us that the advent of the telegraph, with its radically truncated economy of prose, created a whole new language—that of headlines: "sensational, fragmented, impersonal." Postman blamed the telegraph for introducing us to this choppy, discontinuous method of learning that things happen, often far away, with no clear way of making sense of them or weighing their relative importance to our lives or future. "To the telegraph, intelligence meant knowing *of* lots of things, not knowing *about* them."[17]

Newspapers that expanded in number and influence across the world just after and directly because of the telegraph, which allowed for something close to a global awareness, offered some depth and response to the tick-tock nature of the flow of headlines. The context, the adjacent facts, and perhaps the historical background to a story were right there on the same page as the headline. The text of the article had the potential to mitigate the damage that headlines could do to our ability to think about the world, and the wealthier or more responsible newspapers offered the most context and knowledge for readers. No one could offer data saying that people stopped reading after the first hundred words or so. No one could say that a story from Pittsburgh generated more interest (or displayed more "relevance," as they say at Facebook) to an individual reader or an entire community than a story from St. Petersburg. But now, through Facebook, not only do we get just a headline and a scoreboard of "engagement" beneath each item, but the headline is framed and structured in such a way as to deliver as little knowledge as possible. The most successful of them tease or provoke the reader, rather than inform. Juxtaposed with much more dominant and powerful images, the headlines become even less informative than they were in newspapers. After all, in newspapers one did not need to click to read the story. It was right there. And even newspapers with bright, big photos on every page, such as *USA Today* or the British tabloids, offer a much more textual experience than that of scrolling through the series of images that is the Facebook News Feed.

More than forty years ago Susan Sontag described the effect photographs have on our ability to make sense of the world. She used language that almost perfectly describes the problem with Facebook. Photographs have an innate claim to represent "reality" objectively and truthfully. The frequent Facebook comment "Picture or it didn't happen" shows that photography, even in the age of Photoshop editing and Snapchat filters and animations, still carries that power of documentation. Photography collapses any ambiguity of fact claims, questions of context, or helpful framing of a dispute. Every photograph is necessarily and almost by definition out of context. Photographs carry no moral claims. They make no arguments. They don't compare and contrast. They don't by themselves deliver plots or tell stories. But they do tug at our deepest sympathies regardless of the messiness of the world outside the frame. Photographs do odd work over space and time. They bring what happened just then—perhaps yesterday, perhaps in 1914—into our present, leaving us to deal with the image in our own frameworks of judgment and relevance. When photographs scroll across your field of vision as you work your way through your Facebook News Feed they become, in the words of art historian John Berger, advertisements for themselves.[18]

Decontextualized—or, rather, recontextualized as part of a Facebook News Feed—photographs that once carried significant emotional power (even if, as Sontag argued, they lacked explanatory power) lose it as well. Major works of photography can become just symbols of their former power, referring to how they once mattered and now only matter to and through Facebook. When in 2016 Facebook removed a post from the Facebook site of a Norwegian newspaper, *Aftenposten*, that included one of the most famous images of the twentieth century—a naked Vietnamese girl, running and crying in pain because she had just been sprayed with napalm—it received widespread criticism for its clumsy methods of choosing what counts as indecent and worthy of deletion. The image, captured by photographer Nick Ut, of the girl, Phan Thị Kim Phúc, violated the terms of service for Facebook. Facebook's algorithmic scanners noted that the image featured a girl without clothes. In the simplest, most literal sense, it had to go from Facebook. The uproar about the deletion was fascinating, as was Facebook's official reaction. First, the decision was simplistic and unconcerned with the context of the photograph. It ignored the historical and news value of the image. And it reminded people of Facebook's power to limit the spread of certain content or alter the meaning of a message posted on Facebook. But lost in the uproar was the fact that Facebook did not remove the image from the world. It still existed in books, on hundreds of websites searchable by Google, and in newspapers and magazines. Critics were eager to call Facebook to account for a clumsy decision. Clearly, the uproar demonstrated the centrality that Facebook plays in the circulation of images. After the protests and news coverage Facebook unblocked the site that had featured the image. Sheryl Sandberg, Facebook's chief operating officer, explained the error with a stock phrase: "These are difficult decisions and we don't always get it right." She was right on both counts. The image of nine-year-old Phan Thị Kim Phúc carries historical meaning in other contexts, such as in history books. On Facebook, it is now merely a curiosity and a spark to an interrogation of how clumsy Facebook can be when faced with difficult choices at the scale of a global publisher of content from more than 2.2 billion people. [19]

"Recently," Sontag wrote in 1977, "photography has become almost as widely practiced an amusement as sex and dancing—which means that, like every mass art form, photography is not practiced as an art. It is mainly a social rite, a defense against anxiety, and a tool of power." Sontag understood the desire to photograph scenes and events of one's life. Photography is, she wrote, "a way of certifying experience, [but] taking photographs is also a way of refusing it—by limiting experience to a search for the photogenic, by converting experience into an image, a souvenir.... The very activity of taking pictures is soothing, and assuages general feelings of disorientation that are likely to be exacerbated by travel."[20]

Sontag passed away in 2004, the year Facebook debuted and three years before the first Apple iPhone. By 2004 most mobile phones already carried rudimentary cameras. And by 2017 the quality of cameras on most mobile devices rivaled that of the best amateur cameras of the twentieth century. By 2013 Facebook was receiving more than 350 million photographs every day. By 2015 people around the world uploaded an average of 1.8 billion digital images to all the major social media services each day—that adds up to 657 billion photos per year. It's safe to say that sex and dancing have not proliferated as much as photography has since Sontag noted this trend in 1977. Sontag would have understood the ways that Facebook's visual design triggers us to post images habitually, whether cute or horrifying, awe-inspiring or violent. "Like guns and cars, cameras are fantasy-machines whose use is addictive," Sontag wrote.[21]

PERFORMING POLITICS AND IDENTITY

In his two years at Harvard as a computer science major Mark Zuckerberg also dabbled in the study of classics. At his prep school, *Phillips Exeter Academy*, he studied ancient Hebrew, Latin, and Greek. He should have paid more attention to Aristotle. Aristotle, after all, was an early pioneer in the development of logic, the very foundation of the computer code that would 2,300 years later make Zuckerberg rich and powerful.[22]

Zuckerberg could have learned from Aristotle that different forms of friendship have distinct layers and values embedded in them, and operate by different norms. This might have helped Zuckerberg generate a more sophisticated sense of social relationships. We would not all be just Friends with each other and hundreds more. But the most valuable lesson Aristotle could have taught Zuckerberg was to think politically—to be political.

In *The Nicomachean Ethics*, Aristotle describes three types of friendship. The first is based on mutual utility. Both friends derive some benefit from each other. Aristotle acknowledges utility-based friendship as weak and disposable. It's contingent on the needs of each partner in the relationship. It can be easily dissolved or even forgotten. It's friendship of convenience and commerce. The second type of friendship is based on pleasure. Two people are drawn to each other by personality, mutual interest, or just a sense of affiliation. Pleasure-based friendship often grows among the young, as that stage of life is when passions and pleasures are at their highest level of importance, before responsibilities begin to weigh on people. This type of friendship lies somewhere between *eros*, or romantic love, and tribalism, or the bond forged by common experience or condition. Like the utility-based form of friendship, the pleasure-based form might evaporate as conditions in life change for the respective friends. The third and most significant form of friendship is based on recognition of goodness in another person. "Perfect friendship is the friendship of men who are good, and alike in virtue," Aristotle wrote. Such friends admire the other's character and help one another work toward the good life (whatever that may be). Friendships based on goodness are what Aristotle called the highest form of *philia* (φιλία), "brotherly love," and one of the highest forms of love. Aristotle argues that friendships based on goodness of character have the added benefits of encompassing the other two, shallower forms of friendship—they can be enriching and also useful and pleasurable. However, these deeper friendships don't just happen. They certainly don't emerge from a click and a few comments on Facebook. They are infrequent, Aristotle insists. They demand effort, patience, and wisdom.[23]

Whether Aristotle has accurately described the taxonomy of friendship is irrelevant to our examination of Facebook. What Aristotle gets right is that there are taxonomies of friendships. We do relate to different friends in different ways along different terms. We negotiate our levels of trust, the amount of time we invest in others, and the duration of the relationship. Not all friends are Friends, except on Facebook.

Aristotle observed that friendship was political. The polis was forged and supported by a lattice of these three kinds of friendship. A polis may function by resting merely on friendships of convenience and pleasure, but to thrive, a society must have deep, meaningful friendships that allow for virtue to flow forth. "Friendship seems to hold states together, and lawgivers to care more for it than for justice," Aristotle wrote in *The Nicomachean Ethics*. Aristotle based his conception of justice on fair exchange, and did the same for friendship. Friendships work because each friend gives as much as she or he receives. Justice and friendship depend on each other.[24]

Aristotle, famously, declared humans to be "political animals." By this he meant that the distinction, then prominent among Athenian philosophers, between nature (*physis*) and culture (*nomos*) was false. Human desires to deal with others, exert power over others, collaborate with each other, and socialize are essential phenomena, he posited. Humans could know no other way of being. But there was more to Aristotle's idea. Politics was not just a neutral manner of relating to one another. Politics and the formation and maintenance of a healthy polis led people to virtue. The political nature of humans might be essential, but the characteristics of the polis were to be constructed, contested, and debated. Politics have intentions, Aristotle argued. The best political communities operate by consensus or near universal agreement, what Aristotle called *homonoia*. Aristotle was most concerned with local practices and the concept of citizenship within Greek city-states. He did not envision his politics to be applicable to those who lived beyond the constellation of ancient Greece and were not joined by a common language or set of myths and religious practices. By 330 BCE, Alexander, Socrates's most notable and notorious student, ignored Aristotle's distinctions based on tribe (*ethnē*) and spread his rule to include and intertwine Greeks and Persians. Alexander in practice and the Cynics and Stoics in theory (later to influence St. Paul and St. Augustine of Hippo) promoted a very different vision of citizenship, one belonging to the entire world or humanity—cosmopolitanism.[25]

Had Zuckerberg considered the political nature of humans, he might have anticipated the ways that we would use Facebook to act out our politics and that there was a deep connection between how we relate to Friends and how we express and segregate ourselves politically. He might have seen that by creating a durable and ubiquitous forum for affiliation by interest and shared experience, he would enable the further tribalization of Facebook users into something less edifying than even warring Greek city-states. Had Zuckerberg considered the limitation of Aristotle's focus on the local (rather than global) polis, he might have considered that Facebook would be incapable of enriching a sense of global friendship or citizenship.

Aristotle could have shown Zuckerberg that if he wants to make the world "more open and connected" and then "bring the world closer together," the way he designed Facebook would work against those goals.

Zuckerberg, when discussing his company and its effects on the world, commits the same fallacy that Aristotle did when examining the natural world. Aristotle explains the function and structure of plants and animals by their ends (*telos*), or what they are meant to do. Teleology is the explanation of things based on what they are intended to do, not what they actually do. Zuckerberg assumes that Facebook performs a certain type of work in the world because he intended it to do that work. Again, a study of Aristotle's errors might have helped Zuckerberg pay more attention to how people actually use Facebook and how far that use is from his stated intentions. More important, Aristotle could have helped Zuckerberg realize from the start that governance matters. Any collection of friends (or Friends) must have clear and predictable rules by which to maintain itself. It took many years for Facebook to acknowledge and come to terms with the difficulty and complexity of this responsibility.[26]

One key to understanding why we do what we do on Facebook is to see our activity there, right down to choosing which news stories to share, as a public performance of our cultural affiliations. We share content regardless of its truth value or its educational value because of what it says about each of us. "I am the sort of person who would promote this expression" underlies every publication act on Facebook. The "sort of person" I might be might include geographic, musical, athletic, intellectual, or political attributes. We should never forget what Aristotle tells us: the animals who inhabit Facebook are fundamentally political. Their affiliations matter deeply. As circumstances change rapidly and economic and cultural factors churn all around, as platforms such as Facebook disorient us by scrambling our social, commercial, and political lives, we find comfort in declaring our tribal membership. We perform our tribal membership with what we post and share on Facebook. By posting a story that solidifies membership in a group, the act generates social value. If the veracity of that post is questioned, sticking by it, defending it, and criticizing the critic further demonstrate group loyalty. This, again, has social value, even if it has many other costs. Even when we post and share demonstrably false stories and claims we do so to declare our affiliation, to assert that our social bonds mean more to us than the question of truth. This fact should give us pause. How can we train billions of people to value truth over their cultural membership when the question of truth holds little at stake for them and the question of social membership holds so much? If Facebook wants to emphasize, as Zuckerberg declared late in 2017, that posts from family and Friends should mean more to us than posts from *National Geographic* or the *Wall Street Journal*, what hope is there for Facebook to be anything but a forum for tribalism, enhancing some simplistic version of "community" but harming democracy, science, and public health?[27]

The social aspect of social media trumps any effort to build or spread civic responsibility into the systems. Facebook is a pleasure machine. The pleasure is light and fleeting. That's what keeps us coming back. But Facebook is also an anxiety machine, an anger machine, and a resentment machine. The pleasure may be light and fleeting, but the resentment is deep and durable. There is more to this formula. Facebook attracts us, hooks us, encourages us to declare our affiliations, divides us, and tracks every single interaction along the way. Facebook's surveillance system is part of its pleasure system. They cannot be severed.

The Surveillance Machine

n February 2017 an active-duty U.S. Marine Corps cadet stood in line to check in for her new posting at Camp Lejeune, North Carolina. A male infantry Marine stood a few paces behind her. He secretly photographed her. He then posted the photos on a private Facebook page called "Marines United." A call went out for responses and for information about the cadet. Soon comments flooded the image posting on Facebook. The comments went beyond rude. Some suggested forced sexual acts. A few hours later someone, likely a former romantic partner, posted a photo to the group of the woman with her breasts exposed. A retired Marine named Thomas Brennan, working as a reporter for a not-for-profit website called The War Horse, had noticed that the Facebook group that had been founded to help Marines cope with the stresses of combat and return to civilian life had transformed itself into a source of "revenge porn," featuring links to Google Drive folders containing thousands of images of servicewomen from all branches of the U.S. military. A few days after Brennan published his report on the Facebook group, the Marine Corps managed to get the offensive photographs and links removed. The group was shut down by March. But the photos had spread among the group's members and now rested on the phones or hard drives of hundreds of Marines. Women have suffered harassment and ridicule within their workplaces and in their private lives. Those who discovered that their photos had circulated have been weighed down by fear of being humiliated in professional or even combat situations.[1]

This sort of surveillance and harassment occurs every day around the world. Men successfully exploit the power that visual exposure of women grants them. They coordinate humiliation on a massive scale, empowered by the ease, quality, and availability of small cameras attached to mobile devices linked to applications that promise rapid delivery to a targeted and motivated audience. "Social media" quickly become antisocial for the women who are targeted by this practice. Sometimes Facebook is involved. Sometimes Google services host the material. Some revenge porn, often images that originally were captured with the consent of the subject but later were distributed in anger by a former partner, ends up on sites devoted to the phenomenon. The ubiquity of powerful instruments that record images, videos, and sound has enabled malicious distribution of the most humiliating items, injuring the spirit, morale, comfort, and careers of millions of women. According to the research institute Data and Society, 4 percent of American women—and 10 percent of those under thirty years old—have been the victim of revenge porn.[2]

Every one of us who carries a camera attached to a mobile phone is an agent of surveillance. The camera, as Susan Sontag told us long before Facebook and Instagram, calls to us to use it. It demands our attention to render sights around us for later consumption. Sontag could not have imagined that billions of people would have these cameras and that many would abuse others by taking and posting humiliating photographs. But Mark Zuckerberg could. As we have seen, Zuckerberg decided peer photography would be the key to the future of Facebook. Each incident of peer surveillance becomes part of a massive corporate surveillance system once uploaded to Facebook or Instagram. Images are tagged with metadata revealing time and location. People tag photographs with names of the people captured, revealing their presence and movements to others. The cameras themselves sit on a device designed for constant corporate surveillance. Most mobile phones track the users' location with global positioning system connections. And the Facebook and Instagram applications on the mobile phone also gather data about the person holding it. This is systemic surveillance. The key to its power is correlation. If I post a series of photographs taken in Charlottesville, Virginia, and tag three Friends who appear in them, Facebook correlates that information with what it gathers about them. Then Facebook can generate remarkably accurate assumptions about the frequency of our meetings, the nature of our relationships, the next circle of mutual acquaintances, and even our relative income and consumer habits. All of this seems harmless unless a Facebook user wishes to cause harm to another or some oppressive state power gains control over this sort of information. Both of these things happen. Peer surveillance connects to corporate surveillance and to state surveillance.

Revenge porn is perhaps the most troubling aspect, but hardly the only one, of the strange media ecosystem in which each of us plays an active role. Because of its reach and power, Facebook often ends up facilitating not just revenge porn but other incidents of humiliation, harassment, and unwanted exposure. Those who wish to do others harm do not have to work too hard to deploy Facebook in their plans. This is yet another example of good intentions going terribly wrong. Facebook makes it easy for us to gather and share. It favors images over text. It sorts people by interest. And almost 30 percent of the world—including almost everyone in North America and Europe—has a Facebook account. Facebook groups, Mark Zuckerberg's answer to the problem of civic degradation around the world, serve as secret societies through which all sorts of mayhem can go undiscovered and unpunished until it's far too late.

The reason Facebook does what it does so well—including amplifying the malicious and cruel acts that so many wish to perpetrate on others—is that it leverages massive amounts of information about its users to effectively sort and send the content it thinks we want to our News Feeds. What makes Facebook good also makes it bad. What makes Facebook wealthy also lets us be crueler. At the root of all this is a system of surveillance unlike any we have ever seen. And it has reached us in ways we are unprepared to face. Surveillance fosters harassment and humiliation, whether it's from the state or from other people and groups. We can't perform as responsible, informed, engaged citizens of a republic if significant segments of the polis are harassed, silenced, and threatened every time they attempt to engage in matters of public debate. That's the fact right now. And it's perhaps the most acute limitation to the potential of internet platforms to enhance our lives positively.

Facebook has grown into the most pervasive surveillance system in the world. It's also the most reckless and irresponsible surveillance system in the commercial world. If you have been active on Facebook since before 2014 and you interacted with games or applications like Farmville, Mafia Wars, or Words with Friends, then Facebook exported not only a rich collection of your profile and activities on Facebook but also those of your Friends. Facebook has been sanctioned by governments around the world for its practices of collecting, using, and sharing personal data without full or clear disclosure. Yet the company continues to abuse its users, comforted by its popularity and power. In early 2018 when journalists revealed the extent to which a sleazy British political firm called Cambridge Analytica had Hoovered up Facebook data from more than fifty million Americans in preparation for its work to elect a president of the United States, the full range of Facebook abuse finally generated widespread popular attention and condemnation. Social media scholars and privacy advocates had been trying to raise concerns since at least 2010. But before there was a scandal complete with a James Bond–style villainous organization like Cambridge Analytica, few thought deeply about the damage Facebook was doing. A minor movement of Twitter users in the United States promised to #QuitFacebook. Facebook's stock price plummeted during the month of March. Regulators in Europe and the United States took new notice. Thousands downloaded records of what Facebook saved about them only to find that their Android-driven mobile phones had given Facebook records of text messages and calls. The uproar in the United States was strong, but Facebook's global power remained stronger. Still, the revelations of early 2018 presented the best opportunity for reform legislation and public pressure to alter the ways Facebook and other surveillance-based companies would do their business.[3]

DATA FOR DOLLARS

Back in 2008 I was very careful with Facebook. I saw its hazards—and its benefits—as chiefly social. I established (and maintain to this day) a firm rule against interacting with current students on Facebook. I knew that by "Friending" someone I could peer into aspects of that person's life to which I was not invited. And in those early days of social media few people had developed norms and habits to guide their use of the service. I did not want to know whom my students were dating, what they wore to a Halloween party, or—most of all—what they thought of my courses. I was also pretty careful about what information I posted about myself.

I assumed, correctly at the time, that all Facebook could know about me was what I chose to reveal to and through Facebook. My age, relationship status, and sexual orientation fields remained blank during the first two years of my active Facebook participation. Then one day I thought it was time to come out as a straight married man over forty years old. Once I clicked "married," a strange thing happened. The advertising spaces on my Facebook page filled up with advertisements for services that invited me to contact women for the purpose of having an affair. Suspicious, I removed "married" from my profile. The ads disappeared. In the early days of Facebook its data collection and advertising targeting were so clumsy that the site merely filtered for one or two attributes and pushed ads based on them. In addition, the companies that chose to advertise on Facebook in the early days were often unseemly.

That all began to change around 2010. Like for many, my comfort level with Facebook had increased. I had succumbed to the constant prodding and suggestion that I add more Friends. Though I still scrupulously avoided current students, my circles grew. More of my social and political activities moved to Facebook. To be without Facebook by 2010 was to miss out on what seemed to be essential conversations and events. Even my parents signed up for it. Facebook's user base spread to all walks of life and started touching more countries and more languages, leaving would-be and once-dominant competitors such as MySpace with no sense of mission and no way to make money.[4]

Beyond users' lives and habits, something more important was going on inside the company. Mark Zuckerberg had lured Sheryl Sandberg away from Google in 2008 to be chief operating officer in charge of the business side of the company. By 2010 Sandberg had built an effective data collection and advertising system. The ads on my page began to reflect my professional interests and social connections. One regular ad was for a heavy and expensive leather briefcase like the kind professors in movies carry. It was not a perfect match for my interests (or for professors in general, few of whom would spring for a $250 leather case). But it was far better than ads urging me to cheat on my spouse just because I have one. To accomplish the mission of targeting advertisements deftly, Sandberg needed more and better data about what users did, thought, and wanted to buy. So she embarked on a series of expansions of Facebook's capabilities to track and profile users. Not coincidentally, 2010 was the first year that Facebook posted a profit. It's safe to say that if not for Sandberg and her formidable vision and management skills, Facebook might be a broke and trivial company today.[5]

Facebook is the most pervasive surveillance system in the history of the world. More than two billion people and millions of organizations, companies, and political movements offer up detailed accounts of passions, preferences, predilections, and plans to one commercial service. In addition, Facebook tracks all of the connections and interactions among these people and groups, predicting future connections and guiding future interactions. It even compiles contact information on those who do not have a Facebook account.

Facebook exposes us to three major forms of surveillance. We might think of them as three perches or viewpoints. Commercial and political entities are able to exploit the targeting and predictive power of Facebook through its advertising system. Through what we reveal on our profiles, other Facebook users can watch and track us as we build or break relationships with others, move around, recommend and comment on various posts, and express our opinions and preferences. And governments use Facebook to spy on citizens or anyone they consider suspicious, either by establishing Facebook accounts that appear to be those of friends or allies or by breaking through Facebook security to gather data directly.

Facebook itself conducts commercial surveillance of its users on behalf of its advertising clients. Facebook has no incentive to offer any third-party access to the data that it uses to drive user-generated posts and direct advertisements. The commercial value of Facebook lies in its complete control of this priceless account of human behavior. But the interface that Facebook provides to both advertisers and those who run Facebook pages allows them to learn significant amounts about their audiences in general and track the level of response their posts and advertisements generate. To profile users for precise targeting, Facebook uses much of the data that users offer: biographical data, records of interactions with others, the text of their posts, location (through Facebook apps on mobile phones equipped with GPS features), and the "social graph"—a map of the relationships among items on Facebook (photos, videos, news stories, advertisements, groups, pages, and the profiles of its 2.2 billion users). This combination of information allows Facebook to predict user interest and behavior based on what other people with similar attributes and similar connections want, think, or do.[6]

Beyond the data that Facebook gathers from its own core services (Facebook, Messenger, Instagram, WhatsApp, etc.), it allows other firms to connect to Facebook directly through a service called Open Graph. Open Graph is how the music service Spotify interacts with Facebook, using Facebook user names and passwords to enroll and log in to the service. This makes Spotify "social," in the sense that the music one user listens to via Spotify becomes available to her Friends who are also using Spotify, and those Friends' music habits are available to others as well. This creates a mesh of interests that can prompt discovery or recommendations among like-minded music fans. To Spotify, this service amplifies its ability to find new users and maintain established users. To Facebook, it means that more interactions—even outside of Facebook—become part of the larger social graph and thus useful for profiling and targeting. Facebook, through its Open Graph partnerships and the use of tracking cookies that it implants in users' web browsers, is able to gather immense amounts of personal data from people who hardly ever log in to their Facebook accounts. Basically, there is no way to opt out fully from Facebook's ability to track you.[7]

This form of single-firm commercial surveillance seems almost harmless by itself. Facebook lacks a police force, so it can't abuse its power in a way that injures people or denies liberty or property. If it profiles someone inaccurately and targets advertisements improperly, the company just will not generate revenue for that action. When all those data serve Facebook well, leaders of Facebook argue, it provides a more enjoyable and relevant experience to users. No cat owner wants to see a barrage of ads for dog food. No vegetarian wants to see ads for hamburgers. And we generally prefer seeing posts from the people whom we like and think like. There are problems with this sort of filtering, as we will see in Chapter 3. But none of those problems quite qualifies as an immediate risk or danger to users. However, Facebook gathers and deploys much of this information without our knowledge or consent. Facebook does not offer us a full view of how our activities are used. And Facebook does not offer us clear and easy ways to exempt ourselves from this pervasive surveillance. Users might generally understand that the company retains and uses the specific attributes that they post to their profile. But most users certainly do not have a full picture of the depth and breadth of Facebook's activities. Users rarely are informed, for instance, that Facebook buys troves of credit-card purchasing and profile data from the large data marketing firms. A user must poke around or search Facebook's help site to discover this fact. This mix of the information we offer to Facebook, Facebook's ability to track us on the web and in the real world, and the commercial credit data it purchases empowers Facebook and disempowers us.[8]

The chief danger from the Facebook commercial surveillance system lies in the concentration of power. No other company in the world—with the possible exception of Google—can even consider building a set of personalized dossiers as rich as Facebook's. These data reinforce Facebook's commercial dominance in the advertising business (again, mostly shared with Google, which has different ways of tracking and targeting content and advertising but generates many of the same risks and problems). The very fact that we cannot expect another digital media company to generate that much data from that many people and that many interactions means that—barring strong regulation—serious competitors to Facebook will be rare or nonexistent in the near future.

But there are other dangers that come with Facebook having and holding all of this information on us. They come from the two other surveillance positions: peers and states. Many common behaviors of Facebook Friends sever our images or information from our control, regardless of how careful any individual is with privacy settings. Other Facebook users can act maliciously, especially when relationships degrade. And other Facebook users might be more promiscuous in their habits of tagging photographs of people who would rather not be identified beyond a tight circle of known Friends. Beyond this, Facebook profiles can be abused for the purposes of public shaming, harassing, or exposing personal information to outsiders. What we put on Facebook is often carefully selected and managed, a constant if exhausting exercise in self-promotion and self-presentation. That means that Facebook profiles are rarely if ever full and accurate portrayals of our lives and personalities. That's one reason Facebook goes to great lengths to monitor and record our actual activities and movements. We might want everyone to think we are vegan, but we might slip up and eat at Burger King in a moment of weakness. We should not have to reveal such moments to our Friends. But Facebook ensures that it knows us better than our friends and family members do. Still, the fact that Facebook profiles are inaccurate or inauthentic portraits of complex human beings means that actions and reactions by others peering at them can generate unfair or harmful reactions. Jokes can be misread. Declarations of loosely held opinions could blow up into misreadings that cause social conflicts. Facebook was designed to limit our interactions and exposure to the circle of those we trust. It no longer functions that way.[9]

Despite the promises Facebook makes to its users, there are many ways that it ensures users lack control over their information. Privacy journalist Kashmir Hill noticed in 2017 a curious phenomenon. Facebook was recommending that she "Friend" people she hardly knew or did not even know of. She asked her readers if they had had similar experiences, especially any that led to awkward or possibly harmful encounters via Facebook. Social workers and therapists reported being connected with clients despite never exchanging private information with them. A sperm donor was urged to connect to the child of a couple to whom he had donated sperm, despite the parents not wanting the donor to have contact with that child. Hill discovered that a Facebook feature called People You Might Know urged people to upload the address books from their computers or phones. Those email addresses and mobile phone numbers served as identifiers to Facebook profiles. And because Facebook's social graph traced connections among profiles, the People You Might Know feature had the ability to connect people who were quite distant, estranged, hostile, or even violent toward each other. Because no user could control what information lies in another's address book, no user could opt out of the feature. Users are at the mercy of other people and their understanding of how Facebook uses personal information. "A one-night stand from 2008, a person you got a couch from on Craigslist in 2010, a landlord from 2013: If they ever put you in their phone, or you put them in yours, Facebook could log the connection if either party were to upload their contacts," Hill wrote. "That accumulation of contact data from hundreds of people means that Facebook probably knows every address you've ever lived at, every email address you've ever used, every landline and cell phone number you've ever been associated with, all of your nicknames, any social network profiles associated with you, all your former instant message accounts, and anything else someone might have added about you to their phone book." And there is nothing anyone can do about that. Users are tricked at the moment they register with Facebook to upload their contacts for the sake of convenience. Facebook never invites users to consider the consequences of that action.[10]

State uses of Facebook are even more troubling. States do have the power and right to imprison and commit violence against citizens and those they consider threatening. State power leverages Facebook in two ways. First, and most common, we have seen authoritarian leaders in various countries monitor Facebook activity and track suspected dissidents and journalists. They use Facebook and WhatsApp to generate campaigns of harassment against perceived enemies and critics. States can use bogus profiles to infiltrate Facebook groups devoted to reforming or challenging the government, or even groups that offer support to gay and lesbian people. The 2013 revelations by Edward Snowden that the security and intelligence services in the United States and the United Kingdom had managed to tap into the data flows of Facebook, Google, Apple, Microsoft, Yahoo, and other companies showed just how vulnerable Facebook users are to state surveillance power. As long as Facebook retains such a rich source of intelligence, states will try to infiltrate the system.[11]

ENEMIES OF THE STATES

Cinema can help illustrate some of the major concepts of privacy and surveillance. Filmmakers have an understandable interest in the technologies and ethics of surveillance. After all, they watch people for a living and present actions and images to a broad public. There is a long-running conversation about surveillance in cinema. It starts with the work of Fritz Lang. *Metropolis*, from 1927, uses the power of police surveillance for social control of workers as a central theme. *M*, from 1932, is about everybody watching everybody, sort of like Facebook and Instagram today. Recent films about surveillance have included *Captain America: The Winter Soldier*, from 2014, and *The Circle*, from 2017, an adaptation of the dystopian novel by David Eggers about a company not unlike Facebook.

Consider two American films, twenty-four years apart, both starring Gene Hackman as a reclusive surveillance expert. The difference between the work done by Harry Caul, the naive, emotionally stunted private investigator played by Hackman in Francis Ford Coppola's 1974 film *The Conversation*, and the work done by Edward Lyle, the disaffected, cynical former spy Hackman played in the 1998 Tony Scott film *Enemy of the State*, is more than a matter of tools.[12]

Caul uses audio and video surveillance to investigate private citizens, while Lyle deftly deploys the digital tools and techniques that have come to characterize our era of total surveillance. Before choosing to go "off the grid," Lyle did high-level work for either a government organization like the National Security Agency or a private contractor working for the NSA. (The exact truth is never fully revealed.) Lyle seems to be Caul twenty-four years later, with a new name and a deeper sense of nihilism but the same aversion to sharing information with others. Caul's tools, analog and cumbersome, are remarkably effective at capturing the conversations and images of known people. He works on specific targets and is hired by private firms and individuals. He focuses on personal matters, not criminal or national security matters. Lyle, by contrast, introduces both Robert Clayton Dean (played by Will Smith) and filmgoers of the late 1990s to an invisible web sustained by the continuous mining and tracking of digital data. The team of geeky spies assigned to track Dean as he rushes through Washington, D.C., has at its disposal credit records, mobile phone signals, and hundreds of surveillance cameras positioned throughout the city.

Caul lives in a completely different information ecosystem from the one inhabited by Lyle. It's not that the government is more benign or restrained during the Nixon years, or that private firms have more noble motivations. And Caul certainly has the skill and equipment to track individuals and record their expressions in intimate detail. Like Lyle, he has the power to ruin lives through surveillance and revelation. But Caul cannot imagine anything beyond the precisely targeted surveillance of individuals.

Lyle, however, lives at the dawn of the Big Data era. In Lyle's information ecosystem, firms and states maintain massive databases that contain records of commercial transactions, movements, and expressions. There is a permeable membrane between data collected by private firms and data used by state security forces. And our electronic devices, as Dean learns the hard way, facilitate this constant and nearly total environment of discreet surveillance. Data collection is so cheap and easy that it's unnecessary to judge a priori what among the data might be important. Firms and states collect first and ask questions later.

Enemy of the State debuted in the United States the same year that two Stanford graduate students released a stripped-down site called Google that would help people search the World Wide Web with speed and precision, relaying on the data that users would provide through previous searches, links, and clicks. The film appeared three years before the attacks of September 11, 2001, which in turn precipitated a steady increase in state surveillance across the world. The film predated the USA PATRIOT Act by four years. It arrived four years before the U.S. government declared its intention to gather and track massive amounts of commercial and communications data in a program it called Total Information Awareness. The film predated Facebook by seven years, the iPhone by nine years, and by fifteen years the revelations by Edward Snowden that the U.S. and U.K. governments were successfully tapping into and harvesting massive amounts of communication information on their own citizens as well as millions of innocent people around the world. So when viewed today, *Enemy of the State* seems almost comical, as its characters lack the basic awareness and acceptance that we would expect such sophisticated people to have about surveillance today.

THE PROBLEM WITH PRIVACY

Caul's downfall in *The Conversation* results from a moment of weakness. He reveals the wrong details to the wrong person at the wrong time. His own vulnerability awakens his moral sense. Concerned not just for his own privacy, he now feels culpable for the damage he has done to others. In Caul's awakening we glimpse what Georgetown law professor Julie Cohen has called the move from a focus on individual autonomy to the "social value of privacy." Caul's concerns about even other people's individual privacy is inadequate. Theories founded on and bounded by liberal individualism consistently fail to account for how we actually live our lives in a networked world. After all, none of us actually live individual lives. We are embedded in social and cultural relationships, so we live among multiple social contexts. We make and remake ourselves dynamically as we move in time and among others, as our interests and allegiances change.[13]

We can see that privacy is not merely those aspects of our lives that we withhold from others. Privacy is more than the autonomy we exercise over our own information. The word more accurately describes the ways we manage our various reputations within and among various contexts. Those contexts might include school, church, the public sphere, a place of employment, or a family. Each of these contexts shifts and overlaps with others. Borders change. Contexts blend. So configuring a "self" in the twenty-first century is a lot more work than it used to be. The fluidity is liberating, especially for those who seek niches supportive of marginalized identities. But it can be a terrifying and vertiginous liberty—sometimes exhausting and even potentially dangerous.[14]

Contexts in a digitally networked world—a world that Lyle eschews in *The Enemy of the State*—are constantly intersecting and overlapping, like blobs of paraffin in a lava lamp. Our work sphere bleeds into our family sphere too easily, challenging our personal ability to manage our reputations and control the manners of disclosure. Our public contexts blend as commercial data firms collect and then sell our profiles to political parties and campaigns. Facebook brings all of our acquaintances together into one confusing collection of otherwise unrelated profiles that we are forced to deal with without the help of rank or distinction. Friends are just friends. So are lovers, bosses, acquaintances, and high school teachers.

THE CRYPTOPTICON

In the current commercial, political, and regulatory environment, institutions have powerful incentives to collect, save, and analyze every trace of human activity. But there have long been potential payoffs for tracing and tracking subjects (consumers, citizens, criminals, users). To explain the relatively recent turn to Big Data as a tool of choice, scholars and analysts tend to emphasize the availability of appropriate technologies. These include huge server farms, algorithms designed to quickly reveal patterns within otherwise meaningless pools of data, greater bandwidth and faster processing capacities, and so on. But this technocentric analysis misses or downplays the role of significant changes in the global political economy and dominant ideologies since 1980. When securities markets and consultants praise "efficiency" above all other values, when states place "security" above all other public needs, and when mass-market advertising reaps at best murky returns for each dollar spent, the incentives to target, trace, and sift grow in power.

There is little in the current regulatory or market environment that would discourage the use of Big Data. Because it offers clear public benefits, such as, for instance, quicker and broader epidemiological assessments, it would seem foolish to dispense with Big Data and its technological systems and practices. But we should understand the costs as well as the benefits—and not allow its rapid rise and widespread adoption to blind us to the need for critical public and political discussions of its use and abuse. In his influential book from the 1970s, *Discipline and Punish*, Michel Foucault adopted the concept of the Panopticon—Jeremy Bentham's never-realized design for a circular prison with a central watchtower, from which the behavior of inmates could be observed at all times—to describe the programs and techniques used by the modern state to monitor, supervise, and ultimately modify the behavior of its citizens. To Foucault, the Panopticon was embedded in the practices, structures, and institutions of modern society, from government bureaucracies to schools to hospitals and asylums and to the assorted regimes of health, well-being, and citizenship they variously inscribed upon their subjects. Such systems of surveillance left "no need for arms, physical violence, material constraints," as Foucault once said. "All that was needed was 'a gaze,' an endlessly inspecting gaze, which each individual would end up internalizing, thus becoming his or her own constant supervisor. A superb formula: Power exercised continuously and for what turns out to be a minimal cost." The gaze, the theory goes, works as well as iron bars to control the behavior of most people.[15]

Those who write about privacy and surveillance often invoke the Panopticon to argue that the great harm of mass surveillance is social control. Yet the Panopticon does not describe our current predicament. First, mass surveillance does not inhibit behavior: people will act weirdly and willfully regardless of the number of cameras pointed at them. The thousands of surveillance cameras in London and New York City do not deter the eccentric and avant-garde. Today, the example of reality television suggests that there may even be a positive correlation between the number of cameras and observers pointed at subjects and their willingness to act strangely and relinquish all pretensions of dignity. There is no empirical reason to believe that awareness of surveillance limits the imagination or cows creativity in a market economy in an open, non-totalitarian state.

Obviously, coercive state violence still exists, and at times metastasizes. The Stasi in Cold War–era East Germany knew how to exploit the widespread awareness of surveillance to heighten the fear and submissiveness of the general public. But the environment shaped by the Stasi is not the environment in which most of us now live. Unless the Panopticon is as visible, ubiquitous, and intentionally menacing as agencies such as the Stasi made it, it cannot influence behavior in the ways Bentham and Foucault assumed.[16]

In Europe, North America, and much of the rest of the world, governments and businesses achieve their ends in almost the opposite way from that of the Panopticon: not through the subjection of the individual to the gaze of a single, centralized authority, but through the surveillance of the individual by all (in theory, though at least in fact by many). I call this the Cryptopticon: an inscrutable information ecosystem of massive corporate and state surveillance.[17]

Unlike Bentham's Panopticon, the Cryptopticon is not supposed to be obvious. Its scale, its ubiquity, and even its very existence are supposed to be hidden from clear view. So while a CCTV camera mounted over a counter at a convenience store openly warns shoppers to behave or risk being caught, the Cryptopticon relies on browser cookies, data streams retained by telecommunication firms, satellite imagery, global positioning system traces, covert voice surveillance, store discount cards, e-book readers, and mobile applications. Each of these techniques masks its real purpose: to gather or provide data and to track the behavior of millions of people with stunning precision. Beguilingly, though, each technique offers something valuable and convenient—often "for free."[18]

Unlike Bentham's prisoners, we don't—perhaps can't—know all the ways in which we are being watched or profiled. So we don't regulate our behavior under the gaze of surveillance. Instead, we seem not to care. The workings of the Cryptopticon are cryptic, hidden, scrambled, and mysterious. One can never be sure who is watching whom and for what purpose. Surveillance is so pervasive and much of it so seemingly benign ("for your safety and security") that it's almost impossible for the object of surveillance to assess how she is manipulated or threatened by powerful institutions gathering and using the record of surveillance. The threat is not that expression or experimentation will be quashed or disciplined, as they supposedly would be under the Panopticon. The threat is that subjects will become so inured to and comfortable with the networked status quo that they will gladly sort themselves into "niches" that enable effective profiling and behavioral prediction. The Cryptopticon is intimately linked to Big Data. And the dynamic relationship between the two concepts underlines the need to understand both in relation to commerce, the state, and society more generally.

Facebook, Google, and Amazon want us to relax and be ourselves. They have an interest in exploiting niche markets that our consumer choices have generated. These companies are devoted to tracking our eccentricities because they understand that the ways we set ourselves apart from others are the things about which we are most passionate. Our passions, predilections, fancies, and fetishes drive and shape our discretionary spending; they are what make us easy targets for precise marketing. Market segmentation is vital to today's commerce. In order for marketers and vendors to target messages and products to us, they must know our eccentricities— what makes us distinctive, or, at least, to which small interest groups we belong. Forging a mass audience or market is a waste of time and money unless you are selling soap—and a very generic soap at that.[19]

Even modern liberal states such as those of North America and Western Europe want us to be ourselves. They count on subversive and potentially dangerous people to reveal themselves through their habits and social connections, not to slink away and hide in the dark. Repressing dissent and subversion does not eliminate potentially dangerous types. The Stasi lost control over the East German people despite the enormous scale of its operations and the long-lasting damage that inflicted on both the observers and the observed. In the liberal state of the twenty-first century, domination does not demand social or cultural conformity. The state, like every private firm that employs a sophisticated method of marketing, wants us to express ourselves—to choose—because mere expression of difference is usually unthreatening, yet remarkably useful to the powerful.

Florian Henckel von Donnersmarck's brilliant 2007 film *The Lives of Others* demonstrates the corrosive power of constant state surveillance. The protagonist, a playwright loyal to the East German government, enjoys all the perks of stardom, such as it is in a society not overwhelmed with material glitter. Many of his intellectual and artistic friends, however, have strayed from the uncomfortable embrace of the state. Still, he naively trusts that his political loyalty will continue to protect him. When a romantic entanglement places his girlfriend, and then him, under high-level surveillance, his confidence unravels and the depravity of the state becomes clear. The film concludes with a glimpse of the 1991 version of Big Data. The playwright, now trying to reconstruct his life in the wake of the unification of Germany, visits the new archive in Berlin that allows citizens to examine the files that the Stasi collected. This moment leaves viewers with a powerful sense of how detailed, destructive, and all-encompassing state surveillance could be in even an era of non-networked analog media forms.[20]

Companies such as Google and Facebook put Big Data collection and analysis at the heart of their revenue-generating functions, always described by company officials as enhancements to the "user experience."[21] The line between state and commercial surveillance hardly matters anymore, as state security services regularly receive significant data sets on people's movement and habits just by asking for or by licensing the data on the open market.[22] Data collected by one institution are easily transferred, mined, used, and abused by another. So one company might purchase consumer data from a supermarket or big-box retailer and then sell them to direct-mail marketers, political parties, and even local law enforcement. Data firms also collect state records such as voter registrations, deeds, car titles, and liens to sell consumer profiles to direct-marketing firms.[23]

Given the many possible abuses of Big Data, including the long-term tarnishing of personal and professional reputations, citizens need to be fully aware of the flows of information between private firms, governments, and any other institutions that might have an interest in using such data.

SOCIETY

In Michelangelo Antonioni's 1966 film *Blow-Up,* a photographer secretly photographs a couple embracing in a London park. The woman, furious when she notices what the photographer is up to, chases him down. "This is a public place," she says to the man. "Everyone has the right to be left in peace." It is an odd bit of dialogue, at least to American ears. The standard American assumptions about private and public spaces are that everyone has a right to be left in peace in private, but not in public. The seeming incongruity compels most American viewers to interrogate the idea of being "left in peace," and under what conditions someone should be. Because privacy law in the United States has for so long depended on the distinction drawn in the constitutional prohibition on "unwarranted search and seizure," we assume that there are private spaces and public spaces and that our norms and expectations of what is appropriate to each must fall within those demarcations. Privacy ends at the threshold.

Almost fifty years after the release of Antonioni's film, the flimsiness of the American conception of privacy is easier to see. The distinction between private and public spaces is no longer relevant. We might have had privacy when our thoughts and personal information were recorded in papers that we stored at home. But now so much of our essential data sits on servers far from our computers, in a place we nonchalantly and naively call "the cloud." American law does not protect this information from the prying eyes of the state because we have placed it with "third parties." In doing so, we have withdrawn it from the realm of private. As Justice Sonia Sotomayor wrote in her concurring opinion in *United States v. Jones* in 2012, "I would ask whether people reasonably expect that their movements will be recorded and aggregated in a manner that enables the Government to ascertain, more or less at will, their political and religious beliefs, sexual habits, and so on." The case was about the warrantless surveillance of a suspect who was driving around with a global positioning system sensor placed beneath his car. The police argued that they were merely tracking his movements in public. The Court, and Sotomayor in particular, did not find that a persuasive response.

The scene from *Blow-Up*, with its very un-American notion that privacy is not necessarily a spatial matter in all contexts, leads us to recognize that social relations rely on a web of trust. Respecting privacy is high among these norms that facilitate social relations.[24] The unnamed photographer in *Blow-Up* does not work for the state. He does not work for a commercial firm. And it's unclear from the testimony or action of his subject, played by Vanessa Redgrave, what she fears the photographer might use the photograph for. The film teaches us, long before millions of people walked the streets with powerful cameras in their pockets, that one of the greatest threats to personal dignity comes not from large firms or powerful governments. It comes from millions of individuals armed at all times and in all places with audio, video, and photographic recording devices. Fellow members of society have the means, if they are so inclined, to expose, harass, and vilify their neighbors either to satisfy a sense of vigilante justice or simply to amuse themselves. Soon we may have access to "always-on" surveillance technologies such as Google Glass that will not only record all of our public and private interactions in both public and private but also share the images and sounds with Google—thus making them available to businesses and governments as well.[25]

When *Blow-Up* was released, the lone man with a camera in a park capturing images of strangers was an anomaly. Now such behavior is so common that it's unremarkable and even the norm. The new normal deserves remark and reconsideration, not least because it is so ethically and legally fraught. We so precipitously entered the age of (potentially) near-total and continuous mutual surveillance that we failed to weigh our individual consumer desires and personal predilections against the need for certain norms to uphold the common good.[26]

The need for informed debate about the norms, practices, and regulations that would govern how we should treat each other is clearly urgent. Many strong incentives (the desire for ease, efficiency, connection, pleasure) militate in favor of people's tacitly accepting the status quo of maximum surveillance by as many people as possible. And the devices that make this new normal possible are so attractive in so many ways that to criticize them or their users is to encounter a powerful resistance.[27]

How young people manage their reputations within various contexts has been a subject of much poorly conducted debate in recent years. Privacy is as much a matter of social norms as law or technology. Should we, as the pundits warn, assume "privacy is dead" because young people seem to share all sorts of details via social media without regard for traditions of reticence and modesty? In fact, the rest of us might do better to emulate the sophisticated strategies many young Americans actively deploy to protect themselves and engage socially. The studies that danah boyd undertook for her essential book *It's Complicated: The Social Lives of Networked Teens* demonstrate that young people learn early on how to mask the meanings of their social network engagements by developing codes that are impenetrable for parents and others in authority. Just as important, young people are far more likely to manipulate privacy settings on social network services than are their older "friends" (i.e., relatives, teachers, and coaches).[28]

We are beginning to understand the ramifications of rapid change in our information ecosystem. Scholars in such disconnected areas as computer science, science and technology studies, library and information studies, communication, marketing, political science, media studies, and the philosophy of science have been picking away from different angles at the problems and opportunities that Big Data presents. Our thinking about "privacy" and "surveillance" is still overdetermined by American legal history and by the long shadow of Michel Foucault. Focusing on how Facebook uses us might help.[29]

THE ZUCKERBERG DOCTRINE

All of this promiscuous connectivity and data collection does not pose a problem in Mark Zuckerberg's view. He believes that the very process of connectivity is good for us. If some connectivity is good, then more must be better. Facebook employees tend not to use words such as "privacy" when discussing their company's services. There is good reason for this. The term itself is too heavy. It carries too many meanings and can only seem to be the opposite of what Facebook wants to build. After all, privacy implies a denial of communication, a restriction on movement and gaze. Privacy seems to be the opposite of connectivity. As Zuckerberg wrote in a 2010 op-ed in the *Washington Post*, "If people share more, the world will become more open and connected. And a world that's more open and connected is a better world." Facebook has repeatedly and regularly introduced features such as the News Feed, photo albums, and the Beacon program (which alerted one's Friends of purchases) that generated immediate blowback because of privacy concerns. Each time (except with Beacon, which Facebook closed down) Facebook just persisted until its users capitulated and grew comfortable with the new features—or just grew tired of complaining and protesting.[30]

So Facebook's playbook has seemed to be to slowly and steadily acclimate users to a system of surveillance and distribution that if introduced all at once might seem appalling. Facebook has been training us to accept its core principles as matters of habit and practice. Meanwhile, Facebook emphasizes that it gives users "control" over what they share and with whom, even as it steadily erodes resistance to systems and features that remove control from users. And Zuckerberg keeps telling us what he wants us to want. As Zuckerberg told *Time* in 2010, "What people want isn't complete privacy. It isn't that they want secrecy. It's that they want control over what they share and what they don't." He never defines "complete privacy." Facebook documents and Zuckerberg's statements leave "privacy" undefined. Whatever it means to Facebook and Zuckerberg, it's something to be resisted, not protected. It's something to overcome, not something to strengthen. Zuckerberg has decided it is not in our interest. And he has steadily built a system that moves us to accept his vision of a better, more connected, more watched world.[31]

By emphasizing user "control" Zuckerberg is not completely misguided. The essence of privacy is the combination of autonomy and dignity. Privacy is not a substance we can trade away. It's not a state of being that either exists or does not exist. And it can't "die," as too many people have declared. Privacy is a power we exercise—or hope to exercise—when we see fit. It exists when we have control over how information about us is used in various contexts. Early in life we figure out that our social lives are made up of intersecting circles of family, friends, acquaintances, and the people and institutions that exercise power over us. So as children we quickly learn how to manage our reputations among these various contexts. We learn, often the hard way, that some things we can say to our friends we should not say to our parents. Things that we reveal to clergy we should not share with siblings. Teachers and coaches have special knowledge about us that if released to our peers might humiliate us. So we manage who knows what about us. We develop bonds of trust among the people and institutions in our lives. When someone abrogates that trust we suffer. That process of management of reputation among various contexts is what we usually call privacy.[32]

Facebook scrambles our social contexts. If we don't actively partition our collection of hundreds or thousands of Friends and segregate those subcollections, we soon find our contexts melding. A joke meant for friends from university years reaches an employer and degrades our status at work. A political comment meant for a tight circle of peers who have engaged in an ongoing argument gets recast when it shows up in the News Feed of a neighbor. What's entertaining in one context can be embarrassing in another. Facebook offers us rough tools to manage our contexts, but it defines our contexts awkwardly and unhelpfully. So our social contexts quickly collapse. Over time, we give up trying to work so hard at it. Either we accept the social consequences or we temper our expressions under the assumption that the wrong people could read our posts at any time.[33]

By emphasizing "user control," Facebook puts the burden on us to manage the collapse of social contexts that Facebook itself creates. This is the standard position of Facebook, Google, and other Silicon Valley companies that monitor our behavior and record our transactions. They defend their policies by reminding us we may help ourselves if we see fit to do so. We may change the settings on each service to limit the surveillance. While installing the default settings in their favor, they claim they empower us by giving us choices. This spirit of "self-help" teaches us over time that privacy is a personal matter, not a social or political one. The burden Facebook places on us is to protect *ourselves*—not those less aware of how Facebook works or of the consequences of privacy violations, not those more vulnerable, and certainly not the entire ecosystem. Protecting privacy is an environmental problem that Facebook treats as a matter of individual responsibility.

Facebook also treats privacy as an engineering problem that can only be solved using the labor and foresight of its users. As a response to revenge porn, Facebook launched an experiment in late 2017 in Australia. Users who feared they might become victims of revenge porn were encouraged to send nude photos of themselves to Facebook. Facebook employees would examine those images and feed them into a computer to create a unique digital signature for each image. An algorithm deploying artificial intelligence could scan and match the offending images with those others upload to Facebook. Facebook would store the images for a short period (Facebook did not declare how short that period would be) before deleting the original image but retaining the fingerprint. The fingerprinting method, known as "hashing," allows the algorithm to match the original image with an altered version of the image—a move many revenge porn perpetrators make to try to limit the scanning power of photo-hosting sites. Major technology companies use similar processes—a combination of human judgment and algorithmic screening—to identify child pornography.[34]

Because Facebook is so huge, and because the volume of photograph uploads is so massive—more than 350 million each day—there might be no more effective way to address the threat of revenge porn. But that's the problem. Facebook cannot hire and train enough people to do this work preemptively. Plus, looking at thousands of images per day of all the horrible things people do to each other is among the worst jobs in the world. Machine learning is only as effective as the "training data" that go into it— in other words, nude photos. As long as Facebook maintains private groups and allows for the promiscuous and instant uploading of images it must rely on users themselves to police the site. It's not in Facebook's interest to shut down groups or to delay the availability of all photographs for a few hours while computers and people scan them. The "user experience" of most trumps the health and safety of some. The risk and burden lie on us, while the benefits go to Facebook.[35]

This Australian revenge porn experiment highlights the central problem with Facebook's approach to the dark and cruel things people do to each other. Those who have been victimized or fear being victimized by revenge porn are often traumatized. Yet the company is willing to ask those very victims to engage in the most intimate ways with a system that they have no reason to trust and people they will never meet or know. That seems like too large a burden to place on those who have already paid too high a price for these ubiquitous systems of surveillance.[36]

The tension between the ethical demands to protect people from harassment and exploitation and the urge to keep the "user experience" seamless and convenient exists because everything Facebook does is based on the urge to harvest our attention and use it for two purposes: to give us more of what we tell Facebook we want and to help advertisers precisely match their pleas for commerce with those who might be interested in those goods and services. Facebook has mastered the attention economy. It can't operate any other way. Our privacy and dignity ultimately do not matter in the attention economy. They are inconvenient and disposable.

3

The Attention Machine

On July 15, 2015, professional golfer Greg Norman appeared on the American morning news show *Today* and challenged presenter Matt Lauer to sit while colleagues dumped a bucket of ice water on his head. Lauer promised to donate money to a hospice service in Florida's Palm Beach County. Lauer then challenged three friends, including news presenter Brian Williams, lifestyle guru Martha Stewart, and radio personality Howard Stern, to sit for the same bracing experience and pledge to donate to the hospice. At that moment, a fundraising gimmick that had been circulating among professional golfers for months erupted into a craze. Within weeks, all over Facebook and YouTube hundreds of thousands of people posted videos of being drenched in ice water for a cause and then challenging three friends to do the same. The challenge was odd: either the person who had been challenged got soaked in ice water or she or he pledged to donate. Often the subject did both. But just as often, the video of the drenching offered no clue about the destination of the charitable contribution. Many videos never mentioned a cause at all.[1]

Soon after Lauer issued his challenge on American television (which meant, of course, that the video of that event would circulate on Facebook as well), word spread that the Ice Bucket Challenge should support the Amyotrophic Lateral Sclerosis (ALS) Association. Soon all the other charities that had been cited by those who committed the act faded into the background. Facebook made it easy for the challenge to spread, because a person could both name those challenged and "tag" them through the service Facebook provides to link profiles to content. Ultimately more than 2.5 million Ice Bucket Challenge videos circulated on Facebook. More than twenty-eight million people engaged with those videos in some way. Celebrities and politicians joined in. And the trend spread far beyond the United States. In just one month in the summer of 2014 the Amyotrophic Lateral Sclerosis Association gathered $98.2 million, compared to just $2.7 million during the same period the year before. In India, where clean water is scarce and at a premium, the "rice bucket challenge" spread, urging people to donate rice to poor people. And in Gaza, activists posted videos of the "rubble bucket challenge" to raise awareness of the misery of daily life in the severed territory that had seen its infrastructure destroyed during conflagrations with Israel.[2]

By simple measures the Ice Bucket Challenge was a spectacular success. The money it raised contributed to essential research against ALS, a rare condition in which parts of the nervous system malfunction, causing progressive weakness and muscle wasting. As the disease progresses, it hinders basic activities such as walking, speaking, swallowing, and breathing. Life expectancy for about half of those with ALS is three to four years from start of diagnosis, but some can live much longer. The effects of ALS are so powerful that generating compassion for those afflicted was not difficult. The challenge has always been to raise awareness of a disease that affects so few people.[3]

There is a problem with all this success, however. In 2014 a larger amount of money went to ALS research than ever before. Was 2014 a particularly crucial year for ALS research? Was the incidence of the disease rising? No, it was like any other year. ALS, like every other debilitating disease, deserves more money for research and treatment. But a dollar donated to ALS research is a dollar denied to malaria prevention, breast cancer research,

HIV treatment and prevention, or the most deadly affliction of all, heart disease. Who should decide which diseases get more research money and which should get less in any given year? On what should we base that judgment? Perhaps we should consider mortality. Perhaps we should consider the numbers of people afflicted. Perhaps we should consider the likelihood of a breakthrough treatment. Many countries employ councils of physicians, scientists, and epidemiologists to make such judgments about the allocation of public research funds.

But as public funding shrinks in many places, including the United States, private sources of research funding become more important. For private sources, whether in large sums from foundations or wealthy donors or in small amounts from millions of Facebook users, publicity makes all the difference. The associations devoted to funding research and treatment rely on narratives of those who suffer. They offer glimmers of hope that the next drive might push the research to its breakthrough point. And since the Ice Bucket Challenge, they try to attach their causes to spectacles that would spread around Facebook.[4]

The cause that makes the catchiest, cutest, or most clever Facebook campaign generates the most financial support. This is a terrible way to determine where charitable contributions should go, especially when medical science is involved. Nothing in any of the Ice Bucket Challenge videos revealed how well the Amyotrophic Lateral Sclerosis Association spends the money it raises. Few if any of the cold and shivering subjects of the videos, for all their good intentions, explained why ALS was such a debilitating and fatal disease or the good to which the money donated would be spent. Many of the videos omitted any reference to ALS. They became spectacles for the sake of spectacle. In the summer of 2014 the world did not discuss and debate whether ALS was the most urgent or even the most promising of causes. It was just the most fun to think about—even though the thinking remained at the level of watching a person get soaked in cold water. The success of the Ice Bucket Challenge pushed all such philanthropic endeavors to consider more lively ways to engage interest. For many, that meant devoting more attention to Facebook, where attention is the only currency that matters.[5]

THE ATTENTION ECONOMY

Attention is scarce. It is limited by time, of course. Most people find it difficult to pay attention to more than one thing at a time. Yet it's easy to steal. A flash, a movement, or an odd sound can pull attention away from this page to something in the periphery of your field of vision. It takes an active decision to move not only your eyes (because they can glaze over when staring at these letters) but your mental processes back to this book. Attention feeds thought. And thought works in streams. If those streams are limited by duration or not allowed to stay steady and focused, the power of that thought diminishes. Yet attention is also valuable, even—or perhaps especially—when it is brief and shallow. People are more easily tickled or angered when attention is fleeting. They are also more likely to be convinced to click on a link on a web page, application, or email if their attention is shallow and short. To sell something, an advertiser must grab your attention, if only for a moment. Advertisers know that while they have your attention, someone else is trying to steal it away from them. So as our media ecosystem becomes more polluted and fractured, each player in it experiments with new designs, targeting strategies, and stimuli to steal attention and then hold it long enough to convince the potential customer to take some action. Add up all those players seeking smaller and smaller fractions of our attention over long periods and the logic of the market generates cacophony. Few moments are spared from the frantic attempts at attention theft. Few spaces remain unmarked by some effort to pull our eyes from the direction we choose.[6]

As many parts of the world deindustrialized over the past forty years, leaving labor with lower wages and fewer protections, we have been promised that the "information economy" would replace industrialization. Information is not scarce. It's too abundant, in fact. Managing and filtering information has become a valuable function as a result. Google and to a lesser extent Facebook help us manage the torrent of information around us by doing the work of deciding what's valuable or interesting to us. Part of that transition to an information economy involved the rise of industries completely devoted to capturing our attention. Again, Google and Facebook have cornered the market on that. Monetizing our captured attention pays for the labor and technology that enable Google and Facebook to filter the flood of information so effectively. And while those two companies are far from the only players in the attention economy, they are the best at it. Google and Facebook are the most successful of the set of firms that connect advertisers to potential customers. That set includes newspapers, websites, television networks and stations, radio stations, and billboard companies. It now also includes coach and bus services, universities, sports stadia, and hotels, all of which have developed methods of hosting advertising for the patrons and customers who spend time in them. Law professor Tim Wu, who has charted the history of the attention economy, calls this set of firms "attention brokers."[7]

The attention economy emerged from an ideological decision that whole industries made in the late 1990s, when the World Wide Web made it possible to imagine that people would read text and watch video on small LCD screens instead of on printed pages and in dark theaters. Content had to be free. The word "free" carried a lot of weight in those days, signifying the spirit of the age. Capitalism and democracy were ascendant. Libertarianism was no longer considered a fringe ideology. "Free" meant digital content could be cost-free and able to circulate unfettered. To lift the world to new heights of liberty and creativity, the marginal cost of goods and services should approach zero, the theory went. To pay the coders, the utility companies, and the lawyers, however, digital companies would need revenue. Starting with Yahoo in the late 1990s and culminating with Google by the early 2000s, advertising would supply the capital. Once this entire industry decided that content had to be free, it put pressure on industries that had long relied on unit sales or the price of admission, such as music labels, book publishers, and film studios, to drop their prices close to free. These other companies started looking for other sources of revenue that embedded themselves in the attention economy, thus competing against each other not only for the marginal cash in a family's entertainment budget but also for their scarce free time. Culture and entertainment figures strove to make themselves "lifestyle brands" and pushed their images out on YouTube, Twitter, and Instagram. The attention economy has its macroeconomic phenomena, as exemplified by Google, Facebook, and the entertainment and journalism industries. And it has its microeconomic forces, acting upon everyone else who looked at work life as a matter of free agency and a constant hustle for fleeting opportunities.

The ideology that underlies the attention economy also structures individual experience and cultural expectation. When successful private sector managers meet my students, they often tell these aspiring media workers that they must behave as "brands," constantly and exhaustively promoting themselves through Facebook, Twitter, YouTube, and Instagram. Young people are signaled that becoming a "microcelebrity" may lead to bigger and better macrocelebrity later on. The virtues of not being famous rarely have a champion or a fairy tale behind them. The pinnacle of the struggle for attention, which we are promised will surely pay off through wealth and fame, is the TED Talk. Purposely informal and limited to eighteen minutes, these punchy, pithy talks are meant to inspire and entertain. They don't invite deliberation or debate. They don't demand immersion or even background reading. They are capsules of knowledge. To deliver a TED Talk, however, is the apex of self-branding. And, not coincidentally, one of the major ways people discover TED Talks and other self-promotional videos is through Facebook.[8]

On Facebook, everything is an advertisement and advertisements are everything. There are no clear markers that distinguish the lines between items meant to persuade (to vote, to buy, to donate, to play) and items meant to entertain or inform. Even the style of presentation of individual profiles function as advertisements. Facebook scrambles the commercial and the social. Our interaction with Facebook reinforces this. We are frequently reminded that we must groom our social media profiles to offer the most compelling and pleasing image to the world. If we say the wrong thing or post the wrong photo on Facebook, we could find ourselves out of a job or a relationship. The scrambling of our social contexts creates constant pressure to perform and perfect our Facebook selves. We are constantly trying to persuade others on Facebook. We groom our profiles like we groom our hair. We choose what we post to perform our identities and affiliations. It's easy and possible to declare to the people you most want to impress or commune with, "I am the sort of person who cares about Real Madrid, free-market economics, and the European Song Contest." Facebook profiles are advertisements for ourselves. Facebook sorts users' profiles by affiliation and interest, and then more dynamically based on interactions and the flow of "engagement." And users feed clues into Facebook's algorithms that amplify that process further, creating a constantly churning lattice of affiliations.[9]

The more time we spend grooming our self-presentation and declaring our tribal affiliations, the more we grow acculturated to this habit. It becomes a cultural norm. It assumes the soft power of ideology. Companies that desire to break through the flows and distractions all around us find it necessary to detect and play to those affiliations. If I have repeatedly declared myself a fan of the San Antonio Spurs, companies that wish to sell me things would like to know that. To grab my attention away from all the things my Facebook Friends post about the Spurs, both for and against, advertisers have to hook me with something fresh and loud so that they can move me to consider buying something related to my interests. This is not only possible with the massive collections of data about each of us that marketing firms, Facebook, Google, Amazon, and others possess, but it is efficient and inexpensive.

We may have reached "peak advertising." If our information ecosystem becomes completely saturated with attempts to pull our attention toward products and services, we might build up resistance to each effort. News, entertainment, web search, and even social networks would find their marginal returns for each dollar invested in advertising slipping away. If our attention becomes so completely harvested that there is no more for us to give, how would we have dependable and affordable news? There would be no space in our world unmarked by commercial sponsorship. Traditional advertising has had a great run for almost two hundred years. While its practices and technologies have shifted significantly over that time, the basic functions remains the same: grab attention from potential consumers, focus it on a good or service, and have the provider of that good or service pay for that transaction to subsidize whatever media content the consumer had hoped to encounter. The consumer does not have to pay much up front for the content. The media company gets diverse sources of revenue. And the firm that buys the ad gets some faith that it can locate potential consumers efficiently. That's how it's supposed to work. But as each advertisement loses its power in the torrent of draws on our attention, more ads flood our field of vision.[10]

Many public school systems across the United States now allow corporate advertising to target students in exchange for a flow of shared revenue for the schools. Lockers, hallway walls, and meals bear logos. School announcements appear in video billboards amid advertisements. In America in 2018 few spaces are considered sacred or safe from the demands for our attention. The advertisements that seem to work best are those placed through services that precisely target the good or service to the person who might want that good or service, and those that seems least like an advertisement. Facebook accomplished both of these by erasing the cues that help us distinguish between a commercial for a product and a post from one of our Friends. And it accomplished that most powerfully by harvesting data about our behavior and preferences to ensure we see ads that Facebook's algorithms judge to be "relevant" to us.[11]

This is a radical change in how advertising works. Data-driven advertising upends almost two centuries of advertising that's based not on empirical evidence but on a certain faith that the message will reach its intended audience; this earlier type of advertising funded the media systems that enabled many of the changes of the twentieth century. The mania to capture our attention began with the "penny press," which radically altered journalism and commerce in North America. When some nineteenth-century newspaper publishers realized they could sell papers for less than the *New York Times* charged per issue and make up the difference in bulk sales, they traded subscription and newsstand revenue for advertising revenue. All they had to do was demonstrate to local stores that they had a stronger grip on the attention of the rising literate middle class. This move, which never destroyed the *New York Times* yet was led by papers long ago preserved in the amber of library microfilm, served as the model for similar insurgent attacks in other media through the next 180 years. Despite its failure to destroy its rivals, the penny press movement did alter the practices and expectations of all newspapers in America and—more significant—served as a model for how other media forms would deploy advertising in their efforts to reach broad audiences with minimal up-front charges to consumers. Desires to capture and measure consumer attention conflict with dreams of providing the sort of substantive, high-quality culture and information that a thriving democratic republic and dynamic economy need. But overall, advertising has managed to keep alive publications as diverse in depth and seriousness as the *Daily Mirror, National Enquirer, Economist,* and *New Yorker.* Reading markets, like consumer markets, are segmented. Advertisers and publishers have become masters at targeting both content and ads to particular tranches of the American public.[12]

While newspapers and magazines—and thus their advertisers—had long focused on broad segments of a mass market, generally marked by location, ethnicity, gender, and social class, by the 1970s the rise of computer databases and more subtle market research led to some new market segmentation models. These new segments were defined by cultural style as much as gender or ethnicity. Segment names like "Bohemian Mix," "Shotguns and Pickups," and "Young Suburbia" now helped advertisers, marketers, and the publications and programs that depended on advertisers reach audiences with new precision. This data-intensive (for its time) work signaled the end of the assumption that there is a single mass market for just about anything in America. It began the process of the "sorting" of each of us into pockets of like-minded market segments.[13]

In a steady climb over the next forty years, media, marketing, and advertising firms tapped larger pools of data, using more powerful algorithms and processors. Through direct mail they were able to target smaller and smaller tranches of consumers. But the loudest and most persuasive voices were still major publications, commercial radio broadcasts, and television. Market segmentation on television could really only get as precise as a region. So one advertisement for a product might run in Salt Lake City, Utah, while another version for the same product might run in San Francisco. Advertisers rarely employed even that level of segmentation on television because producing and testing targeted ads was expensive and time-consuming. It was more cost-effective to play to the presumed large middle of an audience.[14]

Internet-based advertising offered the ability to label and sort audiences with precision beyond even direct mail. Now advertisers could reach specific members of a household without mailing a piece of paper to the entire household. More important, web advertising creates data that show if the ad actually worked. All other forms of advertising, no matter how scientifically targeted or tested, are leaps of faith. But the advertising system Google invented in the first few years of the twenty-first century operated completely differently. Advertisers would pay for an ad only if a person clicked on it. This meant that if an ad failed, the advertiser could try a different version or target it differently. Digital media allowed that malleability. It's easy to experiment with different ad content, different audiences, and different targeting keywords. Also, Google assigned prices for ads based on instant, computer-driven auctions. The high bidder would pay only the price that the second-highest bidder had offered, ensuring that the auction winner never overpaid for an ad. After Sheryl Sandberg left Google to run Facebook in 2008, Facebook adopted many of the same techniques that had made Google valuable. Then Sandberg directed new experiments and ad services that only Facebook could provide, given the richness of personal data and the graph of social connections. This is the main reason Google and Facebook are the most effective advertising systems ever created. The 1960s and 1970s masterminds behind rudimentary market segmentation, inspired by the ethnic and cultural recognition movements of the 1960s, started a revolution that the Mark Zuckerbergs of the world have seen to fruition.[15]

Advertising in the mid-twentieth century focused on methods of persuasion. Experts in the field promised they could move or inspire people to purchase goods they might never have considered. They promised they could persuade undecided voters to move to support a candidate they might have ignored before. Steadily, as the twentieth century gave way to the twenty-first, advertising became much more about aligning interest with offers. One did not have to try to persuade consumers to buy a good or service if you could find enough new consumers who were already interested or—even better—had already searched for a product or service. Once an advertiser identified that consumer, it required less expense and effort to urge the consumer to make the purchase. Direct marketing had long held out the dream of precise profiling to match the interest to the offer. Not until firms had deep records of searching, shopping, and personal interest behavior could they realize this dream. In an advertising world dominated by Facebook and Google, there is a lot less attempted persuasion. The game is all about matching.

The unrelenting drive to surveil and tag complex consumers and then demand slivers of their attention in hopes that they engage in a series of transactions is more than distracting and exhausting. It's dehumanizing. It treats us each as means to a sale rather than as ends in ourselves. It also undermines centuries of concerted effort to engage in complex collective thought that could enable us to deliberate about the issues we face as a species. It's hard to participate in a republic, let alone face global challenges, when hit network programs such as *The Voice* have our eyes darting from television to iPad to phone, tweeting and cheering and chatting and shopping along.

Not that there is anything wrong with that. Tweeting, cheering, chatting, and shopping are fun. And no one said we signed up for a republic without fun. The difference now is the unrelenting ubiquity of these draws on our attention. Even our political lives are multiscreen affairs. The professional heirs to radio visionary David Sarnoff's NBC empire have spawned the specter that now haunts the party of Lincoln, the constitution of Madison, and the nation of Jefferson—a reality-TV-star-in-chief.

HOW FACEBOOK TURNS PERSONAL DATA INTO PROPAGANDA

In 2016 agents working on behalf of the Russian government used the very Facebook feature that has made the company stunningly profitable and convinced so many businesses to shift their advertising budgets from newspapers to Facebook. The Russian agents targeted content using the Facebook advertising system to mess with American democracy. They created bogus Facebook groups and pages devoted to such issues as opposing gun control, opposing immigration, and pushing for Texas to secede from the United States. Russian agents even ran one Facebook page called "Blacktivist," purporting to support a campaign against police violence. Once U.S. officials pressured Facebook to come clean about the extent to which the company had been hijacked by Russian operatives, Facebook found 470 pages and profiles linked to a Russian company called the Internet Research Agency. The people who controlled pages had purchased about three thousand ads, often paying in Russian currency. Ultimately these techniques reached more than 126 million Americans. These Facebook pages and groups managed to motivate more than 62,000 Americans to pledge to attend 129 rallies and events meant to support Donald Trump, oppose Hillary Clinton, and protest mosques around the United States. Each of these Americans saw these posts because Facebook helped the Internet Research Agency target them through the company's basic advertising service.[16]

Setting up an ad campaign on Facebook is both easy and inexpensive. It's self-service. And there is alarmingly little oversight from Facebook. Such an expansive global system can't easily be controlled. So Facebook leaves it largely uncontrolled. Its chief form of governance is machine learning. As advertisers generate categories of Facebook users to target, or Facebook users cluster through interaction, Facebook's algorithms create new categories to focus the reach of an ad. So there are many categories of targeted users from which to choose. To promote a podcast that I produce, I ran a campaign that spent only $200. I chose to push the notice for the podcast, which is about how scientists who study the brain and behavior do their work and discuss controversies, to a select audience in the United States, Canada, and the United Kingdom. I chose to focus the campaign on those who had expressed interest in psychology and neuroscience. I limited the ad placement to those who had an M.D. or a Ph.D. And I excluded those who were younger than thirty years old. This meant I would only reach about three thousand Facebook users. But they would be the right three thousand Facebook users. Just for fun I also excluded any Facebook user who had expressed interest in the 1970s country music singer Crystal Gayle. This did not change the size of my target audience at all. Or if it did, it reduced it by only a handful of Ph.D.'s who happen to like Crystal Gayle.

This ability to exclude types of people from an advertising campaign is crucial to the success of Facebook ads and therefore of Facebook itself. Only Facebook knows who in the United States, Canada, and the United Kingdom has expressed interest in Gayle. This might seem silly and harmless. It is. Facebook also, notoriously, has allowed advertisers to exclude Jews, African Americans, women, and Spanish-speakers from advertising campaigns, including those for housing and employment.[17]

Facebook's advertising services permit those running an advertising campaign to carry out tests on sections of the audience with different versions of the ad. If one version of the ad, perhaps with a red background instead of a green background, generates better "engagement" (more clicks, shares, comments, and likes), then the advertiser knows to drop the green version. Then the advertiser can test red against blue, or red against yellow, or red in California and yellow in France. Such constant iteration can make advertising campaigns better over time. Without adequate personal data on which to build such a targeting system, Facebook could not offer this service. Without such a targeting service, Facebook would just be running clumsy, ineffective ads—the same kind that newspapers and television stations have run for decades. This is yet another way that Facebook segregates us and creates alternative cultural and political universes for us. It's the core business of Facebook. To reform it is futile. It's Facebook.

FUNNEL VISION

The same logic favors some ads over other ads and some user-generated content (the photos, posts, videos, and questions we all post) over other content on Facebook. Engagement wins. Over time Facebook not only rewards the items that are likely to generate the most markers of engagement (clicks, likes, comments, shares) but also learns to tailor the News Feed of every Facebook profile. The longer you are on Facebook, the more you engage with items on Facebook, and the more you teach Facebook to send you more of the stuff that is very much like what you have already indicated interests you. Both Facebook and Google call this a test of "relevance." Relevance has no relationship to the helpful, the enlightening, the moral, the educational, or the true. That logic works very well for product and service advertising. But when the same logic applies to all posts, whether they are news or news-like items or videos of cats on skateboards, the experience over time is one of a narrowing field of vision. We start to see more items posted by Friends with whom we have richly engaged before. We see more items posted from publications or entertainment outlets with which we have engaged before. It's more than tunnel vision. It's funnel vision.

This phenomenon is what writer, activist, and entrepreneur Eli Pariser dubbed the "filter bubble." Facebook gives us more of the sorts of items we respond to with clicks, likes, shares, and comments, pushing aside things that might not interest us. That's fine if the subject is commercial or trivial. Cat people should not have to see too many items about dog products and vice versa. Pariser noticed in the early days of Facebook that over time he saw fewer posts from Friends who differed with him politically. He suspected that Facebook was algorithmically clustering people, generating this funnel vision. So he interviewed engineers at Facebook and Google and listened to their explanations of the values they embedded in their algorithms. Pariser's suspicions were valid. Once his book *The Filter Bubble* (and the accompanying TED Talk) debuted in 2011 others began to doubt the impact of the phenomenon. The power of filter bubbles remains unmeasured and perhaps unmeasurable, despite many efforts to do so. The intent is clear, however. Both Facebook and Google declare that their algorithms perform the function of delivering "relevant" content based on our record of engagement and what others like us and around us do. The phenomenon is observable on a personal level, as Pariser and others have testified. But the question of whether the filter bubble actually limits our vision or tribalizes us even more than we already do for ourselves remains murky. It's almost impossible to measure the effects of the filter bubble without access to user data that only Facebook has.[18]

In 2015 researchers at Facebook published in *Science* a significant study of political polarization among Facebook users. The study, which can't be replicated or deeply examined because Facebook keeps its data to itself, concluded that "compared with algorithmic ranking, individuals' choices played a stronger role in limiting exposure to cross-cutting content." This means that Facebook researchers found a significant amount of polarization among Facebook users but ascribe it to homophily—a sociological term used to describe our urge to cavort with those similar to ourselves—more than to Facebook's algorithms. It's easy to make too much of these findings. And many did. First, the paper does not deflate the idea that the algorithms sort items along patterns that reflect previous engagement. It just concludes that the algorithmic effect is lighter than the effects of the choices we users make.

The more important lesson to take from this study is that Facebook and user homophily work synergistically to narrow our field of vision. It's wrong to conclude that we have forged "echo chambers" that seal out divergent views, or that Facebook has. That's an extreme and unfounded assumption. But it's reasonable to believe that our vision is narrower than it might otherwise be if we were not engaging with Facebook so often and about such important matters. The choices we make and the choices Facebook makes for us feed each other. We are part of the system. The technology is not distinct from the culture, the politics, and the ideologies in which it operates. The arguments about whether the filter bubble exists or how much it matters too often get bogged down in a false dichotomy: is it the fault of technology or is it the fault of humans? The answer is always yes.[19]

Political segregation, the fraying of civil discourse, and the erosion of trust in civic institutions is a fact of life around the world. So the narrowing of our field of vision, the filtering of information to that which emboldens our confidence in the beliefs we already hold, and the segregation of citizens into polarized camps all steadily undermine the potential for republican governance and reasonable discourse about important matters.[20]

One of the reasons it's easy to doubt the power of the filter bubble is that some have been crying wolf about it since before the problem even emerged. The earliest critique of what became known later as the filter bubble predated Facebook by three years. In 2001 legal scholar Cass Sunstein reacted to a proposition then in vogue among internet idealists: once all of our news content existed on the World Wide Web, we could use various filters and platforms to curate a flow of news that we could customize to our interests. For more than a century we bought a whole newspaper just for the sports section, the comics, or the bridge column. We got the news from Moscow and Melbourne in the package, whether we cared or not. Newspapers had no way of knowing if people read any of their stories from beginning to end. They had no way of knowing if anyone ever opened up the business section. Like the companies that advertised within them, newspapers operated on only the roughest data, total sales, and chose content based on hunches, trends, or even something called news judgment. The web offered readers a chance to encounter only content that they selected. So they might read four stories about the World Cup tournament matches and none about the corruption within FIFA. They could encounter many pieces about the struggles in Puerto Rico following a hurricane and nothing about the suffering in Mumbai after a massive monsoon. Big thinkers such as MIT professor Nicholas Negroponte celebrated this sort of customization. Sunstein was appalled. This reeked of consumerism trumping republicanism, as he wrote in the book *Republic.com*.[21]

Sunstein wrote the same argument with a different set of conditions two more times. In 2007 he updated *Republic.com* with *Republic.com 2.0*. The thing that had changed was the rise of blogs between 2002 and 2007. Then, in early 2017, Sunstein released his third version of the same argument, *#Republic*. This time, the focus was on how social media generated the "daily me," but the concern was the same. The central argument of all three versions is that our growing habit of relying on websites, blogs, and now social media has focused our vision and sorted us into what he calls "echo chambers," ensuring that we fail to see information that complicates our sense of reality and fail to engage with views that challenge our position. Sunstein deserves some credit for identifying this problem many years before other media critics realized it. But he lacked strong evidence for his concern until the rise of powerful algorithms such as those that drive Google and Facebook. The 2001 version of his argument challenged the rhetoric of web enthusiasts who proclaimed that the consumerist vision of a tailored media environment would be wonderful for both individuals and consumers. But in 2001 web pages were still static and fairly new, and the filtering power of Google was only just becoming clear. By 2007 Sunstein was compelled to focus his argument on the blogosphere, just about five years old at the moment of publication. Blogs brought a social dynamic to the web's news, information, and commentary ecosystem through the then-influential blogrolls, which helped readers discover similar blogs recommended by their favorite bloggers.[22]

The problem for Sunstein's thesis was that many of the most influential political blogs at the time regularly and mostly respectfully engaged with ideological opponents in debates that were of high quality. Conservatives such as Glenn Reynolds, Ann Althouse, Mickey Kaus, and Andrew Sullivan mixed it up with liberals including Heather Digby Parton, Jack Balkin, Matthew Yglesias, and Duncan Black. A post on a liberal blog would challenge one from a conservative blog with a link and full quotes. The response on the conservative blog would link back to the liberal one. And each writer would use whatever space it took to outline an argument and offer evidence—also supported by links to sources. Just as important, the high moment of blogs allowed academic experts to exert public voices in ways that had been rare or impossible just a few years earlier. As sociologist Eszter Hargittai found in 2008, the most notable political bloggers across the political spectrum often addressed each other's writing substantively, whether to agree or to disagree.[23]

Two of those newly empowered academic bloggers, Daniel Drezner and Henry Farrell, responded to Sunstein's dour account of blogging with a full-throated defense in *Foreign Policy* of how valuable and important the blogosphere had been to enriching public understanding and discourse. Nonetheless, Farrell coauthored a paper in 2009 that concluded that blog readers tend to read blogs that accord with their political beliefs. Cross-cutting readership of blogs on both the left and right of the spectrum was rare. Farrell and others found strong evidence of polarization among blog readers, who tend to be more polarized than both those who do not read blogs and those who consume television news. Both of these things could be—and were—true: the major political blogs encouraged readers to engage with differing points of view, and regular readers of blogs sorted themselves into clusters by starting their explorations among a core set of blogs with which they agreed strongly. In the age of the blogosphere, no algorithm amplified homophily. But homophily still mattered. Readers segregated themselves, which should be no surprise. We all love to remind ourselves how smart and correct we are. And we are all susceptible to confirmation bias, approving of accounts that reinforce our assumptions and rejecting evidence that runs contrary.[24]

We should look back on the high moment of blogging with nostalgic reverence. The blogging era, roughly 2002 to 2007, was perhaps the richest and most diverse media ecosystem we have ever enjoyed. Google was gaining ground in the advertising market, but the market had not yet moved so destructively away from freestanding publications, both web-based and print-based. Web-based sites such as OpenDemocracy.net and Salon.com grew in status and influence. Diverse opinions and analyses generated by informed and articulate experts found audiences through blogs and the links that appeared on blogs. One interesting blog would lead a reader to another.

Since then, though, Facebook and Twitter have drained the blogosphere of its vitality. Facebook and Google have drained publications of revenue and confidence. Some group blogs such as Huffington Post, Talking Points Memo, and Boing Boing have morphed into influential professional news and commentary sites. But the communal DIY spirit is gone. Much expression that used to fill blog posts now finds itself distilled in 140 characters on Twitter or posted on Facebook and thus subject to the whims of Facebook's powerful algorithms.

The Facebook algorithms made the difference. We chose our Facebook Friends. And most of us have friends, relatives, and colleagues who have different opinions and read different sources than we do. But our habits of interaction—clicks, comments, and "likes"—tell Facebook to reward the sources that earn our "engagement." We get more of the same. We are already creatures of habit and comfort when it comes to our views of the world. Facebook radically amplifies those tendencies. Things posted on Facebook can't easily travel beyond Facebook. And Facebook posts find only the audience that Facebook decides it deserves. Such "choice architecture" is dangerously powerful. We can believe that filter bubbles exist because Facebook and Google tell us what their companies do. They tell us— roughly and without precision or clarity—why we see certain content and not other content. Basically, we tend toward homophily. Our media system can correct for that tendency or it can reinforce it. Our current media ecosystem, dominated by Facebook, amplifies both our weakness for confirmation and our desire to cluster among the like-minded. It's not just the technology. It's not just the cultural proclivities of human beings. Technology is culture and culture is technology. All are part of the same system.

FEEDING THE BEAST

Before Facebook rose to its central role in how people learned about the world around them and performed politics, Google's search algorithms largely determined what got read or seen. Sites that optimized their design and content to satisfy Google's search algorithms could thrive. When people turned to Google as news broke about a mass shooting or a tsunami, the sites that could please Google would earn the clicks. The clicks would justify advertisements. And more clicks and links from other sites would mean more visibility in the future. Success in the "search engine optimization" game could generate positive feedback loops—uphill cascades—so the winners would keep on winning and those sites unable to pander to Google would fall to the dark depths of the second page of search results.[25]

Out of the flurry of homemade and bespoke blogs that proliferated in the first decade of the twenty-first century, Huffington Post, launched in 2005, was the behemoth. Arianna Huffington seemed to be the ideal person to invent a new style of publication for the attention economy. She had, after all, managed to generate attention across multiple media forms (books, magazines, television) about multiple issues (modern art, conservative politics, liberal politics, lifestyle fads). She had written a controversial biography of Pablo Picasso. She had married a millionaire who lost a race for governor of California. She had appeared on talk shows of all sorts. But, having exhibited no significant mastery of anything, no stable ideology, and no business acumen, Huffington was most famous for being famous. Investors gladly bet that the attention economy would reward the sort of person who knew how to make people look and listen. They were not wrong. Huffington's idea was to set up a sort of group blog. Her celebrity friends would contribute posts. People would flock to read what Ted Danson had to say about the state of our oceans or what Larry David had written about the U.S. ambassador to the United Nations. Just as important, the publication that would be dubbed Huffington Post (now HuffPost) offered unknown or yet-to-be-known writers a chance to contribute articles for no remuneration. By attracting writers who did not expect to be paid, Huffington kept expenses low. To keep interest high, Huffington depended on two partners who had already demonstrated a mastery of the new digital environment and who would soon make their mark in the next era of digital media: Andrew Breitbart and Jonah Peretti.[26]

Breitbart was a conservative culture warrior. He had worked for right-wing gadfly Matt Drudge and had mastered the style and substance that made the Drudge Report required reading for the politically obsessed beyond even its core conservative audience. Breitbart, who died in 2012, understood how to push emotional buttons and rile up members of a movement. He had a trickster streak. And he was frenetic and obsessive, making him an uncomfortable business partner for the Huffington Post venture. Soon after the launch Breitbart left Huffington Post to launch his own site, one that would embody his politics and personality: Breitbart. com. That site, taken over after Breitbart's death by another frenetic right-wing populist, Steve Bannon, would master the social media era of the attention economy much the way Huffington Post had succeeded in the search engine optimization period.[27]

Peretti stayed at Huffington Post until AOL purchased it in 2011, but in 2006 he launched what he called a "laboratory" to test how content might flow as the media ecosystem changed. He called that laboratory BuzzFeed. com. Over the past decade BuzzFeed has grown from a source of viral lists, quizzes, images, videos, and cats to a source of viral lists, quizzes, images, videos, cats, and serious, lively journalism. BuzzFeed has investigative journalists. It has bureaus around the world. It has top-notch cultural commentators. And it still has listicles and cat photos. What BuzzFeed learns about testing, revising, measuring, and promoting posts of one kind helps it distribute posts of other kinds. It's a giant learning machine as well as a news and entertainment machine. If any news organization has cracked the code of Facebook, it's BuzzFeed. And by specializing in ethically suspect paid content (advertisements that work like and look like editorial content) BuzzFeed has made a bet on the sort of advertising that Facebook and Google can't and won't do, specially tailored to BuzzFeed readers and distributed via the same algorithmic tricks that Facebook plays on the editorial content. It seems to be working, although the massive tide of advertising moving to Facebook and Google and away from other sites and news organizations has also caught BuzzFeed in a financial bind. If BuzzFeed can't make it in the long run in an information ecosystem dominated by Facebook, nothing can.[28]

Both BuzzFeed and Breitbart are at once tentative success stories and cautionary tales. Breitbart is the source of virulent ethnic nationalistic propaganda that aims to undermine the civic spirit of the United States. It's influential with many people who support President Donald Trump and who work around him. Material that spews out of Breitbart works its way up to cable news shows, often to be denied, debunked, or reported on as a "controversy." So Breitbart performs a disruptive and distracting role in the public consciousness. What Breitbart produces plays very well on Facebook. The people who run Breitbart learned the same lessons that informed Peretti and his associates at BuzzFeed. Separated at birth, both gain and maintain an audience by working with and through the ways Facebook energizes some posts and stifles others.

Their stories also should make us cautious because they signal to other news and entertainment outlets that one should—or must—pander to Facebook to succeed in a shrinking market for advertising revenue and a crowded supply of attention-seeking destinations. Not only do the *Guardian*, *El País*, and *Haaretz* all compete with HuffPost, Breitbart, and the *New York Times* for space and frequency on Facebook News Feeds, they also compete with YouTube videos, games, music, podcasts, and hundreds of other diversions in daily life—all of them more and more precisely engineered to hook us and keep us coming back.

By the summer of 2017, the Pew Research Center revealed, 67 percent of adults in the United States used social media to discover news. That was up from 49 percent just five years earlier. While this is a rough number and might not reveal that much, largely because it's unclear what American social media users consider "news," the upward trend is strong and thus worth considering. Clearly social media and the "choice architecture" that governs them are becoming more important in our lives as citizens as traditional sources of news slowly go broke. To sum up, news organizations are compelled to make editorial choices (which stories to cover, how to craft headlines, whether to favor video over photos or text) to pander to Instagram's or Facebook's algorithms because they can't afford to be invisible on Facebook or Instagram. Yet advertisers flock to Facebook and Instagram and away from the sources of all that essential information about the world. Journalism is feeding the beast that starves it. And there is nothing journalists can do about it.[29]

THE OPERATING SYSTEM OF OUR LIVES

Soon we might not have to pay attention at all. If the five biggest technology companies in the world fulfill their wishes, they will sell us a series of devices, each promising to make our daily tasks a little bit more convenient. These devices would monitor us without our direct interaction. They would capture our intentions and desires at those few moments when we are not staring at screens and typing on keyboards. Some of these devices sit on our counters. Others are embedded in our cars. Some are built into our thermostats and appliances. Others sit on our skin. In 2016 the most successful advertising company in the history of the world introduced an obelisk called Google Home. It's a loudspeaker and a microphone constantly connected to Google's servers and algorithms. Always on, it passively listens to the words and sounds of the home. Google Home melds the information it gathers with the rich dossier that Google already has on its users. It promises to provide personalized responses to verbal search queries and requests to play music. Google Home is a response to Amazon's Echo, which also sits on a counter, constantly listening for voice commands to order more products for quick delivery. The newest version of Apple's Siri is also capable of listening at all times, learning constantly about its owner's desires. Between these devices on our counters and the mobile sensors we increasingly strap to our skin and carry in our pockets, the "attention brokers" need no longer compete for our attention.

Consider the five most powerful digital companies in the world: Facebook, Alphabet (the holding company for Google), Microsoft, Amazon, and Apple. Through most of 2017 these companies were the five most highly capitalized companies in the world. We call them leaders of the "technology sector." Yet they are very different companies that do different things for us. While they compete for highly trained labor, within commercial markets they only compete incidentally. Facebook and Google do compete for web and mobile advertising. But they harvest and sell our attention in different ways because we use these services in different ways. Apple thrives by selling hardware for its core business. Microsoft still sells and leases software to businesses and consumers to make most of its money. Amazon is a retailer of goods that makes most of its money providing web server services.[30]

Yet these companies do compete in a larger, more visionary sense. Each of them has mounted efforts to achieve dominance in the next frontier of digital commerce: the data streams that would monitor, monetize, and govern our automobiles, homes, appliances, and bodies.

They no longer strive to be the operating system of our laptops and desktops. That competition is static and divided between Microsoft and Apple. They don't wrestle as much to be the default operating system of our mobile devices. The duopoly of Apple's iOS and Google's Android has locked out all other competitors, and both firms are thriving in that market. All five of these companies share one long-term vision: to be the operating system of our lives.

The operating system of our lives would measure our activities and states of being and constantly guide our decisions. Data, these visionary companies predict, will soon flow from our clothing, our vehicles, and thus our bodies. Most often this vision of data flowing through everything, with everything reporting back to central, controlling, algorithmically governed computers, is called the "internet of things." But that's not the right term. This new network is about people, not things.[31]

As they steadily introduce personal assistants, new interfaces, self-adjusting thermostats, self-driving cars, internet-connected glasses and watches, and virtual reality goggles, these companies hope to earn the trust of consumers and regulators so that they can set the standards for the transactions that can make this operating system work seamlessly and efficiently. If they realize this vision, there would be no clear distinction between media and non-media. There would be no distinction between content and objects. All objects and all bodies would be mediated content.

Such a prospect should alarm us. How shall we confront such an effort? How shall we muster a vocabulary, a set of theories, and a set of responses sufficient for such a challenge? For one, we should move away from discussing the "internet of things." The abstract vision of "the internet" is that of a network of networks, a set of connections that together create an open, accessible, dependable platform on which others may freely build and send messages without restrictions. The fact is, "the internet" has been a myth all along. The internet has never been a global, open, distributed "network of networks" that can connect all of humanity. In most of the world, digitized network communication is not so open, not well distributed, and not necessarily run through the sort of computer networks that serve as the foundation of internet communication in the United States. When you send a message via the AT&T mobile network, it's not really going through the internet of our dreams. It's going through a highly regulated proprietary system. If you are using an iPhone, that message is going through a highly regulated proprietary device. Because we increasingly send data from and to these machines that sit on our bodies and travel with us throughout the day, these flows of information are not part of some separate sphere or "cyberspace." The basic architecture of the operating system of our lives would be even more closed and restrictive. Firms and governments are quickly learning the hazards of connecting thermostats, robots, cars, and watches to a fairly open network. These networks are insecure and the humans embedded in them are undependable. Malevolent political movements, criminals, hostile states, or pranksters can hijack or bring down a delicate system of data flows. So as the architecture of this system moves on, security will be a priority over interoperability. Data networks are likely to be proprietary and access to them tightly controlled. For such a system of connected objects and bodies to operate properly it would have to be controlled by one company or a conglomeration of a handful of companies. This prospect of concentrated power should overshadow current concerns about the duopoly of Facebook and Google. Whichever company comes to dominate the operating system of our lives will wield massive power and will be an opaque "black box," governing many aspects of life with no transparency or accountability.[32]

We misunderstand this tangle of digital technologies and the roles they play in our lives when we assume that "the internet" has a particular logic, must necessarily have particular attributes (openness, neutrality, etc.), or constitutes a special "place" that operates by its own rules and norms, rather than amplifying some of the rules and norms that we already hold and undermining others. More significant is that we misunderstand the effects of technologies when we pretend that they operate or exist outside of human bodies and human relations. We are all embedded in the data network that would constitute the operating system of our lives. And the data would flow through us. Like with any technological system, we shape these technologies as much as—if not more than—they shape us. And by thinking about "the internet" or the "internet of things" instead of specific technologies and companies and how they interact with our minds and bodies, we miss the real trees for the imaginary forest.

Of these five companies, Facebook is the most pervasive and most dangerous. Facebook plays a peculiar role in the race to become the operating system of our lives. It is the most influential media company in the world. It shapes the messages that politicians, dictators, companies, religions, and more than two billion people wish to send to the world. It increasingly serves us news content, or content that purports to be news. It is the most powerful and successful advertising system in the history of the world. It's increasingly the medium of choice for political propaganda. While Facebook has thus far failed to develop devices that have invaded our homes or attached themselves to our bodies, it has assumed the goal of managing our personal lives, our commercial lives, and our political lives from within its constellation of services and applications. Across the world, more people spend more time during their days staring at their mobile phones, interacting with Facebook, Facebook Messenger, Instagram, and WhatsApp. The data people generate by interacting with these Facebook-owned services shape them. And the design choices that Facebook engineers make for these applications shape how we see and deal with the world. That complex set of feedback loops, the rich flow of personal data, and the way that the ubiquity and utility of Facebook services feel almost given have put Facebook well ahead of the other four companies in the race to be our operating system.

Of the seven most-used social media platforms, Facebook owns four—Facebook, Messenger, WhatsApp, and Instagram. If we consider only social media services that operate outside China, Facebook owns four of the top five; only YouTube, owned by Google, occupies the non-Facebook spot, at number two. Twitter, often erroneously considered a peer to or in competition with Facebook, ranks a distant tenth among all the social media platforms. Twitter has only 350 million registered accounts (compared to 2.2 billion for Facebook in 2018), but some significant portion of those accounts are "bots," or automated accounts that amplify propaganda. In terms of actual influence on actual human beings, there is no digital or social media company with the reach and power of Facebook. It is unique in human history. Yet Facebook has a direct rival. Like all true rivals, it is also an inspiration. Facebook is not the most successful company at grabbing, holding, and processing human attention. That prize goes to Tencent, a China-based firm that makes the most successful social media application in the largest market on earth: WeChat.

With almost a billion users, WeChat has infused itself into their lives in ways Facebook wishes it could. WeChat offers photo and messaging services that resemble Facebook, Instagram, and Twitter. WeChat also performs web search functions similar to what Google offers. Beyond information and communication, WeChat users can use the service to purchase items from vending machines, pay utility bills, exchange gifts, scan QR codes, conduct bank transactions, schedule doctor's appointments, search for and reserve library books, and play augmented reality games such as Pokémon Go. A WeChat user can perform many essential daily tasks without looking up from a phone or even switching among applications. WeChat is the model of one application becoming the operating system of our lives.[33]

Facebook has been building WeChat-like services into its various applications. And Mark Zuckerberg openly pines for an opportunity to operate once again in China so that Facebook can compete directly with or meld services with WeChat. When we consider the role that all those human decisions play in the WeChat or Facebook system, we must recognize that we are being mediated as much as any items of cultural expression or information.

Social media are no longer just social media. All media firms and services are attempting to become "social." Social bonds are "sticky," so they help in fending off others who would try to steal away attention. Social connections are also valuable for segmenting a market and targeting a message. As Facebook becomes more videocentric and superstores such as Amazon move into the business of producing entertainment, media forms converge. Observations and accounts of the political economy of Facebook in 2010 might not be relevant in 2020. What if "social media"—and in fact "media"—become something much more pervasive and powerful in our lives over the next twenty years?[34]

By attaching data-transmitting devices such as phones and watches to our hands we already have made ourselves nodes in the networks, subscribing to one or more companies' efforts to become the operating system of our lives. It could get more intrusive. There is a way for companies to record even more precise measures of our interests and preferences—even our fantasies. And it could grant companies greater feedback control over us in a field that has more addictive stimuli than even the best smartphone. In 2014 Facebook purchased Oculus Rift, one of the more developed virtual reality companies aimed at consumers. Zuckerberg has set a goal of getting one billion people to immerse themselves in virtual reality through Oculus. Toward that end, in 2017 Facebook released a new headset for the service that costs about $200, far less than any previous device. Two days before the company released the device, a cartoon version of Zuckerberg visited virtual Puerto Rico while its residents were suffering greatly after the floods and destruction from Hurricane Maria. The company broadcast a live video stream that managed to combine two ethical violations: disaster tourism and product promotion. He appeared as an avatar that "teleported" to different locations using Facebook's "social VR" tool Spaces. All the while Zuckerberg was sitting at the company's Menlo Park, California, headquarters, dry and safe, with ample electricity flowing around him, wearing an Oculus headset. Zuckerberg half apologized for that stunning lack of compassion by claiming he was trying to "raise awareness" and was motivated by concern for the people of Puerto Rico. The sad truth is that while he *was* concerned, no one in his own ideological filter bubble raised any objections to such a stunt. Zuckerberg, as we will see in Chapter 4, makes no distinction between what is good for Facebook and what is good for humanity. To Facebook, everyone outside the company is a means to demonstrate the world-changing potential of the next big product the company offers. And Facebook, he believes, is a means to make everyone's life better. If he means well, Zuckerberg assumes, he must be doing good.[35]

"The idea is that virtual reality puts people first," Zuckerberg said when he first demonstrated Oculus Rift in 2016. "It's all about who you're with. Once you're in there, you can do anything you want together—travel to Mars, play games, fight with swords, watch movies or teleport home to see your family. You have an environment where you can experience anything." Once you're in there, Facebook would not only track every thought and gesture as you travel to Mars or fight with swords but also track all your social engagements through virtual reality, as it already does through the Facebook app. It would learn even more about you than it already knows. It would push and prompt and move you to feel certain ways and buy certain things more effectively than it already does. Virtual reality is more than a potentially mind-blowing technology for immersive simulation. It's the ultimate Skinner box. You might think you are playing a game with deeper involvement than ever before. But that's what every pawn experiences on every chessboard.[36]

Facebook already monitors our movements and motivations. Through virtual reality it hopes to capture our voices, fantasies, and body movements without our active compliance. If Facebook becomes the operating system of our lives, we could ignore it and it would still respond, monitor, record, profile, sort, and deliver data—and more. We have a long way to go before humanity is constantly connected to and monitored by a handful of companies. Amazon Echo, Google Home, and Oculus Rift are currently just vanity products for the wealthiest among us. But the model is clear: the operating system of our lives would be about our bodies, our consciousness, our decisions. Attention would be optional. Power would be more concentrated, and manipulation constant. That's a world with no patience for autonomy and no space for democracy. It would be a lazy, narcotic world. It would not be some dystopian state of mass slavery, as portrayed in *The Matrix*. It would be kind of dull and kind of fun. It would be an existence like that in *Brave New World*.

4

The Benevolence Machine

"Facebook has always been about building community and relationships," Mark Zuckerberg said at the 2016 Facebook Social Good Forum. "And, in recent years, it's become clear, that a core part of helping grow a community is helping to keep you safe." That's an odd claim for an internet company. How can a company that traffics in data keep a person, let alone a community, safe in the face of floods, hurricanes, fires, or terrorist attacks? Zuckerberg cited two programs that he asserts will help. The first is Safety Check, through which people in an affected area, providing they have access to data streams, can alert Friends that they are safe. "Finally, when a crisis hits, we're also building tools within Facebook, that let people raise money and awareness to help rebuild their communities," Zuckerberg said.[1]

This is an almost perfect distillation of the ideology of corporate social responsibility. A company is willing to provide services that the state can't or won't provide. Those services don't directly benefit the company (except, in the case of Facebook, the more time that is spent with Facebook and the greater the number of people who come to trust and rely on Facebook, the better it is for Facebook in the long run). Those who run and work for the company receive an invisible wage in the form of self-satisfaction. Because the service costs those who use it nothing, and—more important—costs the state or public nothing, there will be little accountability. Few will examine the effectiveness or externalities of such a program. After all, it's free. And it's better than nothing. Such firm belief in one's righteousness is both liberating and powerful. It can create a public message that generates admiration from users, consumers, regulators, workers, and competitors.[2]

Disaster reactions (as opposed to disaster prevention and disaster relief, two domains that only state power can carry out at any effective scale) are part of a series of "socially responsible" programs that Facebook has announced over the years. Others include campaigns to encourage voter turnout in the United States and the Australian experiment to intercede in the distribution of revenge pornography. The specific programs are not as important as the entire orientation of the company. Zuckerberg has stated on many occasions that the purpose of Facebook is to engineer global society in accordance with the values that he espouses. He uses neutral, almost meaningless language to express that desire, so readers and listeners may fill in whatever their own vision of the good might be. Ultimately, Zuckerberg decided which values to impose on his users through the design of Facebook.

"Facebook was not originally created to be a company. It was built to accomplish a social mission—to make the world more open and connected," Zuckerberg wrote in his letter to investors in the company's initial public offering in 2012. Through that letter, Zuckerberg outlined the idealistic vision and the commitment to his own rectitude that would make him unable to consider that good intentions were not just insufficient, they could invite blowback. Zuckerberg combined self-righteousness with naiveté, believing that his fellow humans were inclined to share his values and morals—that the rest of us were basically good and all we needed was a better way to connect and communicate. That better way would be dictated by the power of Facebook's algorithms, which conveniently executed the same values that promote its advertising business. Zuckerberg had built a corporate version of a perpetual-motion machine. It seemed to have no downside. What was good for humanity was good for advertisers. What was good for advertisers was good for Facebook shareholders. What was good for Facebook shareholders was good for Facebook employees. Facebook employees would be well paid to imagine new and better ways to aid and improve humanity. And so on. It looked to Zuckerberg like a virtuous circle. "Simply put: we don't build services to make money; we make money to build better services," he wrote.[3]

"People sharing more—even if just with their close friends or families—creates a more open culture and leads to a better understanding of the lives and perspectives of others," Zuckerberg wrote in the 2012 letter to investors. "We believe that this creates a greater number of stronger relationships between people, and that it helps people get exposed to a greater number of diverse perspectives." Sharing, a kindergarten value, seems so kind and simple. To share is to give and expect nothing in return. Reciprocity becomes a cultural norm. Zuckerberg inherited this value from the hacker community that had emerged as the most compelling force behind the development of free and open source software and the internet during the 1980s and 1990s. Zuckerberg twisted that ethic into one encased within the blue box of Facebook. He even had the audacity to call his letter to investors "The Hacker Way." No actual hackers were consulted.[4]

Zuckerberg's commitment to corporate social responsibility, to making the world a better place through connectivity, has found its fullest expression in his company's endeavors to expand its market into areas of the world in which significant numbers of people lack the access, skills, and money to sustain a digital presence.[5]

Corporate social responsibility has risen in importance to global business culture since the 1970s. It has served as an organizational principle among corporate leaders who were concerned not only about their companies' complicity with the apartheid government of South Africa, environmental disasters such as the deadly chemical accident at Bhopal, India, or struggles against ethnic and gender discrimination, but also about the image of their companies. It emerged at a moment at which a consuming public grew concerned about injustices around the world. Debates around corporate social responsibility have centered on the question of sincerity, of course. Are companies that engage in such promotions really concerned about human rights and a clean environment or are their efforts merely a marketing ploy? Within business culture and the scholarship on corporate social responsibility, the central question has been about the efficacy of such campaigns. Can a company leverage its efforts to be responsible to measurably improve its image and thus its standing in a market? Can companies have it all?[6]

In India, Facebook found the limits of its self-regard. In 2014 Facebook launched a service it called Internet.org. The choice of that brand name indicated that it should be considered distinct from Facebook itself. It would be about the internet itself, rather than one social media company. And it should be considered a not-for-profit venture (.org) rather than a commercial one (.com). The service was essentially an application interface—sort of a mobile operating system—that would work on any mobile device that allowed data connectivity. The operating system would allow access to a handful of Facebook-selected applications including the Bing search engine (Microsoft's competitor to Google), women's rights services, employment services, Wikipedia for reference, and weather information.

It is important to note that these services would be offered at "zero rating," meaning that using data through them would not count against the paid data one would purchase for a mobile account. Using a competing service such as Google or an employment service not selected by Facebook would cost data and thus money for the user. If the user could not afford a data plan—and this service was ostensibly targeted at just those users—they would have to use the services that Facebook selected for Internet.org. Because zero-rating services necessarily favor some data streams over others, they violate the principle of network neutrality, which has been invoked as central to the development and success of internet practices and industries around the world. Regulators have thus been busy trying to determine to what extent zero rating violates their laws and policies.[7]

In each country in which Facebook launched Internet.org (sixty countries by October 2017) Facebook enters into a partnership with one mobile service provider. Facebook promises that offering this service at no charge to consumers who do not currently have mobile data plans will inspire future paid use as users' financial status improves. This pledge rests upon the unquestioned assumption that access to information improves the prospects of users and the communities in which they live and work.[8]

SOCIAL ENGINEERING IN INDIA

In February 2016, the Telecommunication Regulatory Authority of India ruled that Facebook's plan to introduce a free service to underprivileged Indians via a partnership with one mobile company and a handful of commercial application services violated network neutrality, the principle that digital services should not favor one source of content over another. Ultimately, and despite a major campaign promoting the benevolent spirt of the program, Free Basics, as Facebook had re-dubbed its ostensibly philanthropic effort Internet.org, died in a power struggle among a powerful American social media company, resentful Indian technology developers, overwhelmed regulators, sensitive nationalistic politicians, highly organized public interest activists, and rival mobile service providers.[9]

It was a remarkable tale of ideological hubris on the part of Facebook founder and CEO Mark Zuckerberg and the ambitions of Indian citizens and companies, who grew to resent the efforts and claims that Facebook made on behalf of poorer Indians. This story demonstrates the vast complexity of the political economy of social media. Issues such as neocolonialism, cultural imperialism, competition policy, political corruption, digital activism, class struggle, and the ideological foundations of Silicon Valley work to affect how social media function in our lives across the globe.[10]

This challenge to network neutrality thus accompanies a more traditional threat to competition. India, unlike some of the other countries in which Facebook launched Internet.org, has deep traditions of democratic participation and a highly competitive private technology and telecommunications sector. Indian entrepreneurs would like to compete in areas such as mobile health information, search engines, and social media. India has a vibrant collection of public interest activists who have been fighting for free speech and privacy protections through digital networks. They all supported network neutrality and grew suspicious that a big American company had the best interest of Indians in mind.

So when Facebook brought Internet.org to India in 2014, complete with a massive public relations campaign and meetings between Zuckerberg and newly elected prime minister Narendra Modi, it did not expect that it would fail. Facebook officials not only underestimated the opposition within India, they failed to pay attention to the particulars of the Indian political economy. Public interest activists were adept at using social media services—including Facebook but especially YouTube and Twitter—to rally support for network neutrality and opposition to what they saw as an arrogant move by a powerful American company in cahoots with Modi. Facebook officials, in contrast, were not nearly as effective as their opponents at deploying social media in their campaign to convince users and voters that their service would benefit India more than it would Facebook.[11]

Everything Facebook officials did in their effort to thwart a strong network neutrality ruling by telecommunications regulators backfired. Billboards asking citizens to "support a connected India" glowered at motorists stuck in traffic in cities across India. Facebook users in India were greeted by messages on the service asking them to send emails to regulators in support of the newly renamed Free Basics. But regardless of whether a Facebook user actually agreed to send an email to regulators, Facebook would advertise to that user's Friends that he or she had done so. This angered many Facebook users. Ultimately, sixteen million emails reached regulators, but their staff complained that these automatically generated emails failed to address the specific questions they had posed through the public comment process. News coverage focused on the clumsiness and high-handedness of the Facebook campaign. Technology leaders noted the tone that Facebook was using with India and compared it to the promises that British East India Company leaders had deployed in the early days of the colonial project.[12]

Complicating such matters, Facebook officials made tone-deaf statements. Chief operating officer Sheryl Sandberg published an op-ed in the *Indian Express* in which she proclaimed that access to digital services can empower poor women to change their status. Unfortunately for Sandberg, the changing status of women is a controversial subject in India, so the op-ed served to alienate many traditional Hindus who voted for Modi in order to maintain historically male-dominated social relations intact. And economic competition for opportunities and resources is fierce, as India's middle class has swelled over the past thirty years. So the prospect of inviting more poor people into the middle class did not appeal to many families who just recently purchased a scooter or an education. Sandberg and Facebook certainly meant well. But they were dealing with a society they did not understand, and one in which many of its citizens do not mean each other well. The ruling Bharatiya Janata Party represents just those citizens.[13]

DIGITAL IMPERIALISM

Immediately after Facebook lost its effort to stem strong network neutrality in India, Facebook board member Marc Andreessen, the founder of Netscape and a current venture capitalist, sent a tweet complaining about the decision: "Denying world's poorest free partial Internet connectivity when today they have none, for ideological reasons, strikes me as morally wrong." In response to several tweeted replies to this complaint, Andreessen proclaimed, "Anti-colonialism has been economically catastrophic for the Indian people for decades. Why stop now?" This, understandably, set off a storm of resentment against Andreessen. Facebook officials quickly distanced the company from Andreessen's expression. And later that day Andreessen apologized for the tweet and promised to refrain from discussing the history and politics of India on Twitter. The Andreessen affair offered a glimpse into the ideology that too often guides decisions and campaigns dictated from Silicon Valley yet meant to benefit people far from its levels of wealth and power.[14]

Examining the story of Facebook's failures to introduce Free Basics to India demonstrates the need for a sophisticated, multifaceted, and open approach to the study of global corporations. Facebook is not just a social media platform that operates on the internet and mobile devices. It has designs to represent or stand in for the internet and mask its intentions behind proclamations of public service. If it can't get Facebook.com in front of millions of underprivileged people, it will try to convince them that Internet.org is a good enough internet for now. This story is one of a wealthy and powerful company morphing and metastasizing. Facebook's relationships with states, users, and other commercial services are dynamic.

LEARNING FROM ENRON

Facebook is among the most successful and prominent of a new breed of corporations that have emerged in the twenty-first century, in the wake of a significant crisis in corporate reputations the followed a series of collapses of publicly traded companies including Enron, WorldCom, Waste Management, Tyco, and HealthSouth. In each of these scandals, company leaders had committed or allowed some sort of accounting or reporting misstatements, leading to fines and criminal prosecution, and ultimately the collapse of each company and all of the value of their stock. Two lessons emerged from this series of events between 1998 and 2002. First, accounting practices needed to be reformed, and second, it became clear that companies were more likely to push legal and ethical boundaries if their sole motivation was to pump up their stock price. This second lesson led to some deep questioning of one of the central tenets of global corporate culture since at least 1980: that the purpose of a publicly traded corporation was solely to enhance the value of shareholders' stock.

This concept, often called "shareholder primacy," had for most of the twentieth century dominated how business schools taught students to run corporations and how economists explained the ideal role of corporations in the economy. In 1932 two formidable American theorists of business posited opposing visions of the proper role of a corporation. Corporate law professor Adolf Berle (along with his coauthor, economist Gardiner Means) argued that corporations would work best, and society would work best, if they kept their focus on revenues, profits, and the return on investment. They should not worry about solving societal problems or promoting themselves as good civic actors, Berle argued. Environmental, civil rights, and poverty alleviation projects should be reserved for the realms of government regulation and civil society. If companies generated negative externalities such as pollution or exploitative wages and working conditions, countervailing forces in society—chiefly regulations generated through accountable institutions—could correct them. These forces might include consumer activists, labor unions, or state regulation.

Berle was concerned about the concentrations of power—both over markets and over American democracy—that a handful of strong, manager-led corporations exerted in the 1920s. If we look to companies to fix society's ills, we grant them too much power and influence, and the glow of benevolence might shield them from scrutiny. Berle influenced the foundation of New Deal business regulation and pro-labor legislation, even though by the time World War II broke out American companies would find much reason to extoll social values such as patriotism and civic solidarity. Nonetheless, Berle's almost Madisonian vision of the role of shareholder-serving corporations in American life, curbed by other powerful interests, would dominate until the war. After the war and right on until the 1970s, a broader vision of the beneficial role that American corporations could play would prevail in business schools and in the public mind, despite Berle's influence.[15]

In response to Berle, corporate law professor E. Merrick Dodd wrote in the *Harvard Law Review* in 1932 that the idea of companies functioning purely for the interest of absentee shareholders, ignoring the role of business leaders as community members and civic leaders, impoverishes American life and undermines support for enterprise. "That stockholders who have no contact with business other than to derive dividends from it should become imbued with a professional spirit of public service is hardly thinkable," Dodd wrote. "If incorporated business is to become professionalized, it is to the managers, not to the owners, that we must look for the accomplishment of this result." During the postwar years, when the image of the strong, patriotic, civic-minded corporation infused popular culture, when the American economy seemed to reward managers, investors, and workers at rates never before imagined (as long as the workers were white and male and no one accounted for environmental degradation), Dodd's argument prevailed. Berle even conceded as much by the early 1950s.[16]

A distilled and corrupted version of Berle's vision for the corporation would rise again in the 1970s and assume some intellectual currency by the 1980s, but without the countervailing force of government regulation for the public good. This revival was a response to the birth of a full-throated call for corporate social responsibility. Through the 1960s American corporations found themselves confronted by rising social movements promoting environmental stewardship, ending racial and gender discrimination, and limiting involvement in wars. Some companies built marketing campaigns around themes that resonated with younger consumers, in an effort to co-opt their dissent and promote a vision of progress. Others faced the prospect of boycotts and felt motivated to improve hiring and promotion policies. Social movement leaders increasingly put pressure on corporate leaders to live up to promises of justice and progress.[17]

Nobel laureate Milton Friedman grew troubled through the 1960s. He saw this call for companies to serve what he saw as political interests as a violation of the basic laws of markets. Consumers, investors, and managers should all communicate via prices, Friedman believed. The prices of goods, services, and securities should rise and fall as factors change, but should seek some equilibrium as long as distorting factors such as government regulation or what he called "politics"—values such as concern for the environment—don't mess them up. If companies spend time and effort trying to influence their communities or societies, they will have to bake those expenses into the price of the good or service. That might reduce revenues as consumers move toward competitors with lower prices. That might deflate the price of stocks and bonds. A simple decision to support some public value could mess up the beautiful clockwork of the market system, Friedman believed. When Friedman published an article in the *New York Times Magazine* in 1970 he titled it "The Social Responsibility of Business Is to Increase Its Profits." While Berle was concerned that the growing power of corporations had sullied American civic life and democracy itself, Friedman saw "politics" polluting and jamming up the market system. While Berle saw organized labor, organized consumers, and government as countervailing forces that would allow businesses to grow and serve the nation while curbing their excesses, Friedman cleared the debate of any reference to or concern for any other value but the interests of investors.[18]

After Friedman staked his claim for the purity of the market, his colleagues at the University of Chicago worked to further distill vast areas of law and policy into matters of measurable economic analysis. This law-and-economics movement clarified much that had seemed mushy and metaphysical, but it also steadily and almost completely served the interests of investors over any other group—especially labor or the environment. Law-and-economics scholars managed from the 1970s through the present to undermine vast areas of policy, including protections for collective bargaining and antitrust measures. The argument that the core—perhaps only—duty of a publicly traded company was to enhance shareholder value morphed over time from a prescription into an assumption that corporate law in the United States required that companies run themselves for the benefit of their shareholders even at the expense of labor, consumers, the environment, and society in general. This legal claim was a myth, but it so pervaded the general and even professional discussions of the role of corporations that it took a strong, coherent, competing theory to edge it out by the turn of this century.[19]

The response to Friedman and the shallow law-and-economics embrace of shareholder primacy took on the name "stakeholder theory." It first emerged in the business school literature in the 1980s, largely through the work of University of Virginia business school professor Edward Freeman. Freeman posited that corporations can serve their various constituents better over the long term if they work to mediate among distinct parties, convincing each that they would be respected and that the corporation cared about their interests. Corporations should report their impacts along not just one simple axis, that of share price, but several. Companies should report their environmental impact (positive and negative), their effect on their workers (and move to instill a sense of their own investment or stake in the future of the company, thus limiting labor-management tension), and their overall effects on their communities (such as taxes paid, philanthropic efforts made, and cultural effects). If companies consider their workers, their neighbors, and even their regulators among their various stakeholders, they are likely to generate goodwill such that they limit fierce blowback (consumer revolts, strikes, or regulations) when the company seems to have abrogated some norm or law. The core message of stakeholder theory is not defensive or based on public relations. It assumes that people build, run, invest in, and work for companies for more than just remuneration. Freeman articulated a phenomenon that many corporate leaders had for decades promoted: that they did what they did to change the world and make it better, and that making a lot of money along the way was either a happy accident or a means to do even more for the world. This idea would inspire, among others, John Mackey, the founding chief executive officer of Whole Foods Markets. (Amazon bought Whole Foods in 2017 and has given no indication that it plans to continue Mackey's management principles.) One can distill echoes of Freeman's stakeholder theory in the statements and corporate policies of Starbucks head Howard Schultz, who infamously tried to spark conversations about American race relations by asking his employees to engage with customers after serving them beverages. Other global companies, such as Unilever and even Pepsi, turned their corporate cultures toward stakeholder theory in recent years.[20]

Both Friedman's cult of the perfect market and Freeman's stakeholder theory of the corporation emerge from the same well of political thought: libertarianism. By the early 1970s libertarianism was at its nadir. A Republican president, Richard Nixon, had signed the Clean Air Act, the Clean Water Act, and legislation to establish the Environmental Protection Agency. The civil rights movement had by the late 1960s achieved government support for its goals of fighting racial discrimination, and even Nixon endorsed those measures despite campaigning on (and winning in 1968 because of) racial resentment by white voters.

In the era before Fox News and social media, there was no denying that the Cuyahoga River had caught fire in Cleveland, Ohio, in 1969. For any sentient libertarian, there was no denying that racial and gender discrimination had been economically inefficient as well as terribly unjust. So libertarian intellectuals, especially those embedded in business schools, began conjuring market-based ways to address those very real issues. If firms could articulate a way to seek rewards in the market for behaving well—eliminating discrimination, promoting sustainable agriculture, donating to local charities and the arts— not only could they motivate managers who saw themselves as virtuous civic leaders, they could reward workers with an uncountable wage: making a difference. If workers could imagine themselves as partners in the project of improving the world and community instead of as laborers struggling to wrest rewards from the hands of capital, firms could keep hostility in check and perhaps undermine efforts to organize and bargain collectively. If consumers chose the "green" product over the polluting product, firms would compete to improve their reputations and thus, over time, improve the environment. Workers and consumers would exercise the "freedom" to "vote" with their time or their money. No one would be coerced into joining a union or paying higher prices so that all companies in a sector conformed with complex and ever-changing environmental regulations. And over time, managers would figure out that racial and gender discrimination is inefficient and irrational. If the corporation could displace the state as the agent of social change, the world would get better and people would be freer.

In 2005 *Reason* magazine brought Friedman together with John Mackey of Whole Foods to debate the responsibility of businesses from two very different market-oriented perspectives. Their core difference was on the matter of corporate philanthropy, about which Mackey was quite proud. "They were spending their own money, using 5 percent of one part of their wealth to establish, thanks to corporate tax provisions, the equivalent of a 501(c)(3) charitable foundation, though with no mission statement, no separate by-laws, and no provision for deciding on the beneficiaries," Friedman said about the Whole Foods philanthropic system. "But what reason is there to suppose that the stream of profit distributed in this way would do more good for society than investing that stream of profit in the enterprise itself or paying it out as dividends and letting the stockholders dispose of it?"[21]

Mackey's response to Friedman exemplifies both the stakeholder theory of the firm and the powerful new vision for the role of corporations in society post-Enron. "While Friedman believes that taking care of customers, employees, and business philanthropy are means to the end of increasing investor profits, I take the exact opposite view: Making high profits is the means to the end of fulfilling Whole Foods' core business mission," Mackey wrote. "We want to improve the health and well-being of everyone on the planet through higher-quality foods and better nutrition, and we can't fulfill this mission unless we are highly profitable." Mackey described a vision of the firm through which it becomes not only the chief instrument for changing fundamental aspects of life according to Mackey's vision of the good but also the global model of a successful firm. "The ideas I'm articulating result in a more robust business model than the profit-maximization model that it competes against, because they encourage and tap into more powerful motivations than self-interest alone," Mackey wrote. "These ideas will triumph over time, not by persuading intellectuals and economists through argument but by winning the competitive test of the marketplace. Someday businesses like Whole Foods, which adhere to a stakeholder model of deeper business purpose, will dominate the economic landscape."

By late 2017 the five public companies with the largest market capitalization included Alphabet (Google) and Facebook—two firms that exemplify Mackey's vision of the firm (Unilever, a third, sat at number forty in global market capitalization in October 2017). Not coincidentally, Apple, Microsoft, and Amazon were the other three among the top-five global companies in market capitalization. Airport bookstores offered piles of book extolling how more companies could run themselves like these giants. Corporate social responsibility, or the Silicon Valley distillation of it—social entrepreneurship—dominated the global corporate culture in the first two decades of the twenty-first century.[22]

THE HIGH COST OF SOCIAL ENTREPRENEURSHIP

Regardless of the relative success (or lack thereof) of public companies that put civic responsibility first, corporate social responsibility had not completely displaced the standard model of shareholder primacy that had dominated corporate governance since about 1980. But it had emerged within business schools and global business culture as the most exciting and attractive vision of business. Most of the remaining forty-five companies on the list of the fifty most highly capitalized public corporations in the world had visible and vocal corporate social responsibility offices or foundations devoted to public service. Even companies that have been involved in late twentieth-century labor, environmental, and human rights abuses such as Shell, Siemens, and Walmart had fully embraced social responsibility by 2010. Universities began promoting "social enterprise" or "social entrepreneurship" programs for their students. Business magazine covers frequently displayed the faces of Sundar Pichai of Google or Sheryl Sandberg and Mark Zuckerberg of Facebook. Global foundations and TED Talks highlighted social entrepreneurs in their events. The message was clear to any privileged, educated, cosmopolitan young person who desired to improve the conditions of humanity: Don't bother with the clergy, the classroom, or the government. Private enterprise is the more exciting destination. You can enjoy a comfortable and rewarding life, celebrate profits by day, and sleep well at night, just like Mark Zuckerberg.[23]

This was more than a case of a vision or a set of ideas finding an audience on the strength of its arguments—although that should not be discounted. And it was more than the fact that some of the most exciting and successful companies in the world seemed to be addressing some of the world's largest challenges, including sustainable agriculture and climate change. By the twenty-first century the state seemed to be the wrong domain for regulation, reform, and repair. Cynicism about the efficacy of state actions had spread so deeply and broadly since the elections of Margaret Thatcher and Ronald Reagan (sentiments reinforced by the subsequent elections of Tony Blair and Bill Clinton) that much of the world had lost the ability to imagine public responses to common problems.

POLITICS WITHOUT ROMANCE

The emergence of this ideology, generally called corporate social responsibility, coincided with a suspension in much of the world of consideration of the state as a site of effective response to collective challenges. The intellectual roots of the rejection or at least retreat of the state from political imagination lie in public choice theory, a branch of economics and policy analysis that subjected the functions of the state to many of the same assumptions of self-interest to which private sector actors were put. Once public choice theory impressed economists and political scientists, it became awkward to profess the idea that public servants, even low-paid social workers and teachers, were chiefly motivated by a commitment to public service. They were considered operators who would work the system and play games just like any other self-interested rational actor would. James Buchanan, who won the Nobel Prize in economics in 1986 for his work on public choice, wrote that he hoped his work would refresh and clarify debates about policy and politics. His main target was the idealized version of the state, one that offered answers to all problems and often seemed to be described as both omniscient and benevolent. He hoped that "politics without romance" would follow. It certainly did. Public choice was not the only influence on the ideological wave that significantly altered how voters, leaders, and writers viewed the prospect of state action since 1980. But it certainly worked its way into the speeches and policies of both Ronald Reagan and Margaret Thatcher.[24]

While the influence of public choice theory offered scholars, legislators, and regulators some important and bracing lessons by making them aware of real problems such as regulatory capture and rent-seeking, it contributed to a steady reduction of life into a matter of games and rewards. It undermined concern about market failure, when commercial actors and systems cannot provide for an important public good such as education, law enforcement, national defense, parks, basic research, or art. In the 1960s, before public choice and other market fundamentalist ideas gained currency, the United States could create the National Endowment for the Arts and public broadcasting because Congress decided that the public deserved such things and the market clearly was not capable of supporting symphonies, composers, poets, and educational children's television. Once market fundamentalism rose through the 1980s and 1990s, market failure arguments grew rare.

The fact that government science funding generated the basic technologies underlying global positioning systems and internet communication and that a National Science Foundation grant allowed Sergey Brin and

Larry Page to create the PageRank algorithm from which they built Google soon faded from public lore. "Innovation" was a magical force that flowed from lone geniuses working long, odd hours in Silicon Valley garages. More important, our choices about the important things in life were increasingly determined by our decisions about where to shop, what to buy, which companies to invest in, and the cultural and financial power of concentrated wealth. Dollars became votes. Commerce, rather than politics, became the forum. And markets, rather than elections and legislatures, became the aggregators of preferences. The stories of inventors, investors, and impresarios became our myths, their characters our heroes. Elections became exercises in identity proclamation. Policy disagreements degraded into power plays. Expertise grew suspect, sincerity dismissed. Buchanan wished for politics without romance. Instead we got romance without politics.[25]

ROMANCE WITHOUT POLITICS

That's the American story and, to a lesser extent, a Western European story. Sincere political arguments and bold policy proposals still arise in Canada, Germany, Spain, and a few other developed countries with strong republican norms. But the cultural, military, and economic power of the United States pushed much of the world to consider if not accept market fundamentalism. Trade treaties directly imposed it on much of the world through the 1990s and early 2000s. Meanwhile, the earth got warmer. Fresh water became scarce in much of the world. While poverty abated for millions, stagnation rendered millions more frustrated by rising expectations and wealth concentration. Ethnic nationalisms, never absent, grew more vicious as human migration and terrorism spread new fears and deepened bigotry. While market failure became a historical footnote, public failure—the idea that a skeletal or defunded public institution would underperform by design and thus drive support for private actors to assume the role—thrived. Corporations answered the call. Private prisons proliferated. Privatized charter schools pulled public funding away from public schools. Consultants such as McKinsey and Bain instructed state institutions how to outsource their functions to private enterprise. Contractors took on the role that military forces used to—including security and combat. Corporate social responsibility entered the public consciousness. Even the United Nations embraced it as a tool that could be used to help solve global problems. Industry groups short-circuited regulation to address externalities such as low wages, poor working conditions, and environmental degradation.[26]

Relying on corporations to address major global and even local problems is both undemocratic and apolitical. In democratic politics, difference and consensus determine agendas and priorities. Legislatures measure and aggregate public opinion. If corporations or philanthropies set the agenda for fixing the world, they mostly react to the wills of elites or even the personal agendas of corporate leaders.

Consider the most socially responsible company of them all: Hobby Lobby. As a privately held company, it did not need to answer to shareholders. As a retail outlet that faces competition in the market for arts and crafts supplies from the likes of Michaels, Walmart, Target, and Amazon, it has to answer to the whims of consumers. Regardless of consumer sentiment or even public reputation, Hobby Lobby's leaders believe so strongly that birth control encourages social degradation that the company denies its employees health insurance coverage for contraception. Because U.S. law in 2014 required health insurance plans to cover birth control, Hobby Lobby sued the government, claiming the law violated its religious freedom. Hobby Lobby prevailed at the U.S. Supreme Court and created a whole new right for private enterprise that canceled out an important policy generated by a duly elected legislature.

Hobby Lobby fulfills the tenets of corporate social responsibility based on its leaders' vision of social responsibility. It might differ from my sense. It might differ from the sense that other major corporations have. So who is to say what qualifies as "responsible"? One company might consider birth control coverage responsible. Another would consider it irresponsible and even immoral. If every company gets to decide for itself, then solutions to public problems become incoherent and uncoordinated. Some companies, such as Alphabet and Tesla, are led by people who believe that climate change is among the leading threats to our future, and so they devote resources to researching and developing technologies that might stem the trends. Other companies, such as Koch Enterprises, are led by people who believe that climate change is not a great threat and that the greater evil would be regulations that undermine the most efficient work of capital and limit the freedom of people to drive, eat, invest, and invent what they want. Koch Enterprises is socially responsible to those who consider labor unions and environmental regulation to be harmful to the public good. Tesla is socially responsible to those who believe we should be addressing the negative externalities of fossil fuel consumption. This incoherence renders us incapable of addressing climate change effectively—or of protecting the Koch brothers' idea of freedom. It depoliticizes such issues, rendering them among any number of factors influencing consumer choices. Why lobby for a carbon tax when you can buy a Toyota Prius, driving around in a $35,000 signal of your ethical commitment? In a similar way, Zuckerberg addresses the negative externalities of Facebook usage—distractions, depression, disinformation—in purely apolitical terms. These are problems to be managed and designed away. But Facebook remains a force for good because its intentions are good. The rhetorical space of such debates rarely invokes the prospect of effective state action to express the deliberate will of the public on important matters. The conversation never gets that far. Instead, we seem satisfied with simple, painless, impotent choices: to buy a Prius or not; to shop at Hobby Lobby or not; to quit Facebook or not.

The libertarian founders of corporate social responsibility have no problem with that. If consumers (not citizens) are concerned enough about an issue, they will direct their money toward companies that produce goods the way they wish. Imagine a market in which four firms produce paper products. Three do so with little regard for the bodies of water they pollute in the process. A fourth strives to produce paper using recycled raw materials, limits runoff, treats its waste, and thus charges more per ream or roll than its competitors. Consumers who care might seek out the responsible company's products, even if they cost more. Over time, if the responsible company gains market share, the other three might consider improving their behavior to compete. Here is the problem: As long as at least one company undersells the others with products that contribute to pollution, the overall environment fails to improve as much as if the state passed strict regulations on manufacturing methods and runoff. Worse, consumers must incur what economists call "search costs" each time they go to the market. They must constantly research and assess the relative goodness of companies. They must track which corporations produce which products. Which product was the good one again? Can I afford "green" paper towels this week, when rent is due? If I buy organic milk, may I forgo the "green" paper products and still sleep well at night? Putting the burden to save the world on companies means they will pass that burden along to investors, labor, and consumers. Buchanan may have wanted us to abandon the idea that the state was omniscient and benevolent. Now we must all strive to be omniscient and benevolent. Because we are not, little improves.

In the debate between market fundamentalists Friedman and Freeman (or Mackey) the state sloughs away. In reality, the state *has* sloughed away—not as a reservoir of military and surveillance power or a means to shift wealth around society, however, but as the aggregator and mediator of disinterested information and the forger of public interest. The best way forward would be to revive the work of Adolf Berle to encourage a Madisonian balance of interests among firms, labor, consumers, and citizens. If a company pollutes or commits fraud, the state fines it and prosecutes its leaders. Regulations would be based on the best research and the consensus of experts, and would be clear so that private actors could proceed without uncertainty and instability. If a company depresses wages or creates dangerous working conditions, the state should set minimum standards of remuneration and safety, and workers could easily organize into unions and bargain collectively. If an entire industry misbehaves, as the banks did in the run-up to the Great Recession of 2007–9, citizens would demand reform and would expect to get it. If a global advertising company leverages its vast array of dossiers on its two billion users to limit competition and invite antidemocratic forces to infest its channels with disinformation, democratic states should move to break it up and to limit what companies can learn and use about citizens.

BE EVIL

No one should assume that Sergey Brin, Larry Page, Mark Zuckerberg, and Sheryl Sandberg immersed themselves in the works of James Buchanan,

Ed Freeman, or even Milton Friedman. There is no reason to believe any of them supports libertarian policies in general. Sandberg, in fact, worked for former U.S. treasury secretary Larry Summers, who generally takes neo-Keynesian positions on macroeconomic questions. She and Summers did, however, oversee the irresponsible deregulation of the U.S. banking industry during the 1990s. And they all work in Silicon Valley, which has a peculiarly libertarian spirit, as embodied by Facebook board members Peter Thiel and Marc Andreessen. So the idea that companies might exist to change the world for the better is not alien to them. It's almost matter-of-fact. Neither Alphabet nor Facebook is set up along lines of which Milton Friedman would approve. Both companies are publicly traded. But both companies have special classes of shares and particular stock ownership and voting limits such that Page, Brin, Sandberg, and Zuckerberg never really have to answer to shareholders. Returns for investors have been spectacular for both companies, so no group of activist shareholders is likely to question company leaders' vision and practice. Nor do Brin, Page, Sandberg, and Zuckerberg have to fear hostile takeovers. Their companies are theirs, so they get to set the agendas. Because both Alphabet and Google are pervasive and inspirational, they serve as models for those who strive to be engineers and entrepreneurs. Heads of state seek them out for their ideas and opinions. Leaders of Alphabet and Facebook frequent meetings of global elites at Davos, Switzerland. Google's mission statement has long been "to organize the world's information and make it universally accessible and useful." Facebook has long had a declared mission of connecting the world to improve the human condition. Despite all their commercial success and their sincere commitments to the purest forms of corporate social responsibility, the concept of "information" is still up for grabs and humanity grows more fractured and angry every year. For Facebook, its missionary venture to spread information and connectivity to the world's poorest people, Free Basics, has failed spectacularly to improve life on earth.

From its moment of origin in 2004 Facebook promoted itself as a machine that would bring people together. That statement rested on a presumption that bringing people together would make life better. After all, friendship is better than loneliness, knowledge is better than ignorance, and collective action has greater potential to move things than individual action. Before Facebook it seemed difficult to coordinate and collaborate toward collective goals. Calling people to demonstrate or protest, organizing a boycott, or collecting names for a petition used to cost more money and time. The internet generally, and Facebook specifically, lowered the costs of coordination.[27]

Through the early months of 2011, this idea seemed a given, and it seemed almost exclusively positive—if what one wanted was more protest, more coordination, and more turmoil. The presumption, however, was that all of this coordination would come from below, that the dominant forces in a society would be subject to the pressures unleashed by social media. The antiauthoritarian protests that rose across the world between 2010 and 2012 seemed to certify Mark Zuckerberg's self-regard. Perhaps he had created a benevolence machine. And perhaps protest was the fulfillment of that benevolence. "By giving people the power to share, we are starting to see people make their voices heard on a different scale from what has historically been possible," Zuckerberg wrote in his letter to investors almost exactly a year after the dictators of Egypt and Tunisia fled in the face of massive street protests. "These voices will increase in number and volume. They cannot be ignored. Over time, we expect governments will become more responsive to issues and concerns raised directly by all their people rather than through intermediaries controlled by a select few." The initial—and, as it would turn out, incorrect—sense that Facebook had fueled the uprisings in North Africa in 2011 served as the strongest evidence for Zuckerberg's belief in his company's potential to make the world a better place.[28]

5

The Protest Machine

On June 6, 2010, police beat to death Khalid Said, a twenty-eight-year-old middle-class man in the import-export business, in front of his home in Alexandria, Egypt. Police told Said's family that he was involved in the drug trade and had died of asphyxiation. Witnesses to the beating disputed that claim and posted YouTube videos testifying to that effect. Soon autopsy photos of Said's bloody head, his jaw smashed and teeth mangled, spread quickly across Arabic and English Facebook and YouTube pages. People sent the photos to others attached to mobile text messages, so the authorities had less chance of monitoring the communication. Soon Al Jazeera, the international Arabic satellite news channel, noticed the rumblings and posted the images. Other international news organizations recognized Said's death. Demonstrations against the cover-up of his murder and the police corruption that caused it began stirring in Alexandria and Cairo through the summer of 2010.[1]

"I still remember the photo," said Wael Ghonim, a Google employee based in Dubai who helped run the "We Are All Khalid Said" Facebook page.

"I still remember every single detail of that photo. That photo was horrible. He was tortured—brutally tortured to death." The government of Egypt tried to control the story, as it had for similar incidents of brutality for decades. But the presence on Facebook of the image of Said made that task impossible, Ghonim said in a TED Talk he delivered in 2011. Facebook had just recently begun offering its service in Arabic. So no more than five million of eighty-six million Egyptians subscribed to Facebook then. Ghonim was well connected among a small but politically active stratum of cosmopolitan and educated Egyptians. "We Are All Khalid Said" was produced in English and Arabic. The images of both courageous protest and sickening brutality that it spread crossed over between English and Arabic pages and then leaped to other media systems. "It basically gave us the impression that 'wow, I'm not alone,'" Ghonim said. "There are lots of people who are frustrated. There are lots of people who share the same dream."[2]

A locked-down media system, like the one that dominated Egypt for most of its postcolonial history, severs the connections between people. Newspapers never reported on events and issues that brought the state into ill repute. Television was largely under state control. Police infiltrated opposition organizations. The strongest political force to oppose the Mubarak government, the Muslim Brotherhood, had been declared illegal in 1954. Those who had serious grievances against the oppressive state often felt they were alone, or without support. If they or a handful of others made a stand, they would only be easy targets. The state would make examples of them. Protests had erupted before in Egypt. The state had always crushed them.

The massive uprisings in Cairo, Alexandria, Port Said, and other cities in Egypt in January and February 2011 ultimately drove President Hosni Mubarak out of power after thirty years. To those who had not followed the growing public dissatisfaction with Mubarak's authoritarian ways and the highly organized movements against police abuse that had been gathering for almost a decade before 2011, the outbursts came as a surprise. What had changed? Why had the demonstrations of 2011 brought so many people from all walks of Egyptian life into the streets when the protests of 2006 and the general strike of 2008 had not? The answer seemed so simple: Facebook had only been in English in 2006 and 2008, but by 2011 it was available in Arabic. And "We Are All Khalid Said" had served as a beacon for those who used Facebook to find others willing to make a stand. At least that's what Ghonim thought. Ghonim's ability to explain the uprisings to eager journalists meant that many of them credited Facebook for what became known as the 25 January Revolution.[3]

In the heat of the moment, Ghonim, who was as much a member of the global cosmopolitan technological elite as he was an Egyptian, promoted a simplistic idea that stunted a full appreciation of the deep social, political, and economic roots of the Egyptian revolution. That idea also limited full understanding of the power of social media as part of a larger media ecosystem. "This revolution started on Facebook," Ghonim told CNN in 2011. "I want to meet Mark Zuckerberg some day and thank him personally."[4]

A full and measured examination of protests and uprisings around the world since 2007 yields a mixed collection of successes and failures. That's no different from any other global set of uprisings in any other ten-year period of the past 250 years. Sometimes people protest. When they do, they use the communication tools at their disposal. Sometimes they overthrow a government. Sometimes they don't. Sometimes the protest is a one-off event, and it withers as history recedes from it. Sometimes a protest is one small step in a long process of cultural and political change. It's sad that discussions about protests over the past decade have been locked in a shallow and unhelpful prism. The question of whether social media mattered or not, caused change or not, is ultimately silly. We can't run tests on the protests in Athens, Madrid, Cairo, Casablanca, Istanbul, Washington, and New York City between 2007 and 2017 to see if they would have happened, or happened the same way, without social media. They happened. And some people used social media before, during, and after the protests. The use of social media is perhaps the least surprising thing about those protests.

Social media services, especially Facebook, do affect political and social movements, and thus the protests that ensue, in particular ways. The presence of Facebook does not make protests possible, more likely, or larger. But Facebook does make it easy to alert many people who have declared a shared interest in information and plans. It lowers the transaction costs for early organization. Most important, Facebook has the ability to convince—perhaps fool—those who are motivated and concerned that, as Ghonim put it, "we are not alone." Massive protest movements in authoritarian states are possible only when enough people are convinced that enough people will join. Facebook gives them a sense that a movement has hit critical mass. Facebook does not, however, take the place or even bolster the hard work of deep political deliberation and organization.[5]

The plight of Egypt makes this point clear. During and after the 25 January Revolution, Ghonim and others celebrated the leaderless nature of the uprising. Ghonim himself took great pride in the fact that Muslims and Christians protested side by side, offering him a vision of a tolerant, democratic Egypt that certainly appealed to the prejudices of many who cheered him on from comfortable seats in Europe and North America. The reality of the movement that overthrew Mubarak did not match those early, hopeful signs.[6]

Egypt is ruled by a brutal, authoritarian dictatorship once again. It's run by the military. In hindsight, it looks as if the key to the fall of Mubarak was that the military stood down in the first few weeks of 2011, refusing to get involved. Military leaders merely looked on as Egypt's new crop of leaders, an uneasy mix of liberal cosmopolitans and Islamists, forged plans for a new government and held elections. The liberals had only Facebook pages and grand ideas. The only party that had formally organized for decades, mostly in secret, prevailed. The Muslim Brotherhood took control of the government after the elections of 2012. Once in power, the Brotherhood cracked down on efforts to empower Christians and women. Protests broke out against the Muslim Brotherhood government and the rule of President Mohammed Morsi. By November 2012 Morsi had declared emergency powers and begun to imprison critics and journalists. The violence against Christians continued. Larger, angrier demonstrations against Morsi sprouted in April 2013, some rivaling the size and strength of the 2011 protests. In July 2013 the military, under the command of General Abdel Fattah el-Sisi, took control and brutally cracked down on all elements of Egyptian society that had worked to overthrow Mubarak. Sisi has been in power ever since. The idealism of 2011 fades a little more every day.

"We Are All Khalid Said" remains an active Facebook page with more than 285,000 followers in English. It's devoted to spreading anti-Sisi news and propaganda. No one pretends another "Facebook revolution" is likely anytime soon.[7]

NOT ALONE

The key to getting people into the streets, as noted above, is to convince enough people that enough other people are willing to go into the streets. Social media, especially Facebook, can help with that process. The distortions that Facebook users experience when they view the world through Facebook are ideal for fooling people into thinking there is more support for their positions and wishes than there might otherwise be. Facebook, after all, forms filter bubbles, reinforcing confirmation bias. This becomes a self-fulfilling prophecy. If enough people think enough people will turn out to fill a city square, then enough people will turn out to fill a city square. That's the remarkable power of Facebook to motivate short-term, dramatic events. It's myopic power, however. And it dissipates easily. It's much harder to leverage that organizational spark toward more durable political actions, involving the hard work of gathering names on petitions, running meetings, fielding candidates, disciplining messages, and delivering votes. The first step is to make it clear that those who care are not alone. Too often, however, such passion fails to move beyond the first step.[8]

Because of how it is designed and the way the algorithms favor content that generates strong emotional reactions, Facebook is a powerful tool for motivation. For the same reasons Facebook is a useless tool for deliberation. It can be deployed effectively to move people to rise up against oppressive governments. And it can be used just as effectively to move people to rise up against liberal or cosmopolitan governments or in support of oppressive governments. Facebook destabilizes politics more than it enlightens or enhances deliberative politics. For those living in a fairly open, fairly successful, fairly democratic republic, Facebook is dangerous. For those living in a less stable, less open, less democratic environment, Facebook can be very useful in the short term. It's too easily hijacked by forces that would destabilize a weak state. That's why many states ban and block Facebook. A stronger authoritarian state, as we will see in Chapters 6 and 7, can take advantage of Facebook to spread propaganda, monitor the population, and coordinate threats.

It does not take Facebook or Twitter to generate that feeling of being part of a greater movement. Before the spread of digital technology the world witnessed a series of unrelated yet mutually inspiring events that changed history. On June 4, 1989, soldiers of the People's Republic of China slaughtered hundreds and arrested thousands of peaceful demonstrators in Beijing. The protesters had gathered in and around Tiananmen Square for weeks. They were angered and emboldened by the recent death of Hu Yaobang, the former leader of the Communist Party who had signaled his desire to lift some restrictions on criticism of the state. That same day, the labor organization Solidarity defeated the Communist government of Poland in a fair election, thus sparking a series of democratic revolutions throughout the world. At that moment, it seemed anything was possible. It seemed as if democracy, liberalism, and capitalism could spread steadily across a world hungry for freedom and dignity. By November 1989 East German dictator Erich Honecker had resigned, Hungary had become a republic, the pro-apartheid National Party in South Africa announced it would allow full political participation by the oppressed black majority, and the Velvet Revolution began in what was then Czechoslovakia. In late 1989 Brazil held its first free elections after twenty-nine years of military rule. The year ended with Romanian dictator Nicolae Ceausescu being ousted in Romania. Just two years later, with its outer shell crumbled and its empire in ruins, the Soviet Union first invited reform and free speech and then quickly dissolved into chaos and violence. From 1989 through 1992, it was hard not to believe that democracy would grow stronger, with the world finding common bonds and common cause. The free flow of information, it was said, would both enable those trends and benefit from them.[9]

As an American man of twenty-three, I could not have been more optimistic about the world in 1989. As I pieced together stories from these places that were for so long opaque, I began hearing about the central role that new communication technologies had played. The proliferation of fax machines in Eastern Europe and the Soviet Union, for instance, received credit for facilitating activism and awareness among networks of dissidents. These stories were seductive to someone like me. I had only a shallow sense of the history of technology. And I assumed, as many young Americans do, that most of the other young people in the world wanted the same things that I treasured. We just had to find each other and spread good information, and democracy would flower.[10]

Such a techno-optimistic story tracked well with other accounts I held in my mind at that time: that the Reformation and Enlightenment were "driven" or "made necessary" by the emergence of the printing press in fifteenth-century Europe, and that the ability to print and distribute pamphlets such as Thomas Paine's *Common Sense* and the *Federalist Papers* was essential to the birth of the American Republic in the late eighteenth century.[11]

I was not wrong to take account of new communicative methods or technologies as factors in rapid social and political change. But like many others, I put too much emphasis on technology and discounted the years of on-the-ground political struggle that had grown in all of these countries. I ignored the specific historical, cultural, and economic aspects of each country that made each story special and powerful, even if it seemed like they were all coordinated and must therefore share a cause. The rise of new communicative technology was too simple an explanation for the sudden (and, in many places, temporary) spread of democracy and free speech on four continents. Historians of both politics and technology knew the story was more complex than this. But I did not. Neither did most of the news reporters and pundits on whom I relied for information.[12]

The truth is that communicative technologies structured the nature and affected the speed of many of these uprisings. The uprisings turned into revolutions in 1989, when they had failed in 1956 or 1968, because of a few special factors—including both media and non-media factors. The rise of global television news and satellite distribution meant that people all over the world could witness the bravery of young people in China standing up to their military in June 1989. Viewers in Eastern Europe were inspired by the bravery of the protesters and shocked by the bold brutality of the state.

The simultaneity of global television offered them models to emulate. They knew they were not alone. When viewers in Czechoslovakia and East Germany saw their own local uprisings presented on their own televisions in their own living rooms, they experienced what historian Tony Judt called an "instant political education."[13]

There were more important non-media factors that combined to make the revolutions of 1989 seem possible—and thus made them possible. A youthful movement within the Hungarian Communist Party had for several years pushed the government to reform and revealed its weaknesses. In East Germany, the decision to allow Berliners to flow back and forth across the border in late 1989 pushed the Communist Party to the breaking point. The desire to travel or migrate overwhelmed all expectations. And most important, the Soviet Union withdrew its iron fist of support for Communist governments. It showed its own weakness and declared its unwillingness to crush reform movements as it had in Hungary in 1956 or Czechoslovakia in 1968. The Soviet Union's long, brutal, expensive war in Afghanistan had drained the empire of funds and energy and had shown the world that the Soviet military was not omnipotent. In addition, change was rapid within Soviet society itself, regardless of the communicative technologies at work. Soviet leader Mikhail Gorbachev invited the growth of a nascent civil society by engaging in *glasnost,* or a policy of openness, thus allowing dissent to flow in Soviet society through clubs, meetings, and publications. *Glasnost* even liberalized what appeared on Soviet television—a far more powerful and universal medium than the fax machine. Gorbachev himself decided to break the Communist Party's monopoly on information and narrative. Once Moscow was weakened, dozens of other factors—including the efforts of labor unions in satellite states, religious leaders, poets, and criminals—could chip away at the Soviet empire until everything crumbled at what seemed to be the same moment.[14]

By focusing on the novelty of communicative technologies and assuming that their simultaneous arrival in a place *causes* rapid change, rather than merely coinciding with it or aiding it, we ignore the importance of something as obvious and powerful as opening a gate or launching a long, disastrous war in Central Asia. Long wars in Afghanistan have a habit of signaling the imminent decline of powerful empires.

Media can amplify or accelerate a movement as long as that movement already exists—has form, substance, momentum. Technologies don't have radical dynamics of "freedom" or "oppression" built into them. But aspects of particular technologies can make performing certain tasks easier. If some communicative technologies allow like-minded people to find each other and coordinate actions with low cost and high speed, they are going to make a difference. It just might not be a difference that liberates the oppressed.

By the time YouTube, Facebook, and Twitter had arrived on laptops and phones around the world, the soil had been tilled. If email and text messages were effective tools for coordination and messaging, then platforms specifically designed to distribute messages to like-minded people could be even more effective. Technology-obsessed journalists and commenters noted the use of social media platforms in protest movements and uprisings in Moldova and in Iran in 2009. Neither of these "revolutions" came to fruition. By the end of 2010 the idea that social media would revolutionize revolutions, strike a blow against tyranny, and unleash democratic participation was a theory in search of evidence. But the lack of evidence did not prevent U.S. secretary of state Hillary Clinton from embracing its premises and declaring the promotion of "internet freedom" to be the official policy of the United States. Clinton uncritically espoused the power of social media to open up closed societies and undermine censorship efforts within authoritarian regimes. The U.S. State Department began promoting the idea that Twitter had helped undermine the government of Iran (even though the government of Iran made it through the 2009 protests just fine). Clinton made an error that most of those who celebrated the proliferation of social media made during those years. She assumed that when people use social media and rise to protest authoritarian governments, their goals include democracy, human rights, or even basic freedoms. It's hard from afar, just reading tweets and Facebook posts in English, to tell if everyone in the streets even wants the same thing. It's too easy to overlay one's own wishes on those who seem to be using the tools that elites use so well. We use the same platforms. We believe the platforms spread freedom and promote democracy. Therefore if other people are using those platforms they must want freedom and democracy. However, sometimes they want cultural recognition. Sometimes they want access to resources. Sometimes they want cheaper bread. Sometimes they want to rule, exercising their own form of oppressive brutality. And often, for better or worse, and for reasons that are too complex to distill, they fail.[15]

TECHNO-NARCISSISM

As protests against the government of Iran boiled up in the streets of Tehran in June 2009, CNN was all abuzz. Just two years earlier a new service called Twitter had captured the technology and journalistic worlds' attention at the SXSW technology festival in Austin, Texas. Since that time usage among journalists around the world had spiked. Twitter allowed people who could not afford unlimited mobile data plans to post updates in 140-character bursts that would be readable by any other Twitter user who chose to follow the poster. CNN, like most U.S.-based news organizations, had limited access to Iran. Keeping reporters in Iran was dangerous: the government often deported them, accused them of spying, or imprisoned them. A stratum of cosmopolitan activists who knew how to write in English took to Twitter in the summer of 2009 to alert the world about the protests against the government.

On June 18 CNN ran a report quoting from a handful of tweets from English-speaking Iranians, and then interviewed Nicholas Thompson, who at the time was a reporter for *Wired* and has since gone on to become the editor-in-chief of the magazine. "Are we overstating the role of social media in organizing these rallies in Iran?" asked CNN presenter Soledad O'Brien.

"I think we are overstating the role of Twitter," Thompson replied. "I don't think we are overstating the role of cell phones, Facebook, or social networking in general." Thompson went on to explain that while few people in Iran used Twitter for internal communication, its main purpose—and why CNN was paying attention to both Twitter and Iran in the first place—was to inform the world beyond Iran's borders about events within the country. "It's not quite a revolution yet, and it's not quite Twitter," Thompson said. The whole time that Thompson was deftly explaining the limitations of Twitter and why it should not be credited with sparking or even facilitating a protest movement in Iran, CNN ran a graphic along the bottom of the screen that read: "Twitter Revolution: Social Media Explodes over Iran Unrest." It didn't matter that Thompson offered a nuanced and qualified analysis of the role of Twitter in Iran, and that he carefully distinguished how people use Twitter, Facebook, and text messages to communicate and coordinate. What CNN viewers read and heard multiple times in that segment—multiple times that month—was the phrase "Twitter revolution." CNN was not alone in this. News organizations of every kind spent much of June 2009 paying more attention to the idea that people in Iran were using Twitter than to what they were protesting in the first place. Once the government of Iran prevailed and stifled the protests, reasserting its power, the coverage of Iran stopped. If CNN producers could not read tweets, they had little to report. The fact that street protests had occurred many times over the previous decade in Iran, mostly without the use of social media, did not occur to these analysts. The fact that people in Iran had risked their lives to express distress and opposition to the ruling government did not matter as much as the fact that a few had used Twitter.[16]

This pattern would repeat itself for years, and reach its apex during the first three months of 2011, when the misnamed "Arab Spring" sprang. Reporters and pundits would declare that this latest protest eruption was the big one, the one carried by social media, with all the power to connect the disconnected, route around authoritarian media control, and empower people to rise up and promote openness, equality, and democracy. But nothing of the sort happened. At least, nothing like a "Twitter revolution" or a "Facebook revolution" ever happened.

The reductive narrative of the power of social media to energize and organize from below prevented serious and sensitive analysis of crucial political movements and events. It blinded many to the ways social media—especially Facebook—could be used by authoritarian governments to surveil, harass, and suppress dissidents. The obsession with the new prevented a fuller account of the entire media ecosystem that had significantly changed North Africa and the Middle East over the previous decade. The focus on the media at the expense of the messages meant that those places where the uprisings failed never got counted in the tally of success and failure of the impressive and historically important Arab uprisings of 2010 and 2011. Facebook and Twitter users—and internet enthusiasts in general—had imbibed the notion that communicative technologies are necessarily liberating and enlightening, and that the relative openness of internet platforms must work in the direction of free speech, free thought, and democratic reform.

This phenomenon is an example of techno-narcissism. When we are proud that other people seem to be using for important purposes the very same devices and technologies that we use every day, we feel much better about ourselves (and go right back to crushing candy). When we imagine that some part of the world that seems stuck in "the past" bursts into our own moment of technological ubiquity, we cheer them on, convinced that the brilliance of our inventions made all the difference, rather than, say, the price of wheat. Techno-narcissism is both ethnocentric and imperialistic. It assumes that if only people had our tools, toys, and techniques, their lives would improve almost instantly.

That's not to say that social media did not matter in the Arab uprisings of 2011 or any of the subsequent political eruptions around the globe, from Occupy Wall Street to the Catalan independence movement. Social media definitely made a difference, although they did not matter in predictable or idealistic ways and they did not matter in the same ways in every context. Social media did not promote democracy, transform the public sphere, or inspire massive uprisings. Just as had happened with Twitter in Iran in 2009, social media did become one of the chief ways that those outside the countries that experienced uprisings in 2011 learned of events. And they did change the nature of political movements—just in complicated ways.

Basically, Facebook attracts and connects activists with little friction and low transaction costs. It's a powerful platform if one wants to rally supporters for a white nationalist rally, or to protest that a local gym allows members to bring guns into yoga classes (this actually happened with my gym and I participated in a fast, powerful Facebook protest that resulted in a policy change within two days), or to call for the overthrow of a corrupt dictator. For any of these or other such movements to succeed, activists need much more than a good Facebook page. But Facebook does amplify activism for the same reason it amplifies photos of puppies. Items that strike people's emotions are more likely to generate responses and more likely to be shared. And much political activism, even activism meant to disrupt or crush democratic norms, relies on hyperbole and alarm. Facebook does hyperbole very well.[17]

Across North Africa and the Middle East in early 2011, unsurprisingly, people used widely available means of communication to communicate. And the use of Facebook among a small band of cosmopolitan elites in Tunisia and Egypt in early 2011 did affect the nature of the protests and influence the responses of dictatorial states across the region. There is just so much more to the story. In fact, there are multiple versions of the story that were barely recognized in the mainstream narratives that dominated the conversations in North America and much of Europe in 2011.

DEMOCRACY-COLORED GLASSES

Long before the 2011 uprisings in Tunisia and Egypt, people were using text messages, email, and other forms of electronic communication to coordinate protest movements. The earliest example was the deft use of email by the Zapatista movement in Mexico in 1997. In 2000 thousands of protesters in the Philippines filled the streets and squares of Manila to protest electoral malfeasance and government corruption. And the successful 2004–5 Orange Revolution that overthrew the results of a questionable election run by a corrupt government in Ukraine was allegedly coordinated via text messages. That's when the narrative started: this was something materially different and more effective. Coordination without clear leaders, without hierarchy, could emerge from disparate groups and individuals who have grievances against a government as long as they could all find each other. New forms of communication allowed for that discovery and connectivity with low marginal cost, unprecedented speed, and a flexibility that felt significantly different from protest movements of the past.

Protests could emerge faster and overwhelm the powers that be before they had time to muster their forces to crack down. And if information flowed through digital channels, undermining the once-dominant monopoly on information by the state, the political price of a brutal crackdown would be high. That was the theory, anyway. And to some extent, the successful and unsuccessful uprisings between 1997 and 2004 lent support to the theory. Yet none of these uprisings occurred with the help of what we now generally call "social media."[18]

In 2010, just before protesters filled the streets of Tunis to overthrow the Ben Ali government, journalist Malcolm Gladwell stepped up to the question of the power of social media to enhance protest movements. Reflecting on the hyperbole about social media sparking the failed uprisings in Moldova and Iran, Gladwell contrasted them to the long, well-planned, risky, and ultimately successful lunch counter sit-ins in Greensboro, North Carolina, in 1960. The Greensboro protests were one methodical element of a struggle for African American equal rights and dignity that had been going on for a hundred years. Gladwell's point was that the civil rights movement was driven at its most effective moments by what sociologists call "strong ties," bonds of mutual respect and camaraderie that move people to risk their safety not only for a cause but for their fellow activists. Strong ties form among those committed to a cause who imagine a shared fate. Strong ties, Gladwell argued, were better foundations for a political movement than the weak ties on which social media tend to rely. By weak ties, sociologists mean bonds that are merely of mutual recognition or affiliation. They can be very useful, which is why we collect so many weak-tie acquaintances in life (career networking at a conference) and on social media (a friend of a friend recommended an interesting book or a job opportunity). Social media is useful for many things, Gladwell argued, but social and political activism is not one of them.[19]

Three months after Gladwell published his piece in the *New Yorker* a street vendor named Tarek el-Tayeb Mohamed Bouazizi set himself on fire on a street in Sidi Bouzid, Tunisia, to protest stifling corruption and police abuse that had prevented him from making a living. Local protests began within hours in the small, rural town. Demonstrators posted videos of the growing protests to YouTube. The videos were quickly shared on Facebook, which helped the news of the protests move to the capital city, Tunis, where many residents used smartphones and social media. Just as important, the Qatar-based satellite news network Al Jazeera covered the protests via posted videos and phone interviews with participants (Al-Jazeera had been banned in Tunisia for several years). On January 14, 2011, President Zine El Abidine Ben Ali stepped down and fled to Saudi Arabia.[20]

Clay Shirky had long been one of the most influential writers analyzing and advocating for what he saw as a transformative and largely positive role for social media on organization and activism. In his 2008 book *Here Comes Everybody: The Power of Organization Without Organizations*, Shirky had promoted the idea that digital media in general, and social media in particular, allow disparate voices to find each other and join in a chorus. The cost of coordination drops significantly, Shirky argued, when searching for others of like mind becomes cheap, easy, and algorithmically driven. Gladwell had taken a shot at Shirky's book in his *New Yorker* article, claiming that Shirky's case studies work only for the most superficial goals. Shirky responded to Gladwell in an article in *Foreign Affairs* that appeared in January 2011. Shirky, like Gladwell, wrote his article before the uprising in Tunisia. But since both articles circulated in public consciousness as the world watched regimes fall first in Tunisia and then in Egypt in early 2011, their arguments helped shape the frames through which many viewed those events.[21]

Shirky responded briefly yet effectively to Gladwell's claim that social media were useful for the uncommitted who wanted to express concern but useless for the committed who wanted to bring about significant change. "The fact that barely committed actors cannot click their way to a better world does not mean that committed actors cannot use social media effectively," Shirky wrote.[22]

Shirky's article was framed in public discourse as a direct response to Gladwell. It was not. Gladwell was an afterthought to Shirky. Shirky had a larger yet more subtle case to make. Much of Shirky's article was meant to criticize Clinton's "internet freedom" agenda rather than to respond to Gladwell. Clinton's State Department policy had favored funding tools that activists in authoritarian regimes could use to fight censorship and surveillance. Shirky viewed this approach, which he called "instrumental," as "politically appealing, action-oriented, and almost certainly wrong." This policy overemphasized access to information, and thus seemed based on a twentieth-century framework of broadcast media, rather than on tools and platforms that would allow citizens to converse.[23]

The "environmental" view of internet freedom, Shirky argued, would better serve the interests of those fighting authoritarians and of the United States. "According to this conception, positive changes in the life of a country, including pro-democratic regime change, follow, rather than precede, the development of a strong public sphere," he wrote. Conversation would help citizens build organizational capacity, expose corruption and abuse, and use a local dialect and local issues to make the case for change. Reading censored stories from the *New York Times* or smuggled copies of Thomas Paine's *Common Sense* won't accomplish that. Shirky shows concern for the specificity of a political situation and for local concerns. He refuses to see every site of oppression as similar to every other site of oppression. Still, he remained naively optimistic and elided another kind of specificity—media specificity. Shirky defined social media in the broadest possible way, conflating text messaging and email, which are often used for social purposes, with Facebook, which is specifically built for mapping a social grid and exploiting social ties with the power of algorithms. This conflation was unfortunate, because it allowed Shirky to miss or minimize the core reason that Facebook is effective in gathering movement supporters and why it's particularly susceptible to hijacking by the powerful and oppressive.[24]

Gladwell was mostly right. So was Shirky. Social media have limitations in how they can help convert wide expressions of interest into sharp and strong forms of activism that can not only topple dictators but forge effective and disciplined political parties. Social media also foster data-driven homophily, allowing both strong and weak ties to foster the spread of messages across wide arrays of interested people. While Gladwell erred by invoking social theory over lived reality, and by contrasting a specific American civil rights tactic to a general problem of the struggles against corrupt, authoritarian states in places as different as Moldova and Iran,

Shirky missed the fact that communication is not conversation. Social media, and Facebook in particular, do not foster conversation. They favor declaration. They do not allow for deep deliberation. They spark shallow reaction. There is political power in declaration and reaction. But they are not enough to pursue anything more than stronger declaration, fiercer reaction, and strong blowback. Both Gladwell and Shirky considered social-media-influenced political movements to be only those sorts of things that liberal, educated Americans might like. Every *New Yorker* reader loves remembering the courage of civil rights activists. Every *Foreign Affairs* reader dreams of secular democracy in Iran. Neither considered the possibility that Facebook could be used by Buddhist nationalists to spark genocide against a Muslim minority in Myanmar. Neither considered that corrupt leaders such as Ilham Aliyev in Azerbaijan would deftly exploit Facebook and Instagram to promote propaganda and monitor citizens. Neither considered that Facebook does much more than connect Friends: it manages and massages what passes through it.[25]

In the history of protest movements new media were always important, yet seldom crucial or determinative to their outcomes. Global satellite television played a role in the anti-Soviet revolutions of 1989. But satellite television did not play a role in the restoration of civilian rule in Brazil just four years earlier or the Tiananmen Square protests in Beijing in June 1989. Images of Tiananmen Square certainly inspired protesters in Eastern Europe, but not the other way around. Protests and revolutions are complex processes. It's impossible to run an experiment, to remove other variables, to measure the relative impact of a particular media form on a historical event.

So we should just accept that people use the communicative tools available to them when they wish to communicate. This is neither interesting nor profound. It would have been worthy of deep examination had Filipino activists chosen not to use text messages in 2000 or had Occupy Wall Street activists not used Facebook and Twitter in September 2011. However, we should pay close attention to what those tools allow people to do, what they prevent people from doing easily, what sorts of communication they favor, and what sorts of communication they hinder. And we should pay particular attention to the specifics of a political situation.

WHAT'S LEFT?

Wael Ghonim is chastened. The dream of a tolerant, democratic Egypt has been suspended. And Facebook no longer seems to empower the movements that fight for liberty, equality, or dignity. In 2015 Ghonim gave another TED Talk. This time he could not infuse his audience with the spirit of optimism or even reference for technology. "I once said, 'If you want to organize a society, all you need is the Internet.' I was wrong."[26]

Ghonim said that the events of 2011 revealed the great potential of Facebook. "But it also exposed its greatest shortcomings," he said. "The same tool that united us to topple dictators eventually tore us apart." Ghonim noted that the only thing that united the protesters in January and February 2011 was opposition to Mubarak. "We failed to build consensus and the political struggle led to intense polarization," he said. "Social media only amplified that state by amplifying the spread of misinformation, rumors, echo chambers, and hate speech. The environment was purely toxic. My online world became a battleground filled with trolls, lies, and hate speech. I started to worry about the safety of my family." Ghonim outlined five "critical challenges" facing social media: dealing with rumors that confirm people's biases; puncturing echo chambers or filter bubbles; recognizing the humanity of those with whom we interact—and often deride—through our screens; coping with speed and brevity and the limits they place on deep understanding; and the way social media favor declaration over deliberation. Ghonim offered no easy solutions for these challenges. But he identified them by looking at what happened in Egypt as its Facebook use spiked after 2011 and its hopes for a peaceful, tolerant future faded.[27]

6

The Politics Machine

The first surprise arrived on June 23, 2016. Conservative prime minister David Cameron had pandered to his party's hard-line, anti-Europe wing by allowing a United Kingdom–wide popular referendum on whether his country should sever ties with the European Union, of which the United Kingdom was a founding and leading member. Cameron was confident that his party's rank and file, and thus a majority of the nation as a whole, would act conservatively. After all, it was the Conservative Party. He assumed that the sober business community would make the case that the financial, trade, and labor disruptions of leaving the European Union would be devastating. He assumed that those to the left of the Conservative Party would rally their supporters to defend the free flow of labor to the United Kingdom and the reciprocal opportunities for those from the United Kingdom to find work on the Continent. Still, there were loud, hard-line provocateurs within the Conservative Party, and a growing party to the right called the UK Independence Party, or UKIP. Cameron decided that the only way to move on from the constant complaints those factions put forth about the erosion of traditional English culture and the weaknesses in labor markets in the face of steady migration from poorer Eastern and Southern Europe was to once and for all demonstrate that the voters of the United Kingdom do not fear their neighbors and see openness as working to their advantage.

Cameron was wrong. More than thirty million people voted in the referendum, with 51.9 percent voting to leave the European Union and 48.1 percent voting to stay. The two sides had become known by their simple verbs: Leave versus Stay. The victory of the Leave campaign not only shocked conventional wisdom, it surprised many of those who had been issuing and following polls for months. The polls had been very noisy and inconsistent for weeks before the election. But conventional wisdom settled on the prediction that Stay would win narrowly. The British betting markets, which often accurately predict elections, had settled on an 88 percent chance that a majority of the voters would opt to stay. But the very inconsistency and narrowness of the polls demonstrated that they had fairly closely predicted the result—or at least its strong possibility.[1]

The Conservative Party, and thus the government of the United Kingdom, was thrown into turmoil. Cameron resigned immediately. After much shuffling, strutting, bluffing, and palace intrigue among various leading figures in the party, Theresa May emerged victorious and assumed the job of prime minister. May had opposed the vote to Leave, but after it passed she endorsed a vague plan to execute the will of the voters and leave the European Union. Business and finance leaders of the country began planning for the turmoil and the loss of markets for goods and labor. Major firms, including those in banking, began to look for new homes in cities such as Frankfurt now that London seemed unfriendly.

Pundits and journalists quickly searched for explanations. Even if the polls had not botched the prediction, the very fact that so many U.K. voters decided to vote against their own economic interests baffled many. The most visible debates about the merits of the proposal, popularly known as "Brexit," seemed to favor Stay. The major institutions that had for so long managed popular opinion in the United Kingdom had supported Stay. Voters in the media and population centers of England, Scotland, and

Northern Ireland had overwhelmingly voted Stay. But central and northern England and Wales had voted overwhelmingly Leave. How had the Leave campaign so deftly motivated voters in just the right constituencies?[2]

All through the summer of 2016 the Brexit results troubled Americans who were confident that Hillary Rodham Clinton would soundly defeat Donald Trump in the presidential election scheduled for November 8, 2016. There was not a day when Clinton did not lead in the polls. And most prediction services gave Trump only a slim chance to gather more electoral votes than Clinton and almost no chance of winning the popular vote.

The shock of the result was astounding. For most of us in the United States, steeped in the mythology of being the world's foremost and oldest democracy, the fact that for the second time this century a man who had lost the popular vote would become president was both alarming and embarrassing. What a bizarre and absurd system we have, a legacy of compromises the founders of this country made to preserve and extend slavery in the early United States. Nonetheless, this is the system that has—with five exceptions—rewarded the person who convinced the most voters that he should be president. In 2000 George W. Bush lost the popular vote to Al Gore by about half a million votes yet assumed office after the U.S. Supreme Court stopped the recounting of ballots in Florida—a state almost evenly split between the two and the state with the electoral votes needed to deliver the winner. That the 2000 election nationwide and in Florida was close surprised no one, even if the antidemocratic machinations of the Republican Party alarmed many.

However, 2016 was a surprise. It was not supposed to be close. In fact, the popular vote was not close, with Clinton prevailing by almost three million votes. Trump, however, won the Electoral College vote, in which each state is granted between three and fifty-five votes depending roughly on population (although many states with the minimum of three votes have a sliver of the population of states such as Nebraska and Iowa, which only have five and six votes respectively).

Somehow, without spending much money on the classic forms of political advertising and campaigning such as television advertisements or door-to-door contact with voters, Trump had managed to squeak out victories in three states that he was not supposed to win and that had gone to Democratic president Barack Obama four years earlier. Trump won Wisconsin by 22,000 votes out of 2.9 million votes. He won Michigan by 10,700 votes out of more than 4.8 million cast. He won Pennsylvania by just 44,000 votes out of almost 6.2 million ballots. Those three states delivered the Electoral College majority to Trump. They did so by a total of just 76,700 votes across the three states. That's how slim the margin was between President Donald Trump and President Hillary Clinton.[3]

Other states, including Arizona, North Carolina, and Florida, were also close. Trump won Florida by just 112,911 votes out of a total of 9.5 million votes. Had Clinton prevailed in Florida and North Carolina she would now be president of the United States. Because Trump's campaign was able to pull all of these very close states to his side he won the Electoral College by a sizable margin, 304 to 227 for Clinton.[4]

How did Trump pull off such a feat without spending as much money as Clinton did, without performing the time-tested rituals of American electoral politics, and without the experts and seasoned journalists realizing what was going on? Elections are complex phenomena. Hundreds, maybe thousands of variables can swing something as messy and dynamic as an American election (essentially fifty distinct elections). One thing became clear, and the Trump campaign was blunt about it: Facebook made a difference. It allowed Trump to target advertisements at voters in select states with remarkable precision. In some cases, Facebook ads were meant to dissuade potential Clinton voters. In others, the Trump team carefully tailored and tested Facebook ads to motivate small segments of potential Trump voters so they might show up at the polls. It worked. Facebook turned out to be a more powerful tool in the hands of Trump than it had ever been for allegedly technologically savvy candidates such as President Barack Obama. The only question was, did Facebook need help in the form of detailed data about voters supplied from outside consultants to target these voters? Or did Facebook provide all the tools that Trump needed to nudge three key states from Clinton to him? Either way, what does it say about the fate of American democracy that national elections would be decided based on motivation rather than deliberation?

What would democracy look like if Facebook's algorithms governed the art and science of persuasion?

PSYCHOGRAPHICS, *QU'EST-CE QUE C'EST?*

A prospective villain quickly rose from obscurity, and it seemed to explain both the Brexit and the Trump upsets. On September 27, 2016, a man named Alexander Nix gave a presentation called "The Power of Big Data and Psychographics." Nix was the chief executive officer of a market research firm called Cambridge Analytica, a part of the larger SCL Group, an American-based company owned by billionaire investor and computer scientist Robert Mercer. The board of Cambridge Analytica included one of Mercer's friends, Steve Bannon. Bannon left the board in the summer of 2016 to take over the management of Donald Trump's failing campaign. And Cambridge Analytica staff members were involved with the campaign to convince U.K. voters to choose to leave the European Union.

"It's my privilege to speak to you today about the power of big data and psychographics in the electoral process," Nix told the audience of the Concordia Summit, a European global affairs forum that encourages limited government and private-public partnerships. At the urging of Mercer, a little-known and little-liked U.S. senator from Texas, Ted Cruz, had hired Cambridge Analytica to consult on his effort to win the Republican presidential nomination.[5]

Cruz, Nix explained to the audience, had little chance of competing against a field of better-known opponents such as Jeb Bush, the brother of one former president and the son of another, and reality television star and failed casino owner Donald Trump. That Cruz stayed in the field of contenders for many months longer than Bush or almost all of the other challengers to Trump spoke to his use of Cambridge Analytica's data sets and the precisely targeted advice the company gave him, Nix claimed. Cruz's campaign had survived more than a year, until he ran out of money after losing the Indiana primary to Trump in May 2016. Ultimately Cruz won the second-largest number of committed delegates in his unsuccessful effort to wrest the nomination from Trump. After Cruz retired his campaign

Bannon convinced Mercer to support Trump, so Trump's San Antonio, Texas–based digital team quickly made room for new partners from Cambridge Analytica.[6]

"Most communication companies today still segregate their audiences by demographics and geographics," but those markers of identity only roughly predict a person's opinions about the world, including products and politics, Nix said. "But equally important—or probably more important—are psychographics, that is, an understanding of your personality." With the use of psychographic profiling, a marketer or campaign could precisely address an individual even if he or she stands out from the larger groups to which she belongs. So psychographic profiling uses character designations such as "openness" (how welcoming a person is to new experiences), "conscientiousness" (how much one prefers order and regularity or change and fluidity), "extroversion" (how social a person is), "agreeableness" (one's willingness to put other people's needs above her own), and "neuroticism" (how much a person worries). This is known in the trade as the "OCEAN" model.

Then Nix made a bold claim, one that he has not been able to support: "By having hundreds and hundreds of thousands of Americans undertake this survey (of personality traits) we were able to form a model to predict the personality of every single adult in the United States of America."[7]

This boast was stunning in its breadth and scope, and alarming in its potential. If this claim was true and psychographic data could be used to reliably predict the precise political inclinations of individual Americans, then a campaign could manipulate voters based on single or narrow issues, prejudices, or a lack of information. In a close election such power could sway the result if a few thousand people who would otherwise vote for a particular candidate or issue could be persuaded either to switch votes or—just as valuable to a campaign—not vote at all.

"For a primary, the Second Amendment might be a popular issue amongst the electorate," Nix explained, referring to the provision of the U.S. Constitution that grants American broad rights to own firearms. "If you know the personality of the people you are targeting you can nuance your message to resonate more effectively with those key audience groups."

A different collection of personality traits might demand a different sort of advertisement, Nix said. So some voters might be moved by a warm and family-oriented video that reminds a voter about the pleasures of hunting with a grandchild, for instance. Some voters need to be nudged to the left to support a particular candidate, while others might need to be nudged to the right to support the same candidate. With enough data and subtle psychographic profiles, Nix explained, a firm or campaign could develop just the right message for a particular voter or narrow set of voters.[8]

Again, the implications of this, if Nix's claims are true, are substantial. They raise some serious questions. What possible platform could deliver dozens or hundreds of precisely targeted ads to individuals? Television and radio only broadcast. A campaign could use one video advertisement in New York and a different one in Texas, or one in Dallas and a different one in Houston, but getting more granular than that would be impossible. Radio allows more precision and ads are cheaper to produce, as some people congregate around certain genres of music or news. Newspapers and magazines are slow and static, offering limited ability to use narrative or hyperbole. The only platform that could deliver powerfully manipulative text or video ads so precisely to almost every potential voter is, of course, Facebook.

Just how did Cambridge Analytica gather all the personality data that filled its system? Much of it is available for sale from private data aggregators that have served marketing firms for decades. These vendors have dossiers on millions of consumers around the world, based on their purchasing records and demographic features. If Cambridge Analytica had only data from those private sources and some publicly generated data such as voter registration and voting history, Nix would be making weakly supported but bold claims about standard and well-developed techniques. His almost revolutionary boasts would not hold up to scrutiny.

The day after Trump declared victory, Nix made another bold claim. "We are thrilled that our revolutionary approach to data-driven communication has played such an integral part in President-elect Trump's extraordinary win," Nix wrote in a press release from Cambridge Analytica. "It demonstrates the huge impact that the right blend of cutting-edge data science, new technologies, and sophisticated communication strategies can have." While the press release did not include the word "psychographics," to anyone who had followed Nix's recent speeches and his company's embrace of psychometrics, it was easy to assume that "our revolutionary approach" meant that Cambridge Analytica had done for the winning Trump campaign what Nix had claimed it had done successfully for the losing Cruz campaign.[9]

Within a month, some people who followed the intersection of data and politics would make that connection explicitly, even if Nix did so only obliquely. In December 2016 an article appeared on the Swiss website *Das Magazin*. It generated some interest in Europe. But interest in it spiked six weeks later when the U.S.-based website Motherboard published an English-language version called "The Data That Turned the World Upside Down."[10]

The article opens with an account of a young researcher named Michal Kosinski, who started his career at the University of Cambridge conducting research on psychometrics. Psychologists had forged the area of study in the 1980s and had generated the five personality traits that supplied the initials to OCEAN. Before this century a researcher could tag a person on the OCEAN matrix only after the person agreed to sit for a long questionnaire. That meant that the potential application of psychometrics was limited to those who agreed to participate in studies. From a sample of data, researchers could generate predictive models. But there was for a long time a shortage of good data to feed into and thus test and refine models. That all changed when Kosinski thought about Facebook.[11]

On Facebook, users were more than willing to take "personality quizzes." These seemed harmless and fun. Tabloids had long run attractive stories about how certain preferences or behaviors "revealed your personality." And there was a major personality testing industry, albeit specious and lacking any empirical support, devoted to personality testing to help employees perform, managers to manage, and recruiters to recruit—the Myers-Briggs system.[12]

Kosinski realized that he could create an application that would run within Facebook that Facebook users would gladly share. They would opt in to letting Kosinski scrape their record of likes from Facebook as well as the answers to the test. Kosinski could then correlate the record of likes with the answers that millions of users were giving to his personality quiz. Through this method, which Facebook now forbids, Kosinski was able to generate predictive models that could indicate many aspects of identity beyond the OCEAN scale scores. Finally, a psychometric laboratory had more data than it ever imagined it would have. People volunteered these data, although it's not at all clear that those who took the quiz fully understood the implications of allowing such deep surveillance of their social and political interactions. Still, the data came from a more "natural" setting, someone sitting at a computer or staring at a phone in an office or on a bus, not in some contrived setting such as a university office or classroom. The model proved remarkably effective at predicting attributes. "The model correctly discriminates between homosexual and heterosexual men in 88% of cases, African Americans and Caucasian Americans in 95% of cases, and between Democrat and Republican in 85% of cases," Kosinski and his co-authors wrote in the paper they published in 2013.[13]

After summarizing Kosinski's research, the article in *Das Magazin* then describes an uncomfortable incident. Once of Kosinski's colleagues at Cambridge approached Kosinski about licensing the quiz and model to SCL, which owns Cambridge Analytica. Once Kosinski realized SCL was in the business of political consulting he refused to engage in any such collaboration or licensing agreement.[14]

Kosinski discovered after the surprise Brexit vote that Cambridge Analytica had boasted about using data from Facebook and the OCEAN scale to generate a model that could predict personality traits for millions of voters. The article in *Dan Magazin* does not state or imply that Cambridge Analytica took and used Kosinski's quiz, model, or data. We found out in early 2018 that Cambridge Analytica relied on a different University of Cambridge researcher, Aleksandr Kogan, for that Facebook data.

After months of investigating the sources of Cambridge Analytica data, the *Observer* and the *New York Times* released reports simultaneously in March 2018 that Kogan had, in fact, given data on more than 87 million American voters to Cambridge Analytica. Reporters had found a former

Cambridge Analytica data engineer who had developed misgivings about the role and purpose of the firm. "They want to fight a culture war in America," said Christopher Wylie, the engineer-turned-whistleblower. "Cambridge Analytica was supposed to be the arsenal of weapons to fight that culture war." Wylie revealed that Kogan had copied the user data from Facebook under the guise of performing academic research, but had sold access to the data to Cambridge Analytica. The company had built models to predict voter behavior and had convinced campaigns in the United States and around the world that the models would help target and persuade voters. When the news broke of the breadth and depth of data that Facebook had allowed out, and the fact that Facebook took no effective measures to punish companies that exploited data like that, political and commercial pressure on Facebook built to a level the company had never before experienced or expected. A movement began on Twitter urging Americans to delete their Facebook accounts. Legislators and regulators in Europe and North America launched investigations into Facebook and its data practices. And Cambridge Analytica was further exposed as a bad actor both in the methods that its leaders claimed to use and in the utter ineffectiveness of the company's efforts on behalf of campaigns.[15]

VAPORWARE EVERYWHERE

Almost immediately after the *Das Magazin* article appeared in English, critics of the article and of Cambridge Analytica spoke up to undermine the association of psychometrics with electoral success. Perhaps most damning, officials who ran voter targeting and contact programs for the Cruz campaign bluntly dismissed the scheme as useless. Cambridge Analytica's data and advice were so bad that the firm was wrong about identifying Republican voters as Cruz supporters about half the time. The Cruz campaign stopped using Cambridge Analytica after it lost the South Carolina primary to Donald Trump on February 16, 2016—three months before the Cruz campaign closed up for good. And when the Trump digital team tried to use Cambridge Analytica data, it found the older, more basic data sets offered by the Republican Party to be more reliable and useful.

Much of that standard Republican Party data derived from publicly available voter records and responses the party had gathered from voters over the previous three years.[16]

As political scientist David Karpf wrote in the aftermath of the psychographic moral panic, "Targeted advertising based on psychometrics is conceptually quite simple and practically very complicated. And there is no evidence that Cambridge Analytica has solved the practical challenges of applying psychometrics to voter behavior." In addition, the concept that Nix describes in his talk from October 2016 implies that any campaign can and would generate hundreds or thousands of tailored pieces of campaign advertising to match every combination of psychometric labels. Such a campaign would require a creative team of hundreds of writers, producers, and editors working around the clock to test various versions of an ad and quickly swapping it out for some voters and not for others. This could be done among a small number of roughly targeted set of voters—those who prioritize gun rights, others set on stopping abortion, still others who wish to stop immigration, and so on. But that targeting can and has been done for more than a decade using voter data compiled by both major parties. "The simple explanation here is that Cambridge Analytica has been engaging in the time-honored Silicon Valley tradition of developing a minimum viable product (vaporware, essentially), marketing the hell out of it to drum up customers, and then delivering a much more mundane-but-workable product," Karpf wrote. "The difference here is that [Cambridge Analytica's] marketing has gotten caught up in our collective search for the secret formula that put Donald Trump in the White House."[17]

Soon even Nix and Cambridge Analytica backed down on previous claims. Many recent statements by Cambridge Analytica clearly state that the company did not engage in psychographic profiling for the Trump campaign. And for some reason the company spokespeople now insist they did nothing to help the Brexit Leave campaign. To the Trump campaign, Nix now insists, the company provided more conventional consulting advice and data analysis. There is not much evidence that Trump campaign officials appreciated even that more conventional advice from Cambridge Analytica.

This did not stop some people from continuing to draw the specter of an evil cabal of Mercer, Bannon, and Trump using our personal data and personalities to steal an Electoral College victory and vacate the will of the American voting public, which overwhelmingly supported Clinton. The *New Yorker* ran a story by Jane Mayer in late March 2017 recounting the story from *Das Magazin*. Mayer's story was a deep and deft account of Robert Mercer's rise as a factor in extreme right-wing politics. And Mayer mentioned Karpf's debunking of *Das Magazin*. But the moment the claims of psychographic voter targeting appeared in one of the most respected magazines in the world, the issue took on new life among readers who might not follow political scientists on Twitter.[18]

Even Hillary Clinton fell for the irresistible story of Cambridge Analytica practicing the dark arts of psychometrics on American voters. In May 2017 Clinton gave one of her most frank and revealing interviews after the election debacle. Speaking with technology journalists Kara Swisher and Walter Mossberg, Clinton said, "I take responsibility for every decision I made. But that is not why I lost." Clinton told the journalists that her campaign tried to replicate the data tools developed and used so successfully by Obama in 2012. "The other side was using content that was just flat-out false, and delivering it a very personalized way, both above the radar screen and below." Clinton explained that the Republicans had reacted to their 2012 loss by upgrading their data infrastructure so that they had drawn even with the Democrats and perhaps surpassed them. "Then you've got Cambridge Analytica," Clinton said.[19]

In England the Cambridge Analytica–psychometrics story also refused to die and, in fact, grew in visibility. On March 4, 2017, the *Observer* ran the first of what would be several stories linking psychographic voter targeting and Cambridge Analytica to the Leave campaign. The article cited a February 2016 article by Nix in the election-professional trade magazine, *Campaign*. "Recently, Cambridge Analytica has teamed up with Leave. EU—the UK's largest group advocating for a British exit (or 'Brexit') from the European Union—to help them better understand and communicate with UK voters," Nix wrote. "We have already helped supercharge Leave.

EU's social media campaign by ensuring the right messages are getting to the right voters online, and the campaign's Facebook page is growing in support to the tune of about 3,000 people per day."[20]

A dogged reporter and essayist, Carole Cadwalladr, has since followed up with a series of articles for the *Observer* that describes the growing influence of large pools of data on politics. Cadwalladr draws the same connections among Robert Mercer, Cambridge Analytica, the Leave campaign, and the Trump campaign that others have. Cadwalladr justifiably raises serious questions about the legality of potential "in-kind" contributions of consulting services by Cambridge Analytica to the Leave campaign. And she has been a fervent critic of the data industry that feeds so much personal information to those who would manipulate government for their own ends. Reporter Jamie Bartlett of the BBC has been similarly enchanted by the connections between Cambridge Analytica and the Leave and Trump campaigns. He has produced long video reports about Silicon Valley and data and how they affect our lives. In one segment Bartlett showed the empty San Antonio offices of Trump's digital team with the side office where Cambridge Analytica staff worked. But neither Bartlett nor Cadwalladr can offer evidence that psychographic targeting per se works for campaigns. In June 2017 BBC *Newsnight* reporter Robert Gatehouse presented an in-depth segment on the same issues, leading off the report with spooky silent film images of hypnosis to imply that there is some sort of mind control at work in British politics. While Gatehouse's report is ultimately fairly blunt in his dismissal of the efficacy of psychographics, it does open, close, and center the segment on the dark arts of psychographics. It's just too good a hook for reporters to resist. All of this journalistic work has value. And because of it the UK Information Commissioner's Office launched an investigation in 2017 into the use of private data by the Leave campaign, including its possible links to Cambridge Analytica. But by invoking psychographic profiling and manipulation as powerful and this frightening, Gatehouse, Bartlett, and Cadwalladr obscure the very real problems with the use of Big Data in politics and governance.[21]

THE DAMAGE

It's not clear that Mercer, Nix, SCL, and Cambridge Analytica have succeeded in generating useful models at all, despite all the boasting Nix has done about them in an effort to seed new business. It's also clear that by 2018 there had been no evidence that psychographics performed any better than the more standard data-intensive techniques used by the Obama and Romney campaigns of 2012 or the Clinton campaign of 2016. Leave and Trump victories were troubling and perplexing to elites and analysts. So many desperately wish to identify a magic bullet to explain complex systems generating slim differences. There were no magic bullets. There were many forces at work for both Leave and Trump that were largely unacknowledged before those votes were cast. And there was Facebook. Still, Cambridge Analytica captured all the attention, making public issues concerning Facebook, data, surveillance, and politics that had been boiling in scholarly circles for a decade.

It sounded like the stuff of spy novels. A secretive company owned by a reclusive genius billionaire taps into sensitive data gathered by a University of Cambridge researcher. The company then works to help elect an ultranationalist presidential candidate who admires Russian president Vladimir Putin. Oh, and that Cambridge researcher, Kogan, worked briefly for St. Petersburg State University. And his research was designed to develop ways to psychologically profile and manipulate voters. Before we go too deep down the rabbit hole, let's recognize that the data Cambridge Analytica gathered to try to target more than 87 million Facebook users in the United States was not stolen from Facebook or removed after some security flaw or "data breach." The real story is far less dramatic but much more important. It's such an old story that the U.S. Federal Trade Commission investigated and punished Facebook back in 2011. It's such a deep story that social media researchers have been warning about such exploitative practices since at least 2010, and many of us complained when the Obama campaign in 2012 used the same kinds of data that Cambridge Analytica coveted. Obama targeted voters and potential supporters using software that ran outside of Facebook. It was a problem then. It's a problem now. But back in

2012, the Obama story was one of hope continued, and his campaign's tech-savvy ways were the subject of "gee whiz" admiration. So academic critics' concerns fell silent. Just as important, Facebook in 2012 was coming off a peak reputational moment. Facebook usage kept growing globally, as did the glowing if misleading accounts of its potential to improve the world after the 2011 revolution in Egypt. Between about 2010 and 2015, Facebook was a data-exporting machine. Facebook gave data—profiles of users who agreed to take one of those annoying quizzes that proliferated around Facebook between 2010 and 2015, but also records of those who were Facebook Friends with those users—to application developers who built cute and clever functions into Facebook. These included games like Mafia Wars, Words with Friends, or Farmville. You might have played, and thus unwittingly permitted the export of data about you and your Friends to other companies. Until 2015 it was Facebook policy and practice to let application developers tap into sensitive user data as long as users consented to let those applications use their data. Facebook users were never clearly informed that their Friends' data might also flow out of Facebook or that subsequent parties, like Cambridge Analytica, might reasonably get hold of the data and use it however they wished.

The Federal Trade Commission saw this as a problem. In 2011 the agency released a report after an investigation revealed that Facebook had deceived its users over how personal data was being shared and used. Among other violations of user trust, the commission found that Facebook had promised users that third-party apps like Farmville would have access only to the information that they needed to operate. In fact, the apps could access nearly all of users' personal data—data the apps didn't need. While Facebook had long told users they could restrict sharing of data to limited audiences like "Friends Only," selecting "Friends Only" did not limit third-party applications from vacuuming up records of interactions with Friends. The conclusions were damning. They should have alarmed Americans—and Congress—that this once huggable company had lied to them and exploited them. Through a consent decree with the commission, Facebook was barred from making misrepresentations about the privacy or security of consumers' personal information. It was required to obtain consumers' affirmative express consent before overriding privacy preferences. And Facebook was required to prevent anyone from accessing a user's material more than thirty days after the user has deleted his or her account. Most important, Facebook had to proactively police its application partners and its own products to put user privacy first. The consent decree put the burden on Facebook to police third parties like Kogan, the Obama campaign, and the makers of Farmville. Facebook was responsible for making sure fourth parties, like Cambridge Analytica, did not get and use people's information. We now know how well Facebook lived up to that responsibility. Facebook shut down this "Friends" data-sharing practice in 2015, long after it got in trouble for misleading users but before the 2016 election got into high gear. Not coincidentally, Facebook began embedding consultants inside major campaigns around the world.

For 2016 Facebook would do the voter targeting itself. Facebook is the hot new political consultant because it controls all the valuable data about voter preferences and behavior. No one needs Cambridge Analytica or the Obama 2012 app if Facebook will do all the targeting work and do it better. This is the main reason we should stay steady at the rim of the Cambridge Analytica rabbit hole. Cambridge Analytica sells snake oil. No campaign has embraced it as effective. Cambridge Analytica CEO Alexander Nix even admitted that the Trump campaign did not deploy psychometric profiling. Why would it? It had Facebook to do the dirty work for it. Cambridge Analytica tries to come off as a band of data wizards. But they are simple street magicians, hoping to fool another mark and cash another check.[22]

We should be wary of the practice of data-driven voter targeting in general—whether done for the Trumps of the world or for the Obamas of the world. The industry devoted to rich data targeting and voter manipulation is far bigger than SCL and Cambridge Analytica. It's growing on every continent. And it's undermining democracy everywhere. Facebook is doing the data analysis internally. Facebook is working directly with campaigns—many of which support authoritarian and nationalist candidates. You don't need Cambridge Analytica if you have Facebook. The impact of Facebook on democracy is corrosive.[23]

By segmenting an electorate into distinct sets, candidates move re-sources toward efforts to pander to small issues with high emotional appeal instead of those that can affect broad swaths of the electorate and perhaps cross over presumed rifts among voters. It's not necessary—and may be counterproductive—for a campaign to issue a general vision of govern-ment or society or to articulate a unifying vision. It's still done, but it's not the essence of the game anymore. Voter targeting, even without the power-ful black magic of psychographics, encourages narrow-gauge interventions that can operate below the sight of journalists or regulators. A campaign like Trump's can issue small, cheap advertisements via platforms like Facebook and Instagram that disappear after a day or get locked forever in Facebook's servers. That's bad for transparency. That's exactly what hap-pened. That story has not echoed as far as the one about Cambridge Analytica and psychographics. But it's the real story.

Since 2000 American political parties, campaigns, and consultants have been experimenting with two forces that are transforming the methods of communication, persuasion, and organization and threatening the spirit of a democratic republic. While the interventions have yet to yield consistent and durable results for campaigns, the damage they do is already clear. These two forces are political engineering and the managed citizen.

Political engineering is like social engineering. It is the process of har-vesting data about citizens (proprietary consumer behavior records, census information, voter records, poll data) and generating algorithmic tools that efficiently focus resources on those most likely to be moved by tailored messages. The citizen under target need never know that her information is being processed and that she is being profiled. This can be done without psychographics because consultants have learned to correlate these data with records of the effectiveness of messages. This means that a campaign need not have a consistent overall theme or message for all the citizens it is trying to move. Campaigns can shift tactics in something close to real time. This is all standard practice for commercial marketing. Since at least the 1960s political consultants have borrowed tools and tactics from the pri-vate sector, and many have worked in commercial marketing as well as po-
l communication. This synergy has never been healthy. And it has had

its critics since Joe McGinnis revealed the influence of Madison Avenue opinion merchants on the Richard Nixon campaign in *The Selling of the President, 1968*.

As marketing has grown more intrusive and data-driven, so has political communication. As marketing has moved to social media, so has political communication. Marketing has changed from something like poetry to something like engineering. So has politics. The changes in private sector marketing are troublesome because of the ways people can now find their reputations out of their control as information leaks into new contexts. But the changes in political communication undermine the principles of a democratic republic and the autonomy of citizens. Citizens can (and are) deliberately misled and confused. They are pushed to react to narrowly tailored issues and concerns and to ignore the larger needs of society. The culture of politics, therefore, has become customized: each of us is asked whether a candidate or platform is good for us and our immediate gratification rather than good for our community, nation, or world. Any thematic connection to the commons—or to our common fate—is inefficient. Political engineering quashes inefficiency and thus undermines efforts to seek broad support to address problems that cut across our narrow demographic channels. Political engineering also amplifies and accelerates the dynamics of motivation and activism, bolstering efforts to push political positions and candidates. Activists and interest groups (including political parties) can summon action for less money, in less time, and with less effort because of these technologies and tactics. And, of course, the better-funded a movement or party is, the greater the potential for effective political engineering. The trade-off is a diminished ability to convene a polis to compromise and collaborate. Politics becomes bitter and opaque.[24]

HYPERMEDIA

The twenty-first-century media environment, even before Facebook rose to dominate every aspect of it, was structuring citizenship in some dangerous ways. Back in 2006, when Facebook was just one of many social network sites battling for the loyalty of young Americans, Philip Howard called the

new political media ecosystem "hypermedia." As Howard observed political operatives harvesting consumer data, profiling voters in narrow tranches
based on issue interest rather than just demography and geography, and
rapidly adjusting strategy, tactics, and messages for these narrow segments
of potential voters, he foresaw a remarkable transformation in how citizens
would relate to politics and government. Hypermedia encourage redlining,
excluding or ignoring segments of the polis that are deemed unworthy of
the application of campaign resources because of the unlikelihood of a desired response. More important, as voters receive customized messages
that pandered to their top or pet concerns, there could be no larger political
conversation about common good or common fate. Hypermedia allow
campaigns to conceal core policy positions or make them "strategically am-
biguous." So every narrow, targeted message would not only motivate potential supporters but also distract voters from other policies to which they
might object. Everything becomes a distraction from everything else. This
fosters single-issue campaigns and encourages single-issue candidates (or
so it would seem to single-issue voters, because they would only see the
messages targeted to them). Hypermedia facilitate the rise of formerly marginal political actors, ones the traditional filter mechanisms of political parties fail to exclude. That's exactly what we have seen across the world over
the past decade—most recently and dramatically in the United States.[25]

Through hypermedia campaigns, governments in power are able to
"manage" citizens. They can manipulate and precisely target flows of information or propaganda. There is no public or polis, only tribes that can be
combined or divided depending on the needs of the moment. Any hope of
developing a politics of depth or sincerity, or of encouraging collective sacrifice for the common good, evaporates as the culture of political communication rewards immediate response and gratification. Citizenship grows
"thin," as too much information lies within convenient reach but is cacoph-
onous, confusing, and contradictory. Contacts from political actors, including journalistic institutions, are easy and frequent. They do not demand
of a citizen that she carve out some time, appear in person before a group of
fellow citizens, or recognize the needs of others or the nuances of complex
issues. Every political interaction is a quiz, a poll, a click, a share, a comment,

a like, an email, an online petition, a donation via text message, or a request for more attention. "Thin citizens do not need to expend much interpretive labor in their political lives, because they use information technologies to demark political content they want in their diet," Howard wrote. "Political hypermedia are designed to deny universal, collective needs and to accept diverse individual needs." This is, as we have seen, wonderful for movements and organizations. For little marginal cost and over little time they can identify and motivate the motivatable. But it undermines deliberative democracy.[26]

We must also consider how hypermedia feel to the citizens themselves. For many years in the late twentieth century those who monitored the health of democracies were concerned about citizens growing disaffected as power seemed to lurch further from their influence and become more concentrated by capital and within capitals. Hypermedia can have the opposite effect, which might not be positive in the long run. Citizens energized and motivated through hypermedia can seem conditioned to be alert to slights or slippage in status. Status slippage, after all, is a great motivator. Citizens can be pushed to support issues and candidates that threaten entrenched elite power. They can also be prompted to support demagogues who fool them with populist promises yet govern like oligarchs. Either trend (or both simultaneously) can emerge from a hypermediated environment. But a polis could grow more polarized as hypermedia structures distinct rhetorical fields and separate bubbles of perceived reality, rendering the process of meeting in the middle, mediating differences between elections or violent clashes, close to impossible. Hypermedia are constant, alarming, exhausting, and disruptive. Hypermedia limit collective thought and hollow out moments of public debate into performances of sincerity rather than engagement with a different point of view and set of values.[27]

The rise of hypermedia offers citizens a sense of emotional connection with matters of public concern and politics. Before Facebook, Twitter, YouTube, online polls, and other digital methods and platforms that let citizens "talk back" to those in power, or just among themselves, it was easy to feel voiceless. Hypermedia, by indulging and pandering to the desires of segments of the polis, simulate empowerment. Finally, someone might listen, someone might watch, someone might care what I think. If this sense of empowerment constituted actual empowerment, democracy would be richer. All indications are, however, that few places in the world (Tunisia being the most obvious example) have a democracy richer and stronger than it was in 2004, when Zuckerberg first coded a social network service for his fellow Harvard classmates. The constant expressions of affect and the constant feedback that those in power deliver based on expressions of affect have generated a poverty of politics that overrides and exploits the sincere desire for people to matter to their governments.[28]

The sudden recognition of dynamic manipulation of the voting public made people susceptible to buying the nightmarish story of Cambridge Analytica deploying the darkest of psychological arts. But this model for such manipulation has existed for almost twenty years. It was just not perfected until the rise of Facebook. Just as important, before the 2016 election the practice of political engineering in the United States relied much more on public records of demography and voter habits (frequency of voting, party registration, duration of registration, etc.) than on expensive proprietary databases. Attempts by both major American parties to generate a powerful tool to deploy proprietary data had either underperformed or proved incompatible, undependable, and unwieldy. Political engineering was still data-intensive and getting more so during the second decade of the twenty-first century. But campaigns were still deploying the sorts of data they had had available in 2000. That changed in 2016, but not because of Cambridge Analytica. The Donald Trump campaign had another, more opaque partner in its effort to move voters. That partner was Facebook.[29]

IT'S COMING FROM INSIDE THE HOUSE

Much of what scholars have analyzed about trends toward political engineering and the management of citizens have occurred within campaigns and public interest groups themselves, and are executed by phone, in the streets, or through traditional media and advertising systems. But something has changed since about 2014, when Facebook restricted the ways its advertising partners could extract, analyze, and deploy Facebook user data.

Now Facebook executes the political engineering and the management of citizens. And the company boasts of these efforts, as if it were some sort of civic obligation to manipulate citizens.

In 2014 an article in the *New Republic* by Harvard law professor Jonathan Zittrain asked us to imagine if Facebook were led by a political partisan—perhaps Mark Zuckerberg, perhaps his successor. Facebook in 2010 ran experiments on how the service could use social prompts (messages that your Friends have voted, so you should as well) to increase voter turnout. Zuckerberg had never been shy about his—and thus the company's—level of political engagement in the United States, having hosted President Barack Obama several times for speeches. Given the vast collection of valuable personal and political data that Facebook has on what was then only about one billion users around the world, such a partisan corporate leader could sway or motivate more than a few voters in more than a few key districts, precincts, or states. In a close race (or set of close races) Facebook could make the difference. But the public might never discover the extent of such manipulation. Facebook has no obligation to reveal what data it has on us or how it uses those data. Facebook is unlikely to face any regulatory restrictions in the United States on how it might use its data for persuasion. It is, after all, primarily in the business of selling advertisements. So persuasion is its purpose. The only thing keeping such manipulation from occurring, Zittrain wrote, was Facebook's belief in the value of the trust of its users. But if that manipulation occurred clandestinely, and there is no reason to believe it could not, then there would be no accountability short of an employee willing to violate a stern nondisclosure contract. Zittrain endorsed an idea promoted by Yale law professor Jack Balkin that Facebook, Google, and other such companies be treated by federal regulators as "information fiduciaries," required by law to use our data only in ways that do not harm us. Lawyers, doctors, financial advisors, and others are required by law and professional canon to act only on behalf of their clients. If Facebook were required by law to consider us clients instead of (or in addition to) products to be sold, it would have to generate clear, public, enforceable protections against political and other sorts of manipulation.[30]

By 2014 Facebook had decided to move forcefully into the realm of political advertisements. The company had set out to move much of the lucrative market away from television and radio, where expensive ads had dominated for five decades, driving up the cost of running a major campaign. Facebook did not hide its intentions. The company boasted about its abilities to target voters and prepared for the 2016 U.S. elections by describing its systems to the few journalists who were willing to listen. More important, Facebook joined Twitter, Microsoft, and Google in marketing efforts to urge political consultants, parties, and campaigns to work closely with the companies to maximize return for both the campaigns and the companies. Facebook made it clear to political professionals that advertising with it, rather than with television stations around the country, would be both less expensive and more effective. Most of the major presidential and congressional candidates in both parties in 2016 took Facebook up on the offer.[31]

Political professionals had for more than a decade dreamed of an ideal data system for targeting voters. It would meld commercial consumer behavior data, census data, public voter records, and records of party and political interactions (donations, volunteering, etc.) to code every voter in the country with an indicator of likely behavior. If a campaign deemed a voter a potential convert, that voter would receive one kind of message. If that voter was a true believer in that party or cause, she would receive a different kind of message. If that voter was a Spanish-speaker, she might get only messages in Spanish.

It turned out that while proprietary and commercial data proved to be expensive, unreliable, out-of-date, and in forms that made it difficult to merge with other types of data, Facebook solved all those problems in its own systems. Proprietary data sets in the hands of parties and campaigns could not predict a voter's ethnicity, religion, or sexual orientation. But Facebook could do all of that. Facebook users, after all, regularly declare on their profiles those attributes and many more—never having any idea that such expressions of opinion and affiliation might be used by political campaigns. That was the key insight that Kosinski made when he pulled all of that data out of Facebook through his personality quiz. Self-reporting via Facebook was just about the richest, broadest, and most dependable data any social scientist or psychologist could ever hope to acquire. And Facebook would no longer let it get out. All those data are too valuable. The company would let its advertisers—and thus political campaigns—in to use the data, but always under the control of the Facebook advertising system.[32]

HOW FACEBOOK HELPED MAKE TRUMP PRESIDENT

When Donald Trump put together his campaign team in the summer of 2015 he had few Republican veterans from which to choose. There were sixteen other candidates for the nomination, all but two of whom had held elected office before, all but one of whom had never run for elected office before. Among these Republicans, Jeb Bush, the former governor of Florida and the son of one former president and brother of another, seemed to have locked up most of the most generous donors and most experienced campaign advisors. There was not that much money and talent to go around, and Trump's lifelong aversion to committing to one political party or another (he had donated to campaigns of both Republicans and Democrats—including to the Senate campaign of Hillary Clinton), his ideological inconsistency (he had at various times supported and opposed the right for women to have abortions safely and legally), and his endorsement of overtly racist positions kept both potential donors and professional campaign advisors wary of him. So Trump filled his campaign staff with longtime friends and loyalists, only a few of whom had any relevant political experience.

Short of cash, short of experience, but invested in loyalty, Trump turned to his son-in-law, real estate heir Jared Kushner, to put together his digital strategy. "I called somebody who works for one of the technology companies that I work with, and I had them give me a tutorial on how to use Facebook micro-targeting," Kushner told *Forbes* after the election. To execute a lean strategy, Trump and Kushner hired the same person who had done the internet marketing work for many Trump companies in recent years, Brad Parscale. While Kushner operated out of an office in Trump Tower in Manhattan, Parscale saved money by adding to his company's regular staff and working out of a modest office near the airport in San Antonio,

Texas. Parscale, like Kushner, had no experience with political campaigns. Kushner was not bound by the conventional wisdom of consultants and party leaders. Parscale knew how Facebook worked. So he worked Facebook for Trump.[33]

Parscale's digital operation from San Antonio spent $70 million per month on Facebook and had three functions: promote the candidate on social media and YouTube, sell merchandise to support the campaign, and solicit donations from supporters. Facebook, Parscale knew from his commercial experience, could accomplish all three tasks with minimal overhead. "Facebook was the single most important platform to help grow our fundraising base," Parscale told BuzzFeed after the election. The campaign took in more than $250 million in donations from Facebook and other online sites. Parscale dubbed his digital fortress "Project Alamo." (The Alamo is a former Catholic mission in the center of San Antonio at which proslavery immigrants from the United States in 1836 lost a two-week siege to the antislavery forces of President Antonio López de Santa Anna of Mexico. The legend of the Alamo lives on in Texas lore as a tale of bravery and sacrifice to a lost cause, one redeemed six weeks later when Texas won its independence from Mexico and preserved slavery in Texas for another nineteen years.)[34]

Every person who donated money or purchased a "Make America Great Again" hat through Facebook or the Trump campaign website gave the campaign a name, address, and email address. Facebook's Custom Audiences from Customer Lists function allows advertisers to upload files of customers' email addresses to Facebook. Facebook then matches the email addresses to its collection (generated when people first joined Facebook). This way, advertisers have precise ways to reach those it knows are likely customers or, in the case of the Trump campaign, voters. Custom Audiences also serves as an effective way to contact previous donors with targeted, immediate appeals for more money via Facebook. Parscale knew that by using Custom Audiences, he could maintain strong relationships with Trump supporters in key states. He could give them early notice if the candidate was going to appear on Facebook Live. He could urge them to travel many miles to a Trump rally. He could nudge them to vote on election day.

Facebook's Custom Audiences from Customer Lists also gives campaigns an additional power. By entering email addresses of those unlikely to support a candidate or those likely to support an opponent, a campaign can narrowly target groups as small as twenty people and dissuade them from voting at all. "We have three major voter suppression operations under way," a campaign official told Bloomberg News just weeks before the election. The campaign was working to convince white leftists and liberals who had supported socialist Bernie Sanders in his primary bid against Clinton, young women, and African American voters not to go to the polls on election day. The campaign carefully targeted messages on Facebook to each of these groups. Clinton's former support for international trade agreements would raise doubts among leftists. Her husband's documented affairs with other women might soften support for Clinton among young women. And by connecting Clinton to efforts to increase criminal incarceration under President Bill Clinton's administration, Trump hoped to soften the commitment that some African American voters had for Clinton. The campaign could quickly test and then change Facebook-hosted videos meant to deliver these messages if they failed to generate reactions. They could test dozens of versions on each theme. The Trump campaign had no illusions that they could pull these voters over to support Trump. That was a lost cause. The campaign merely wanted to seed enough doubt among just enough of these core supporting demographics that turnout for Clinton would be slightly lower than expected in a few key states. It was a long shot. But for most of the campaign Trump was running more than eight percentage points behind Clinton in nationwide polls. Trump's only shot at an upset victory was to pull just the right states into his column by suppressing just enough votes. Notoriously, the Trump campaign targeted the families of immigrants from Haiti who live in South Florida with reminders that Bill Clinton had failed to sufficiently aid Haiti both as president and as head of a relief effort after a major earthquake in 2010. The fact that Trump lost Florida by only 112,000 votes indicates that if even a few thousand potential Clinton voters in Little Haiti stayed home instead of voting for Clinton, the inexpensive Facebook ads made a difference.[35]

Custom Audiences is a powerful tool that was not available to President Barack Obama and Governor Mitt Romney when they ran for president in 2012. It was developed in 2014 to help Facebook reach the takeoff point in profits and revenue. Because Facebook develops advertising tools for firms that sell shoes and cosmetics and only later invites political campaigns to use them, "they never worried about the worst-case abuse of this capability, unaccountable, unreviewable political ads," said Professor David Carroll of the Parsons School of Design. Such ads are created on a massive scale, targeted at groups as small as twenty, and disappear, so they are never examined or debated.[36]

THE NEW CONSULTANTS

For the 2016 elections, Facebook, Twitter, Microsoft, and Google all embedded staff in the digital headquarters of major presidential candidates. Two scholars of political communication, Daniel Kreiss and Shannon McGregor, interviewed many of those employees who served the campaigns. They discovered that these companies not only supplied basic guidance about how to use their services (and in the case of Microsoft, that was largely about cloud software and server installation and configuration). These companies also worked as de facto unpaid consultants for the campaigns of both major U.S. parties. Of these, Facebook and Google (which owns and runs YouTube) had the most influence. Search-based advertisements on Google are proven ways to generate interest and raise money. YouTube is the most powerful source of political video in the world, as it hosts campaign ads, amateur video with political content, and clips from major news outlets. YouTube videos are easy to embed and share—especially on Twitter and Facebook. But Facebook, with its superior penetration across every facet of the American electorate and its powerful advertising targeting services, became the most important and powerful ally in the 2016 U.S. presidential election.

The companies assembled partisan teams made up of practitioners with backgrounds in Democratic and Republican politics to advise campaigns and parties of the same political affiliation. Understandably, campaign officials and party operatives are more likely to trust people who share their views. This means that in the heat of a campaign, as news breaks and the candidate's standing rises and falls, the Facebook, Twitter, and Google employees embedded in those campaign headquarters sympathize with their hosts. As a result, these embedded technology workers meld their interest in promoting their company's services with the goals of their client. They soon find themselves advising the campaign on content and strategy. This was particularly acute in the Trump campaign. While the Clinton campaign carried a large digital staff, most of who had ample political experience and thus trusted their own professional judgment on matters of strategy and content, the Trump campaign had no veterans of previous campaigns, so they relied on the guidance and feedback that the embedded Facebook staff could offer it. The line between generating content that spiked the "metrics" and generating content that promoted the goals of the campaign simply did not exist. "For technology firms, this meant more revenue," Kreiss and McGregor write. "For campaigns, the better performance of ads meant more attention to their messaging among targeted groups, more sign-ups to their email list, and more donation." The synergy was clear and irresistible. By denying that Facebook plays an active political role in the world, and treating the campaigns as just another set of advertising and marketing clients, Facebook staff effectively granted a major advantage to the Trump campaign.[37]

For the 2016 campaigns, and for Trump much more than any other Republican candidate or Hillary Clinton, Facebook was an active partner in shaping the electorate. It was the conduit for fundraising, message shaping, message delivery, volunteer recruitment, merchandise vending, and—most perniciously—voter suppression. Facebook served as both a political consultant and a distribution outlet. To Facebook, this collaboration is more a confluence of interests than a conflict of interests.

Because, as we have discussed, Facebook is designed to favor content that is of high emotional power, is quick to digest, is image-heavy and preferably videographic, and flows through a person's field of vision among a weird mixture of decontextualized social, personal, and entertainment-based items, it is the worst possible forum through which we could conduct our politics. Donald Trump's success deploying the tools Facebook offered in 2016, and the fact that Facebook will certainly update and add new tools for 2018 and 2020, means that the next series of political campaigns in the United States will be even more dependent on and influenced by Facebook.

By timbre, temperament, and sheer force of personality, Donald Trump is the ideal manifestation of Facebook culture. Trump himself uses Twitter habitually both as a bully pulpit and as an antenna for reaction to his expressions. Twitter has a limited reach among the American public, and his off-the-cuff, unpracticed, and untested expressions could do him more harm than good. But Facebook, with its deep penetration into American minds and lives, is Trump's natural habitat. On Facebook his staff makes sure Trump expresses himself in short, strong bursts of indignation or approval. Trump has always been visually deft but close to illiterate. His attention span runs as quickly and frenetically as a Facebook News Feed. After a decade of deep and constant engagement with Facebook, Americans have been conditioned to experience the world Trump style. It's almost as if Trump were designed for Facebook and Facebook were designed for him. Facebook helped make America ready for Trump.

Trump, however, is as much a symptom of the degradation as a cause. Had Hillary Clinton won the Electoral College in 2016 we would still be facing the same problem: the privatization, hollowing, and fracturing of political culture fostered and amplified by Facebook. Once Trump leaves office the United States and the entire world will be left with a desiccated political ecosystem. It will be more dependent on Facebook than ever before. Facebook will win. Democracy could lose.

The Disinformation Machine

In September 2016 Facebook revealed that advertising accounts based in Russia had precisely targeted advertisement at segments of American voters with propaganda intended to undermine support for Hillary Clinton's presidential campaign. Immediately speculation renewed about the depth of Russian meddling in American democracy. Was Cambridge Analytica involved with Russia? Who supplied the data that these ad accounts might have used to target so many Americans? Was there a connection between these ads and the Trump campaign?

While much of the discussion and speculation focused on Russia, it became immediately clear from that moment that Facebook has contributed to—and profited from—the erosion of democratic practice and norms in the United States and elsewhere. The audacity of a hostile foreign power trying to influence American voters rightly troubles us. But it should trouble us more that Facebook makes such manipulation so easy and renders political ads exempt from the basic accountability and transparency that healthy democracy demands.

Alex Stamos, who was at the time head of security at Facebook, wrote on a blog post, "We have found approximately $100,000 in ad spending from June of 2015 to May of 2017—associated with roughly 3,000 ads—that was connected to about 470 inauthentic accounts and Pages in violation of our policies. Our analysis suggests these accounts and Pages were affiliated with one another and likely operated out of Russia." The majority of ads did not directly mention either U.S. presidential candidate but "appeared to focus on amplifying divisive social and political messages across the ideological spectrum—touching on topics from LGBT matters to race issues to immigration to gun rights." Stamos's statement did not say whether this would be the last or only revelation of Russian interference via Facebook. Nor did he reveal how many Facebook users saw the advertisements. The ads, according to an expert on Facebook's advertising system who spoke to BuzzFeed reporters, likely were seen by between twenty-three million and seventy million people, based on the $100,000 ad buy alone.[1]

Stamos announced this revelation as a supplement to a report that he had coauthored in April 2017. That report, in the wake of the 2016 U.S. election and the growing controversies over the proliferation of false news stories and other forms of propaganda, had conceded that Facebook had hosted and delivered significant amounts of suspect content that served to undermine deliberation and democratic practice. "Our mission is to give people the power to share and make the world more open and connected," the Facebook report read. "Yet it is important that we acknowledge and take steps to guard against the risks that can arise in online communities like ours. The reality is that not everyone shares our vision, and some will seek to undermine it—but we are in a position to help constructively shape the emerging information ecosystem by ensuring our platform remains a safe and secure environment for authentic civic engagement." The report did not quantify or offer any examples of what it called "information operations" by states and nonstate actors. It just said that there had been some. The report also did not specify what Facebook could do to "constructively shape the emerging information ecosystem" beyond pledging to deploy machine learning to recognize accounts that seem automated. "In brief, we have had to expand our security focus from traditional abusive behavior, such as account hacking, malware and financial scams, to include more subtle and insidious forms of misuse, including attempts to manipulate civic discourse and deceive people."[2]

The September revelation, which came as government officials began raising questions about the internal data Facebook had that might show whether the Trump campaign had actively colluded with those within or working for the Russian government, was the first specific Facebook disclosure of "information operations." The specific offending elements, according to Stamos, were what the advertising industry calls "dark-post ads," seen only by the narrow intended audience, obscured by the flow of posts within a Facebook News Feed, and ephemeral. Facebook calls its dark-post service Unpublished Page Post Ads. The service is popular among advertisers for its low cost, ease of use, efficiency, effectiveness, and responsiveness. Facebook gives rich and instant feedback to advertisers, allowing them to quickly tailor new ads to improve outcomes or more granularly customize messages. There is nothing mysterious or untoward about the system itself, as long as it's being used for commerce instead of politics.[3]

One week after Facebook revealed the presence of these Russian-based advertisers, it admitted that Russian operatives had put up event pages on Facebook to attract attendees to anti-immigrant rallies in the United States. Another report showed that Russians had put up a Facebook page encouraging Texas to secede from the United States. Three months earlier Reuters had reported that a Russian think tank controlled by the Kremlin, the Russian Institute for Strategic Studies, had generated an elaborate plan to influence the 2016 U.S. presidential election. The document recommended the Kremlin launch a propaganda campaign via social media and Russian state-backed global news outlets to encourage U.S. voters to elect a president who would take a softer line toward Russia. As the campaign rolled on and it looked as if Clinton would win easily, the institute proposed that the social media propaganda effort turn toward undermining faith in the American electoral system by spreading false stories of voter fraud. Back in late November 2016 the *Washington Post* had reported on internet experts warning that Russian-based organizations and companies had seeded Facebook with disinformation intended to undermine faith in American democracy. These earlier reports helped put pressure on Facebook to finally reveal what it knew. As of September 2017, Facebook had revealed only a slim portion of what others have alleged.[4]

As it turns out, we need not spend time wondering who gave these Russian firms the data needed to target specific American audiences. Russian operatives did not require any help from Trump or Cambridge Analytica. Facebook does all the targeting work in-house. Facebook officials, who seem not to grasp the difference between commercial advertising and political propaganda, have repeatedly refused to reveal details of or data from political advertising campaigns. Rob Sherman, deputy chief privacy officer for Facebook, told Reuters in June 2017 that Facebook holds such data in strict confidence because it is "sensitive," the equivalent of trade secrets. "In many cases, [advertisers will] ask us, as a condition of running ads on Facebook, not to disclose those details about how they're running campaigns on our service," Sherman said.[5]

In other words, those who purchase political ads on Facebook enjoy far greater respect for privacy than those of us who use the service every day. Our records of web use, purchases, locations, and interactions with friends and family are all mined for the benefit of advertisers. This pervasive level of surveillance is unmatched in human history. Facebook has created one of the most profitable advertising machines ever created—one that has drained many millions in revenue away from the very news organizations we depend on to foster democratic deliberation and accountability. When a campaign or interest group buys an ad in a newspaper or on a cable television channel the ad could be seen by broad segments of society. It's also expensive to run even one version of an ad, let alone a dozen different versions. And there is usually a persistent record of the televised advertisement. In the case of federal campaigns in the United States, the 2002 McCain-Feingold Act requires candidates to state they approve of an ad and thus take responsibility for its content. The Federal Election Commission has, so far, neglected to extend the regulatory framework that governs political advertisements on television or radio to web-based or social-media-based political ads.

That tradition of accountability and transparency does not matter to Facebook. Ads on Facebook meant for twenty- to thirty-year-old home-owning Latino men in Virginia would not be viewed by anyone outside that niche. The ads would be ephemeral. Ads could promote falsehoods or misinformation. No one could respond to or even question the claims made in such ads. No one could criticize a group or campaign for its practices or run a response ad. And there would be no public record of campaign themes, arguments, and strategies for present-day political scientists or future historians to analyze. The potential for abuse is vast. An ad could falsely accuse a candidate of the worst malfeasance forty-eight hours before election day and the victim would have no way of knowing it even happened. Ads could stoke ethnic or gender hatred and no one could prepare or respond before serious harm occurs. This should not surprise us. Anyone can deploy Facebook ads. They are affordable and easy. That's one reason that Facebook has grown so quickly into a financial supernova, taking in $27.6 billion in revenue in 2016 by serving up the attention of two billion Facebook users across the globe.[6]

Daniel Kreiss, a communication scholar at the University of North Carolina, proposes that services such as Facebook, Twitter, and YouTube maintain a repository of campaign ads so that regulators, scholars, journalists, and the general public can examine and expose ads. This is a noble idea and one that deserves exploration. But the very fact that campaigns can make hundreds of versions of the same ad and that so much political propaganda comes from people and firms outside the traditional campaign and party system would render such a repository limited in its effects. In the absence of a legal requirement, companies have no reason to agree to and coordinate with such an archive. Beyond that, the U.S. Congress is unlikely to reform a system that their election campaigns are just learning to master.[7]

Facebook has pledged to install better filtering systems using artificial intelligence and machine learning to flag accounts that are run by bots, fake accounts (run by people who misrepresent their identities or interests), or accounts that otherwise violate Facebook's terms of service. These are just new versions of the technologies that have caused the problem in the first place. And there would be no accountability beyond Facebook's word. The fact remains that in the arms race to keep propaganda flowing, human beings only review troublesome accounts long after the damage has been done. The prospect is stronger for reform in Europe and the United Kingdom. In 2017 the Information Commissioner's Office in the United Kingdom launched an investigation into the role played by Facebook and its use of citizens' data in the 2016 Brexit referendum and 2017 national elections.[8]

DISINFORMATION

We are in the midst of a worldwide, internet-based assault on democracy. Scholars at the Oxford Internet Institute have tracked armies of volunteers and "bots," or automated profiles, as they move propaganda across Facebook and Twitter in efforts to undermine trust in democracy or to elect favored candidates in the Philippines, India, France, the Netherlands, the United Kingdom, and elsewhere. We now know that agents in Russia are exploiting the powerful Facebook advertising system directly. Russian disinformation has worked its way into the social media feeds of voters in France, the Netherlands, and the United Kingdom in the past two years. Armies of volunteer social media activists, working on behalf of authoritarian-minded parties around the world, have flooded Facebook, Twitter, and Facebook-owned Instagram and WhatsApp with disinformation, propaganda, and threats against critics and journalists.[9]

This disinformation takes many forms and has many different motivations. Some of it was designed to attract clicks to generate advertising revenue. Some of it was designed by a political party, government, or nonstate actor to generate political pressure, to undermine trust in the institutions that make democracy function, or to disrupt democratic deliberation. And some of it seems to have been created just for the entertainment value of those who promote it. It's a mess, and it's difficult to discuss the phenomena as a single field or subject. Investigations of the various modes of disinformation require a wide array of scholarly and journalistic tools, including ethnography, data science, and digital forensics. Facebook itself, with its global span and rich collections of user and advertising data, is the one actor that could help us accurately assess the impact of these behaviors on publics around the world. But Facebook has the most to lose if the data reveal that the company could have stemmed the flow of disinformation long ago and did nothing, or that—more likely—there is nothing Facebook can do to fix the problem, that it's endemic to the very core design of Facebook. So Facebook remains silent, leaving the rest of us to fumble around, trying to make sense of what seem to be rather severe threats.[10]

Facebook is hardly the only domain of disinformation. And it's rarely the birthplace of it. Other platforms such as 4Chan and 8Chan have been known to launch many of the most troubling campaigns of harassment and disinformation. Reddit, blogs, and websites that serve far-right nationalist groups often sprout it as well. Profiteering websites in places such as Macedonia have produced thousands of bogus stories and used Facebook and Twitter to attract readers to their sites, where advertising services generated revenue for them. Twitter is infected with bots that amplify false narratives and other forms of disinformation or distract critics of authoritarian leaders by harassing them with garbage.

To grasp how disinformation works in the world we must consider the entire ecosystem. Those who push this content start from the fringes, such as Reddit and 4Chan, where publication is easy and they can test various forms of their message among like-minded and motivated peers. They can generate catchy new hashtags for Twitter or join new content with established and popular hashtags.

They can post videos on YouTube, which then allows for easy redistribution via Twitter and Facebook, and which, thanks to Google's search algorithms favoring its own services, is a powerful social distribution platform in itself. Once items or issues rise in visibility on Twitter, editors of established online news and commentary sites such as BuzzFeed, Breitbart, Salon, or HuffPost can take notice. These sites are often starving for lively content that can connect to the hot issue or controversy of the day. So editors eagerly push young, underpaid reporters to echo each other with "hot takes" or sly commentary on whatever that issue might be—even to deflate or debunk the claim. It hardly matters if the story is important or even true once this level of content-hungry news site amplifies the story even more. Each of these rather recently established news organizations has optimized its headline writing, image placement, and writing style for social media distribution. If they have not noticed the items already, more established news services such as the *Guardian*, the BBC, Fox News, CNN, and the *Washington Post* soon catch on to the buzz of the day and might prepare new versions of the story as well—again, often to debunk claims. But it hardly matters. At this point, the specious content has moved completely up the chain of the media ecosystem. At every link in the chain, Facebook, the largest and most powerful media system in the world, plays a role in amplifying the disinformation. But by the time the content reaches the level of HuffPost or Breitbart, it's irresistible to many Facebook users. Those who buy into the claims of the disinformation share it gleefully. Those who are appalled by the existence of the disinformation share it out of disgust. Whether intended to signal acclimation or disgust, comments and sharing work the same way and generate the same result. Facebook reads both negative and positive comments as "meaningful engagement," so it amplifies the message, pushing it into more News Feeds and making it appear higher up in the feed and more frequently. The effect is the same: chaos reigns. And the disinformation artists laugh at just how easy it all is.[11]

The media ecosystem includes humans and machines, minds and algorithms, and operates through a series of similarly distinct and innocent choices: read this; report on this; share this; comment on this; click on this. As danah boyd, president of Data and Society, put it, "We've built an information ecosystem where information can fly through social networks (both technical and personal)." Having followed disinformation and harassment campaigns that emerge from gaming, misogynist cabals, white nationalist groups, and pornography internet subcultures for years, boyd warned that the technological interventions that Facebook promised to introduce would do little to stem the flow. Facebook amplifies and enables the phenomenon. But it originates among us—particularly among the most alienated of us. We built an attention economy, boyd argues. So we should expect people and groups to exploit that economy—ruthlessly and mercilessly.[12]

Beyond the algorithm, the very fact that we choose to perform our identities for others on Facebook amplifies the potential for disinformation to spread. "Sharing" an item on Facebook is an act that is both social and performative. Sharing is a declaration of identity. Sharing items about the San Antonio Spurs or FC Barcelona places me in particular circles. It also separates me from indignant fans of rival sports clubs. The act of sharing divisive material bonds me with some and separates me from others. But mostly it defines me to my circle of Friends.

So while Mark Zuckerberg thought he was forging a social network to connect people, by encouraging us to share content from other sites so easily he actually divided us by connecting us. These divisions are fluid, and some matter more than others. But over time, as Facebook structures our feeds to reward those who interact most frequently with us, our tribes solidify. Because we yearn for those small bolts of affirmation—the comment, the like, the share—we habitually post items that have generated the most response. We teach ourselves what sort of material will satisfy our tribe and will generate applause. Facebook also rewards us for that and pushes that rewarding content out farther, faster, and more frequently. If the item is false, hateful, or completely absurd, it hardly matters to the community. In fact, highly disputable, divisive, or disreputable content can become even more valuable as a signal of identity. Even if one loses Friends over it, or perhaps especially if one loses Friends over it, edgy or false or hateful content has the power of certifying that the person who posted it cares more for the identity marker than for the relationship.[13]

THE DISINFORMATION ABOUT "FAKE NEWS"

As the 2016 U.S. election campaign moved into the fall, American journalists became aware of a proliferation of fiction circulating on Facebook, disguised as legitimate news. Many, but not all, of the items spread false stories that could have helped expand or solidify support for Donald Trump, including false claims about Hillary Clinton, Muslims, or Mexican immigrants. A notorious case involved a frequently shared item claiming Pope Francis had endorsed Trump for president. American journalists quickly—and unfortunately—dubbed the phenomenon "fake news." BuzzFeed and its lead reporter Craig Silverman generated many of the most notable accounts of the "fake news" phenomenon. Silverman had been tracking the rise of such sites since at least 2014.

One of the keys to the success of "fake news" is that often these pieces were designed expertly to play both to the established habits of rapid sharers of Facebook content and to Facebook's EdgeRank algorithm. They reinforced existing beliefs among a highly motivated subset of Facebook users. Absurd or controversial posts are likely to be shared and cheered by those willing to believe them and dismissed, commented upon, argued about, and shared by those who dismiss the veracity of those posts. If someone sees an obviously fraudulent claim on a Friend's Facebook site and responds to it, it's likely to flare a long and angry argument among different camps. As we know all too well, Facebook is designed to amplify that sort of engagement. So the pieces spread. BuzzFeed was the ideal news organization to dig deeply into this dynamic, as it was founded to generate similar levels of engagement for both its news posts and its lifestyle features, listicles, and quizzes.[14]

However, the right-wing mediasphere quickly tried to discredit Silverman, BuzzFeed, and the term "fake news." An article in the conservative magazine *National Review* questioned Silverman's methodology when he tried to determine if "fake news" stories had been shared more heavily than more traditional sources of news. And the ultranationalist site Breitbart ran a story accusing Silverman of manufacturing a moral panic around "fake news" to advance his career.[15]

Despite these efforts to undermine the reporting on the proliferation, the epithet of "fake news" carried some meaning for about six months, until about January 2017, when the Trump transition team and his supporters co-opted the term by using it repeatedly to characterize news produced by professional organizations that operated within the traditions of verification and correction. In other words, Trump and his band flipped the meaning of "fake news" almost completely, making it hard for any serious examination of the phenomenon to start with that term. In early January 2017 *Washington Post* columnist Margaret Sullivan, formerly the public editor of the *New York Times* and editor-in-chief of the *Buffalo News*, declared the term useless and meaningless. "Faster than you could say 'Pizzagate,' the label has been co-opted to mean any number of completely different things: Liberal claptrap. Or opinion from left-of-center. Or simply anything in the realm of news that the observer doesn't like to hear," Sullivan wrote.[16]

"Pizzagate" was a term applied to a weird story that circulated among extreme right-wing news sites and social media users in the United States. It referred to a rumor that the email that had been stolen from the computer of John Podesta, a top Hillary Clinton campaign official, contained records of a child-sex ring run out of the basement of a pizza restaurant in Washington, D.C. Believing the false stories, a man bearing a gun entered the pizza restaurant in December 2016 to investigate and free the abused children he was convinced were being held in the nonexistent basement.[17]

The term "fake news" never covered the problem adequately in the first place. Not all of the troublesome items on Facebook were purely false. Sometimes they included elements of truth, even links to respectable news outlets, but took those elements and framed them in distorted or inaccurate ways to promote a partisan agenda. This is a classic technique of propaganda. In that way, this phenomenon was not new. Only its alarming amplification by its most fertile medium was new.

If the term "fake news" does not do the job, because it has been co-opted by the very forces that seek to undermine legitimate, professional news reporting practices and institutions, what terms can capture and describe what is going on? Searching for a better way to describe the variety of troublesome reports and doctored images floating down News Feeds, Caroline Jack, a researcher at the New York–based think tank Data and Society, set out to categorize and clarify the problem. Her report, entitled, "Lexicon of Lies: Terms for Problematic Information," walks through the pros and cons, strengths and limitations of terms such as "propaganda," "agitprop," and "misinformation." Jack described "disinformation" as "information that is deliberately false or misleading." Disinformation has the added feature of being often irresistible to the clicking fingers of Facebook users and thus the distributive power of Facebook algorithms. After all, the most incredible stories are the most emotionally powerful despite being—literally—incredible. The motives for such misleading can be pranksterish, selfish, or just malevolent. It seems that "disinformation" describes the widest set of phenomena with the most accurate description.[18]

The obsession with identifying, filtering, and quashing "fake news" distracted many from the larger, deeper problem of disinformation. "Fake news" is a trivial problem compared with the general assaults on civic and democratic norms that have been at work for many years in the United States and around the world. Whether for laughs, blood, or profit, disinformation campaigns share a goal: to undermine trust in civic norms and institutions. Disinformation divides and debilitates a polis. With enough exposure over enough time, the idea of trust becomes comical, the idea of truth becomes irrelevant, and the idea of justice melds with tribal vengeance or retribution. Society devolves into a craven, selfish state in which, as in the title of journalist Peter Pomerantsev's revealing book about Russia under Putin, "nothing is true and everything is possible."[19]

THE AUTHORITARIAN PLAYBOOK

If you wanted to design a media system to support authoritarian leaders and antidemocratic movements, you could not do much better than Facebook. Katy Pearce, a scholar who studies social media use in Azerbaijan and other post-Soviet states, has deflated the idea that Facebook chiefly serves the cause of liberation and the promotion of democracy. From the 1980s right through the years during which Secretary of State Hillary Clinton promoted her "internet freedom" agenda, pundits and politicians promised that the introduction of digital media would create cracks in the systems of information control that authoritarian leaders had traditionally used to maintain power. The theory held that by connecting dissidents and nascent civil society movement (churches, labor unions, human rights groups) to allies and information from democratic societies, the former group would grow larger, bolder, and more effective. Even Ronald Reagan, who served as president a decade before the internet achieved global recognition, said, "The Goliath of totalitarianism will be brought down by the David of the microchip." This theory has not held up to empirical scrutiny,

Pearce argues. Social media, especially Facebook, are certainly designed to aid civil society to organize efficiently, but they are also designed for authoritarians to exploit with better resources than their opponents have.[20]

There are five major ways that authoritarian regimes exploit Facebook and other social media services. They use it to organize countermovements to emerging civil society or protest movements. They can frame the public debate along their terms by virtue of having greater resources and technical expertise than their opponents and critics. They can allow or even manage social media as a stage for citizens to voice complaints without direct appeal or protest, thus letting citizens vent about corruption or governmental incompetence (as China allows citizens to use WeChat). Regimes can use social media to coordinate among elites to rally support as well.[21]

The fifth and most pernicious way authoritarian regimes use social media—especially Facebook—is in the surveillance and harassment of opposition activists and journalists. It's easy to plant a fake "Friend" with an activist group or an activist's profile page, allowing access to rich personal and organizational information. It's also easy to doctor photographs and video purporting to show an activist or journalist in a compromising situation, thus discrediting or at least distracting her or him and undermining the reformist effort. Once a sensational item about a well-known person arrives on Facebook, it gets around. And again, debunking it only enhances the story's penetration and influence. While most of the world was focusing on how social media helped insurgent groups in what became known as the 2011 "Arab Spring," the governments of Bahrain and Syria quashed nascent protest movements and thus avoided being grouped in with Tunisia and Egypt by deploying these tactics.[22]

Vladimir Putin's regime has mastered these tactics and deployed them both domestically and internationally. Much of the pro-Trump and anti-immigrant material that showed up on American Facebook News Feeds came from a St. Petersburg–based company called the Internet Research Agency, which employs hundreds of people to generate and spread disinformation that could serve the interests of the Russian government. And the Russian state propaganda outlets RT and Sputnik have positioned themselves to seed anti-immigrant, anti-Muslim, and anti-establishment disinformation into Germany, the United Kingdom, France, Ukraine, and the United States in a concerted effort to undermine trust in journalistic, governmental, and civil society institutions. Domestically, Putin's allies have spread abusive and harassing messages about critics, dissidents, and journalists. The Russian success at these efforts has made it a model for other authoritarian leaders and has brought attention to the matter within the United States and Western Europe. But the real masters and early adopters of pro-authoritarian social media use now rule two more populous countries than Russia: India and the Philippines.[23]

The rise and consolidation of the Bharatiya Janata Party, or BJP, under Prime Minister Modi has been historic. Earlier in its history the BJP had formed weak coalition governments in India, but never before did it have the overwhelming parliamentary majority that it gained in the 2014 elections. The party had solidified a coalition of regional ethnic and religious nationalist parties that it called the National Democratic Alliance. No party had controlled a clear majority in Parliament since 1984, when India was essentially a one-party state under the control of the Congress Party of Indira Gandhi and her sons. The overwhelming BJP victory surprised pollsters and pundits. Much credit for it went to reports of endemic corruption within the Congress Party. But Modi's fervent embrace of social media did not go uncredited.[24]

The BJP originated as the political wing of a militant Hindu nationalist movement called Rashtriya Swayamsevak Sangh (RSS). The RSS has long insisted on traditional roles for women, restricting immigration from majority-Muslim Bangladesh, a ban on celebrations of Valentine's Day because it signifies a degradation of morals by promoting "Western" ideas of love, and prohibitions on the slaughter and consumption of beef. One of its most fervent followers assassinated Mohandas Gandhi in 1948 because Gandhi and the Congress Party embraced a secular vision for India and tolerance of the 20 percent of the country that was Muslim. The RSS is the chief promoter of the idea of Hindutva, a protofascist vision of India as a Hindu homeland and theocracy. It has promoted a cleansing of history books, harassment of historians who describe India's multifaith past and traditions of tolerance, and a call for Hindu men to be strong and virulent in the defense of their identity. Anti-Islamic politics and policies have been central to the RSS and thus the BJP. When Modi, a longtime member of the RSS, was chief minister of the state of Gujarat in 2002, an anti-Muslim pogrom broke out. More than 1,000 people died, 790 of who were Muslim. Although cleared of malfeasance by a subsequent investigation, Modi clearly failed to act on behalf of his Muslim citizens, and other BJP officials participated in the pogrom. Human Rights Watch accused Modi's government of covering up the government's role in the atrocities. The United States and the United Kingdom banned Modi from entering their countries until he assumed the prime ministership.[25]

For a candidate so historically embedded within violent, nationalist forces, Facebook was the ideal platform to motivate potential supporters. The most caustic messages could fly below the view of journalists and international observers. Messages could rile up anti-Muslim passions and channel people to the polls. Not only did Modi develop a formidable social media team for his campaign, but his BJP continued to run a social media team staffed by both professionals and volunteers after the 2014 victory. The chief purpose of this team was to spread propaganda in favor of BJP policies. But it also had orders to destroy the reputations of journalists, civil society activists, critics of anti-Islam policies, and political enemies. In her book *I Am a Troll*, journalist Swati Chaturvedi tells the story of a woman who became enchanted with the BJP's Hindu nationalism while living in the United States. Upon her return to India, the woman enrolled as a social media worker at the BJP digital headquarters. At first she gleefully spread pro-BJP and anti–Congress Party items via WhatsApp. But after a while the negative messages struck her as cruel and unwarranted. "It was a never ending drip feed of hate and bigotry against minorities, the Gandhi family, the journalists on the hit list, liberals . . . anyone perceived as anti-Modi," the woman told Chaturvedi. "I simply could not follow [the social media director's] directions any more when I saw rape threats being made against female journalists like Barkha Dutt." The woman quit the BJP soon after.[26]

Facebook staff worked with BJP officials during the Modi campaign. India has more Facebook users than any other country, with more than

250 million in 2018, about 30 million more than the United States has. That 250 million is less than one-quarter of the population of India, while the 220 million Americans on the service constitute more than 60 percent of the U.S. population. So not only is the future of Facebook in India, the present of Facebook is as well. Modi's Facebook page has more followers than that of any other world leader, 43 million, or almost twice what Donald Trump's Facebook page has.[27]

Rival parties in India have established similar social media teams to mimic the BJP success. And now a slew of independent "troll farms" offer their services to private citizens, politicians, and companies that wish to destroy people's reputations. These services create fake videos of targets engaging in sex, drug use, or religious desecration. As the BJP solidifies its political standing the overall political culture of India has degraded through social media harassment and intimidation.[28]

FREE BASICS ENABLES OPPRESSION

While Narendra Modi has managed to distance his personal reputation from the damage done by his supporters, the president of the Philippines, Rodrigo Duterte, has ridden his army of social media warriors from the position of longtime mayor of Davao City to president in May 2016. At each step, Duterte and his supporters engaged in virulent character assassination, threats, and harassment. Unlike India, the Philippines in 2015 invited Facebook to spread its Free Basics service. That means for the half of its 103 million citizens who regularly partake of social media on their mobile phones, Facebook use does not count against the monthly data allotment they pay for. Visiting reputable news sites costs data and thus money.[29]

"We're one step closer to connecting the world as we launched Internet. org in the Philippines today," Zuckerberg wrote in March 2015. "Now everyone in the country can have free access to internet services for health, education, jobs and communication on the Smart network. Here's a photo of Jaime, a driver in Manila who uses Facebook and the internet to stay in touch with loved ones who moved to Dubai." It was a sweet, lovely post. Facebook was bringing Jaime's family closer together, at least virtually, and on Facebook's terms. Zuckerberg showed no awareness that by unleashing this service on the Philippines he was inviting brutality and misery to descend on innocent Filipinos.[30]

The dominance of Facebook in the media diet of Filipinos because of Free Basics was instant and timed perfectly for Duterte. The first move Duterte made when launching his campaign in 2015 was to hire a social media director and team. That team quickly leveraged the new connectivity created by Facebook's Free Basics service. Duterte's team of paid social media supporters, up to 500 volunteers, and thousands of bots have manufactured and spread false stories, and undermine trust in professional journalists. They deploy fake accounts to multiply the effects of the disinformation they share.[31]

Duterte's social media army during the 2016 campaign was divided into four groups, and each group was given a group to target: overseas Filipino workers, residents of the island of Luzon, Visayas, and Mindanao. Each group created its own content to express the daily narrative dictated by the Duterte campaign headquarters. Often these teams targeted university students they identified as Duterte critics. They shared and released students' mobile phone numbers. One Facebook post threatened a student with death. Other students received rape threats. Once Duterte assumed office he proceeded to shun interviews and encounters with professional journalists, choosing instead to communicate via Twitter and Facebook.[32]

Facebook itself made all of this possible. In January 2016 Facebook sent three employees to Manila to train the various presidential candidates and their staffs how best to use the service. The Facebook team met Duterte's campaign staff at the Peninsula Manila Hotel. The campaign staff learned the basics of setting up a campaign page, getting it authenticated with a blue check mark, and attracting followers. Duterte's campaign constructed a social media apparatus unlike that of any other candidate in the race. Every day the campaign would create a message for the next day. The teams of volunteers would then pump the message across both real and fake Facebook accounts, some with hundreds of thousands of followers. Facebook almost immediately received complaints about inauthentic pages. Soon, however, the company fielded complaints about Duterte's Facebook army circulating insults and violent threats. The Duterte campaign instructed its followers to circulate bogus stories, including a false endorsement by Pope Francis, with the phrase "Even the Pope Admires Duterte" pasted under the pope's image. Truth ceased to matter. Following a pattern familiar to those who watch politics in India, Russia, Ukraine, and even Estonia, the troll-army-driven propaganda dominated the political conversation. Any discussion of policies or choices or compromises became impossible. Opponents, journalists, and civil society leaders were left gasping at the audacity of Duterte's stunts. By April 2016, just one month before the election, a Facebook report called him the "undisputed king of Facebook conversations." Duterte occupied 64 percent of all election-related conversations on the Facebook pages in the Philippines.[33]

After Duterte won, Facebook extended its partnership with the administration, helping Duterte execute his violent, nationalist agenda. Duterte banned the independent press from covering his inauguration live from inside Rizal Ceremonial Hall. He didn't need journalists. He just had the inaugural events streamed live on Facebook. With the rise of Duterte, Facebook solidified itself as the only media service that matters in the Philippines, a country of more than 105 million people, rich with resources, a multilingual and globally dispersed population, and a rich history of anticolonial resistance.[34]

Duterte's direct communication with his supporters through social media has been powerful and effective. Since his election, Duterte has openly fostered a culture of vigilantism. More than fourteen hundred people have been killed by police and civilians because they were accused or suspected of selling or using illegal drugs. The Philippines was not long ago known as a country with a strong civil society and stable democratic values. A popular uprising in 1986 called People's Power expelled corrupt dictator Ferdinand Marcos and installed reformer Cory Aquino as president. People Power in the Philippines, following the fall of the military junta in Brazil in 1985, was among the first of a series of largely nonviolent revolutions between 1985 and 1991 that swept away authoritarian governments from South Africa to Poland to the Soviet Union. Filipinos rose up again in 2001 to peacefully reject a corrupt leader, President Joseph Estrada.

At the time, the 2001 uprising was among the first during which activists used SMS text messaging to coordinate the movement. Since 2001, the political culture of the Philippines has degraded. But it took its most serious downturn just as Facebook introduced Free Basics and Duterte took full advantage of it.[35]

In November 2017 Facebook announced a new partnership with the Duterte regime. Facebook will work with the government to lay underwater data cables that will bypass the Luzon Strait, where typhoons and earthquakes have often damaged standard cables. Facebook will fund the underwater links. The government will build cable landing stations. The Philippines has been moving for some years to become the central hub of optical fiber cables to facilitate digital data flows for East Asia and the South Pacific. A deep and profitable partnership with Facebook, while Facebook serves as the chief propaganda and harassment platform for the Duterte regime, means that Facebook will not have much choice but to continue to support Duterte as he expands his campaigns of terror.[36]

Like Duterte, Hun Sen, the dictator of Cambodia, has become a Facebook star as he has leveraged the power of Free Basics to harass his opponents and promote his image. He has used the classic authoritarian playbook: develop a following; ensure that independent media can't compete with state propaganda on Facebook; make sure Facebook is the equivalent of the internet itself; and employ a troll army (in Hun's case, hired from firms based in India and the Philippines—two countries with experience in just such methods) both to push items that show him in a positive light and to terrorize and humiliate opponents and critics. Most important, Hun's staff works directly with Facebook staff to silence critics and maximize the influence Hun's Facebook pages can generate.[37]

In October 2017 Facebook changed how news provided by professional news services would appear on the pages of users in Cambodia, Slovakia, Sri Lanka, Bolivia, Guatemala, and Serbia. Professional and independent news items would no longer run in the main News Feed along with advertisements, personal posts, and music videos. Instead news would sit on a separate, harder-to-see tab on the Facebook page. The results were predictable. Traffic from Facebook to independent news sites in all of these countries plummeted. Hun got an even better experience from Facebook. In angry response to this change, Serbian journalist Stevan Dojcinovic wrote an op-ed in the *New York Times* called, "Hey, Mark Zuckerberg: My Democracy Isn't Your Laboratory." In it, Dojcinovic wrote, "The major TV channels, mainstream newspapers and organized-crime-run outlets will have no trouble buying Facebook ads or finding other ways to reach their audiences. It's small, alternative organizations like mine that will suffer." In every country in which Facebook made this change, Facebook dominates the media ecosystem. Even small changes in Facebook's design or algorithmic emphasis can alter the political fortunes of an entire nation. Zuckerberg presented Internet.org and Free Basics as tools that would bring people together. The malevolent consequences of this benevolent concept have been all too clear. Facebook canceled the journalism experiment after the uproar. But its willingness to use small, poor countries as laboratories should trouble anyone who cares about global peace and stability.[38]

In perhaps the most alarming account of how Facebook has further empowered violent, oppressive state power, Free Basics has also transformed Myanmar, a country that has just recently emerged from decades of military rule. In 2014, only a year before the country's first free elections since 1960 elevated the human rights advocate Aung San Suu Kyi to power, the first mobile phone companies established data connections in Myanmar. Government policy pushed for rapid adoption of mobile phones. And by 2016 Facebook introduced Free Basics, ensuring that—like in the Philippines—for many Burmese there was no distinction between Facebook and the internet. To be connected means to use Facebook. Any other service costs money. The country has not had time to develop a mature and professional media system or a tradition of professional journalism. So the chaotic nature of Facebook is even more pronounced than in most of the rest of the world. In a country so recently opened up after more than fifty years of military control of every facet of daily life, Facebook seems like a gift. Now Burmese people can read and share news and rumors, experience music videos, share jokes, and, of course, spread hate.[39]

Under military rule, rumor was the dominant form of "news" and the chief subject of discussion. So through Facebook, old habits thrive.

Buddhist nationalists have spread rumors of a global Muslim conspiracy bent on ridding the world of Buddhism. Through Facebook they have called for boycotts of Muslim-owned businesses, a ban on interfaith marriages, and limitations on rights for Muslims who live in Myanmar. Anti-Muslim riots broke out in 2015 in cities across Myanmar. By 2017 Buddhist attackers, supported by the military, carried out genocidal attacks on the Muslim Rohingya minority in western Myanmar, driving many into neighboring Bangladesh, which had no ability to absorb them. Many Rohingya refugees proceeded west into India. In September 2017, as the world took notice of the genocide, Aung San Suu Kyi posted a message on her own Facebook page declaring the genocide a myth and blaming "terrorists" for unrest in western Myanmar. She then went to India to meet with Modi to enlist his help. Modi concurred with her assessment of the Muslim threat.[40]

Atrocities such as the slaughter and expulsion of the Muslim Rohingya people of Myanmar are hardly new. They have been a constant in human history. And, like with the various uprisings of 2011, people are going to use the communicative technologies available to them. So we should not be surprised that authoritarians, religious bigots, and ethnic nationalists push out disinformation via Facebook. We must, however, carefully consider what specific features and structures of Facebook make it so useful in such a consistent way by authoritarians and the movements that support them. Facebook allows authoritarian leaders and nationalist movements to whip up sentiment and organize violence and harassment against enemies real and imagined. It's like nothing before. Its ubiquity and ease of use in countries that are still struggling after centuries of colonial rule—Kenya, Philippines, Cambodia, and Myanmar—offer the most destructive forces an ideal propaganda system. Facebook does not favor hatred. But hatred favors Facebook.

The Nonsense Machine

n August 2017 my town became a hashtag. Charlottesville, Virginia (population forty-five thousand) became #Charlottesville. My Facebook News Feed swelled with images and insight into events that occurred just two miles from my house. People who lived states and even oceans away pontificated on the greater meaning of a conflagration between thousands of white supremacists and antiracist residents of Charlottesville, Virginia. The experience of having my small town turned into international news and a social media barrage, to see it become a symbol and an allegory while people I knew and loved took blows and took a stand, was bizarre and deeply troubling. All the while I was mourning for my town and country and fearing for my neighbors' safety I was finishing this book, pondering all the various social, intellectual, and political effects of Facebook.[1]

Jason Kessler, a local white supremacist leader, had used a Facebook page to announce and recruit for the planned Charlottesville demonstration scheduled for August 12. Kessler, like fellow white supremacist leader Richard Spencer, had long deployed major social media platforms including

YouTube, Facebook, and Twitter to present a clean-cut image of the new racist in an effort to earn a measure of mainstream respectability. Much of the organizational communication among the white supremacist groups did not occur on YouTube, Facebook, or Twitter. Those were the outward-facing messages meant for fellow travelers, potential recruits, the general public, police, and journalists. The real work was being done on other, meaner social media and discussion platforms such as 4Chan, Reddit, and a chat application called Discord.[2]

For months before the attack on Charlottesville, these forums churned with bold claims of a growing and energized movement. Young white men who felt disrespected or disaffected found solace and solidarity. Leaked chats from Discord revealed that before August 12 some white suprema-cists were fantasizing about inflicting violence, including "driving over pro-testers." On August 12 a car crashed into a crowd of antiracist protesters, killing thirty-two-year-old Charlottesville resident Heather Heyer. At least nineteen others were injured, some severely, in that crash. Countless others were hurt that day and the previous night by white supremacists wielding clubs, fists, and baseball bats.[3]

These different levels of communication—closed chat apps, Reddit forums in which users speak in code and euphemisms, YouTube videos by racist leaders and the comments made by their followers, Twitter threads, and Facebook pages and groups—all work in concert to recruit, motivate, alert, and organize white supremacists. Like many other social (or antiso-cial) movements, these groups have mastered the methods of working their expressions "up the chain" through these platforms, to blogs and propa-ganda sites such as Breitbart.com, and finally into mainstream media sources. They have also generated deft methods of masking their intentions and memberships when they find that appropriate; when they are accused of being violent racists, they claim they are posing ironically or merely pro-moting edgy speech as entertainment.[4]

Antiracist activists deployed many of the same platforms and some even infiltrated white supremacist discussions to gather intelligence on their plans. The recent boldness of American white supremacist groups, especially on social media, have allowed antiracists to keep tabs on their growth and activities with remarkable success. Beyond those who took direct action against the white supremacists, residents of Charlottesville had for months discussed the rolling racist demonstrations and how we should react to them. There had been extreme right-wing events in Charlottesville in May, June, and July 2017, all building up to the explosive events of August 11 and 12. My neighbors discussed plans and responses in churches, community meetings, neighborhood associations, and on Facebook. At the local level, among like-minded Charlottesvillians, Facebook worked well. We invoked work written by community members and those from elsewhere. We shared information and perspectives on the best responses to such events. We debated the virtues and vices of "Antifa" activists, some of whom were willing to launch violent responses in defense of people of color. As it had in response to a Ku Klux Klan rally in July, leaders from the city government, religious organizations, civic groups, and the University of Virginia planned alternative programs scheduled for August 12 to give residents a way to converse, convene, and contemplate questions of justice in our town and beyond. Much of this civil response was organized via Facebook. But all those alternative events were quickly canceled on August 12 after heavily armed white supremacists sparked violence that morning, forcing the governor of Virginia to declare a state of emergency.[5]

The role of Facebook in planning and organizing these events, like the role of Facebook in the misnamed "Arab Spring," is easy to overstate. Once again, people who wanted to communicate with others of like-mind used the most effective methods with which to do so. It's unremarkable that Facebook was among those tools. So while Kessler used a public Facebook page to announce the plans for the August 12 invasion of Charlottesville, he did not have to. The fact that he did spoke to his confidence and his assumption that his event would have some measure of popular support and significant mainstream attention.

Immediately after the brutal attacks of August 12, many social media platform companies announced moves intended to stem the distribution of white supremacist propaganda on their services. These moves were cosmetic and futile. Filtering and moderating content on a global scale, given all the conflicting values at work and the diversity of human relationships, is impossible. At a scale of more than two billion people linked across most of the world, Facebook simply cannot pretend it can improve the conditions of any part of it. Holding Facebook responsible for filtering too strongly or not strongly enough misses the point. The problem is the very idea of Facebook multiplied by more than two billion users.[6]

STOP AND THINK

The influence of Facebook on the violent attacks on Charlottesville is difficult to trace but important to address. I live in a nation that no longer seems able to filter out of its public sphere the most odious calls for an ethnically pure state, that has a major political party that can no longer resist fringe elements, and has a media ecosystem that rewards the most alarming and spectacular claims and is now willing to take seriously the claims of white supremacists. One man sympathetic to white supremacists even assumed the presidency in 2017 because the established filters all failed. Facebook did not generate these problems. It did amplify and normalize them by scrambling our senses of truth and justice and fracturing a sense of collective national fate.

Mostly Facebook makes it hard to think. That's somewhat true for us as individuals, but as individuals, we can deploy strategies and tactics to cope. We can delete an app or turn off a mobile phone. There are no such strategies for the harm Facebook does to our ability to think collectively. When we are informed of a challenge or threat, Facebook invites us to express ourselves in the most succinct and shallow ways, even if only by clicking on an icon for anger, laughter, or love. Facebook fools us into thinking that problems can be addressed by harnessing individual donations into some impressive grand total, without any sense of what difference that money ever makes over the long term. Facebook indulges us by making us believe we matter to events and people at a great distance and can make a difference with just a click or two. Mostly Facebook makes it difficult for us to convene and address our greatest challenges with agreed-upon facts and shared agendas. This problem goes far beyond the looming threat of ethnic or religious nationalism in the United States, Austria,

Hungary, or India. Our inability to think through our problems collectively threatens our lives collectively.

As I type this in early September 2017 much of the fourth-largest city in the United States, with a metropolitan population of more than five million people, is under water. After catching the edge of a massive hurricane that made landfall about one hundred miles to the south of the city, Houston sustained massive floods that immersed houses and schools, closed hospitals, separated families, and caused more than two hundred deaths. Meanwhile, Mumbai, with its population of almost nineteen million people, suffered even more after monsoon rains pushed all its drainage systems to failure. Bangladesh was also struggling to emerge from a similar monsoon drenching that displaced forty-one million people and killed more than twelve hundred people. Almost two million children across South Asia were shut out of schools because of flooding affecting four countries. In July 2017 Lagos, Nigeria, also suffered from torrential rains and subsequent flooding. Later in the summer more than a hundred thousand people were displaced by floods in the Nigerian state of Benue. And on this very day another powerful hurricane is threatening Puerto Rico, the Dominican Republic, Haiti, Cuba, the Bahamas, and Florida, promising more suffering and death.[7]

Flashes of human suffering and appeals for relief appear regularly down my Facebook News Feed. Most of them reveal glimpses of problems in southeast Texas, where I have many family and friends. More than a few appeals for attention called out about Nigeria, Bangladesh, and Mumbai. Despite the many opportunities to donate money to help those who lost homes or worse in these floods, the flow of images and testimony deepened my sense of helplessness. Did we have the collective will and imagination to help all the people harmed and, more important, reduce the chances of such damage reoccurring or occurring elsewhere? Are we stuck in a cycle of intense disaster relief because we are unwilling to confront the causes and invoke solutions to such vulnerabilities?

There is little doubt that human-generated climate change amplified the frequency and intensity of the storms that immersed much of the world in the late summer of 2017. By human-generated, I mean machine-generated. Humans invented, improved, and deployed machines that would burn carbon-based material that stifled the earth's ability to disperse heat. So the oceans are warmer and more turbulent. The atmosphere is heavier with moisture. Winds are stronger. And because of internal combustion engines farms are more efficient and productive, people are more mobile, and thus cities are more crowded. This renders many more people vulnerable to the eruptions caused by the very engines that made their presence possible in and around cities such as Lagos, Mumbai, and Houston.

What an absurd situation we find ourselves in as a species. Here in the early years of the twenty-first century we have powerful tools that can take us from one side of the world to the other in one day, project our images and voices across screens at any distance, spread ideas and arguments without loss of signal, mimic reality so we can imagine ourselves flying or having sex merely by putting goggles on our heads and connecting to a computer, move money instantly, and remove the tops of mountains and dig great craters from which we can extract the hardened remains of ferns and dinosaurs.

Yet we cannot have a serious global conversation to improve life and safety in our large cities in anticipation of great storms or earthquakes. We can't address public health before pandemics break out. We can't curb our production of carbon dioxide, which melts polar ice caps and washes away islands. We can't revive a global ethic to resist ethnic nationalism effectively because it's now too easy to exploit fears to assume power.

And so we are helpless. We are vulnerable. We face threats that remind us of the fate of Pompeii or Krakatoa—yet are far from "natural." Our very tools and techniques threaten to wipe us out. We display unlimited talents but no mastery. We process infinite data but display no wisdom.

This is the problem (among others) that consumed Hannah Arendt after World War II. Our assumptions about the "progress" of "civilization" and technology proved faulty as totalitarian regimes rose across Europe and Asia after both world wars. As a species, we seemed both brilliant and stupid. We were spectacular at making things (we were, Arendt declared, *Homo faber*), especially disposable items for personal consumption and technologies of death and oppression. We were terrible at thinking things through and then doing those things, especially things that might improve our collective plight. While it is understandable that many since the rise of

Putin, Modi, Erdogan, Trump, and others have revisited Arendt's classic works on totalitarianism, I would urge a rediscovery of her thoughts on society, thought, and action. They speak to our inability to face vital challenges and are as relevant today as they were in the 1950s. One of Arendt's key insights was that totalitarianism can take hold where people without power are kept too busy to consider the greater ramifications of their actions—especially actions that are complicit with massive crimes against humanity. One of Arendt's favorite English phrases was "stop and think" because she believed one had to stop all movement to think clearly.[8]

Through our markets and our cultures we have focused our technological and mathematical prowess on placing irresistible advertisements before potential consumers and voters and on generating new forms of financial assets that spread or shift risk while concentrating rewards. What a waste of our collective intelligence. While we have rendered ourselves incapable of collectively thinking our way out of our problems we have enriched and empowered those who would deliver to us the intellectual equivalent of junk food. We complain we are drowning in data. But because we refuse to put down our phones and look away from the screen, many of us are drowning as city streets fill with dirty water.

THE RATIONALIST PATH TO THE IRRATIONAL PRESENT

Here is the painful irony. We have invited into our lives a complex system that promises to relieve us of inconveniences and streamline decisions and actions. It's the culmination of remarkable human achievement. We have harnessed and coordinated the powers of mathematics, metallurgy, linguistics, logic, material science, behavioral psychology, and economics. These are among the great results of the scientific revolution and the Enlightenment. Yet, not for the first time, market and political forces have turned products of the Enlightenment against enlightenment.[9]

These new technological systems are designed in such a way, amplified by market forces that favor the immediate and the gratifying, that they undermine efforts to deliberate deeply about important matters. They could have been designed differently. They could have been rolled out carefully, with more public discussion and debate. We could have generated cautious regulatory impediments to rash investment and deployment. We've done that with other technological systems such as automobiles, although often too late to avert the long-term damage they do. The problem does not lie in the application of technology per se. And the problem certainly does not lie with pure science or the scientific method. It lies in the irrational ways we think about science and technology. When we make a cult of technology and welcome its immediate rewards and conveniences into our lives without consideration of the long-term costs, we make fools of ourselves. When we ignore or dismiss unapplied science, the search for knowledge for its own sake, we also make fools of ourselves. Somehow—in the United States, at least—we have managed to do both of these things.

By removing friction from so much of our lives, by lifting our gaze from the local to the virtual, these systems have made many lives easier (ignoring, for a moment, those poisoned by runoff from heavy metal mining in Africa or those injured in electronics factories in China). But the constant, daily effect of these technologies is narcotic and neurotic. We are anxious when we don't connect through our screens. We are restless and exhausted despite brief moments of entertainment and distraction. So when confronted with the suffering our phones and tablets have created, we spend only fleeting moments shaking our heads, and then move on down the News Feed for something to counter that brief discomfort—something to mask our complicity.

Because these products are relatively inexpensive (the cost of living without them is so much higher) and so many of the services are allegedly "free," we quickly and thoughtlessly agree to let ourselves be tracked and profiled by hundreds of companies, many of which we have no direct relationship with, and by powerful states. We have become data-producing farm animals, domesticated and dependent. We are the cows. Facebook clicks on us. "That data is woven into an invisible lattice of coercion and control—not to mention as a source of enormous profit when sold to advertisers or other interested parties," wrote Ian Bogost, the creator of Cow Clicker, the dumbest game ever.[10]

The success of Facebook, enabled by its almost global ubiquity, feeds itself. Except for those places in the world excluded (for now) from Facebook use, such as China and Iran, there are social costs to opting out of Facebook membership. Those not connected might miss the news of the birth of a nephew or a call to a meeting of concerned citizens. Even if being disconnected has slight personal costs, the social pressure of not missing out on something makes an impact on the daily lives of those who live among Facebook users. There are other social media services. But none of them have the reach, the features, and, most important, the gravity of Facebook. That scale means that just about everyone has a reason to participate, putting bigots into contact with like-minded bigots and often into conflict with the targets of their bigotry. Abuse and harassment, unsurprisingly, flow freely on Facebook. Yet Facebook puts the burden of managing hate and threats on the targets and victims. That's regrettable yet understandable. Facebook is simply too large and the variety of human depravity too vast for the company to deploy enough people or computer code to anticipate and regulate the misbehavior of millions. The global scale of Facebook invites such danger. The global scale of Facebook prevents it from effectively confronting the problems it has created. Facebook is too big to tame. The ideology of corporate social responsibility prevents Mark Zuckerberg from even acknowledging the malevolence set loose by his invention.

PROGRESS VS. INNOVATION

It was not supposed to be this way. This was not the plan. Before Facebook there was a dominant and seductive story of "the internet." This new network of networks and all the people who built it and built things on it had collectively pledged its power to Enlightenment principles—chiefly that of progress.

Progress was such a strong part of eighteenth-century Enlightenment thought that the drafters of the U.S. Constitution instructed Congress "to promote the Progress of Science and useful Arts" via copyright and patent law. Sometime in the late twentieth century "progress" dropped out of fashion. Today, those who advocate for increased investment in or protection of technology do so in the name of "innovation." Now it's almost embarrassing to invoke progress. The grand mega-projects of the twentieth century—dams, highways, national parks, public universities—seem as distant from our current collective imaginations as pyramids and the Taj Mahal. The 1893 World's Fair in Chicago was devoted to marking the technological progress since Columbus landed in the New World, and its grand exhibit featured the power of electricity. The 1939 World's Fair in New York described the "World of Tomorrow." And the 1964 World's Fair in New York boasted of the imminent coming of world peace through "Man's Achievement on a Shrinking Globe in an Expanding Universe." We are still waiting for that. In 1996 the television show *The Simpsons* mocked the pretentions of World's Fairs by sending Bart and his buddy Milhouse to Knoxville, the decrepit site of the 1982 fair. Today a fair promising grand public projects or technological wizardry would get ignored as much as the 1982 fair is forgotten. We still get massive sports stadia, but no one pretends they mark "progress." They are merely publicly funded temples to commerce and spectacle.

Innovation differs from progress in many ways. Innovation lacks a normative claim of significant betterment. It emerges from many small moves rather than grand, top-down schemes. Innovation does not contain an implication of a grand path or a grand design of a knowable future. It makes no claim on the future, except that it always exists in that future, just out of reach of the now. And innovation always seems to come from the distributed commercial world rather than from grand, planned policies engineered from a strong central state. States are now encouraged to innovate rather than solve big problems or correct for market failures. The ultimate goal of innovation seems to be more innovation.

"Innovation" is everywhere today. You can't peruse a copy of the *Harvard Business Review* or *Inc.* without sliding by multiple uses of "innovation." Universities large and small boast of new "innovation centers" and programs devoted to unleashing "innovation" in their students as well as their libraries and laboratories. Everyone is expected to innovate. Those who raise questions about the wisdom of a policy or technology are quickly dismissed as anti-innovation. The use of "innovation" in published books, as measured by the Google Ngram Viewer project, surged in 1994, just as the internet entered public life and the dot-com boom started. Harvard Business School professor Clayton Christensen's use of the term "disruptive innovation" has dominated debates about management in both public and private sectors since the 1997 publication of his book *The Innovators' Dilemma*. That book, sloppy in its use of cherry-picked anecdotes posing as evidence and devoid of historical complexity, has been thoroughly discredited by scholars including Harvard historian Jill Lepore. Yet Christensen's influence has not waned. Some fairy tales are too good to stop believing, even after you grow up. Innovation, especially the disruptive kind, has become a religious concept, immune to criticism.[11]

Even UNICEF leaders have felt compelled to launch UNICEF Innovation, "an interdisciplinary team of individuals around the world tasked with identifying, prototyping, and scaling technologies and practices that strengthen UNICEF's work. We build and scale innovations that improve children's lives around the world." It's not clear to me how that mission differs from all the other work that UNICEF does and has done for sixty years. But UNICEF Innovation web pages certainly deploy more buzzwords than the standard UNICEF pages do. "In 2015, innovation is vital to the state of the world's children," the page reads. "Challenges have never been larger, or coming faster—urbanization, climate change, lack of employment opportunities, broken education systems, increased disparities and digital divides."[12]

That historical claim is impossible to substantiate, of course. Temporal narcissism demands that we must always live in the most crucial, most urgent, most dangerous, yet most opportunity-rich time in human history. Technology must always be "moving faster than ever before." And law and policy, of course, must "not be keeping up with technology." So while recent decades are generally described with bombast (note all the alleged "revolutions" we have endured in the past twenty years), the dominant terminology of our time is steeped in modesty. Modesty is a virtue. In many ways the focus on modesty instead of progress is refreshing. A belief that progress is definable and inevitable became hard to maintain by the turn of the twenty-first century as we confronted the efficient dehumanizing brutality of slavery, the gulag, the killing fields, and the final solution.

Like with innovation, progress could be the locus of debate for two completely opposed policies. Historian David Brion Davis has written that appeals to progress were used by both advocates of expanding slavery and those who fought it. Davis identifies three aspects to the ideology of progress: a belief that historical change is not governed by chance or that historical events mesh in a meaningful pattern that reflects the principles of the natural sciences; a belief that the overall trajectory of history bends toward the better; and a prediction that the future will necessarily improve on the past, either through faith in human reason or through divine providence.[13]

Ecology has dealt perhaps the strongest blow to the ideology of progress. Ecological historians have charted the ways that humans have burned through their habitat, rendering much of it denatured and fragile, and improving crop yields through fossil-fuel-burning machinery and fossil-fuel-based fertilizers. So progress for some, such as an escape from the Malthusian trap of population outstripping food production, could mean devastation for all at some later date as the entire agricultural system collapses like an abandoned coal mine.

So perhaps the small-bore appeals to innovation are slightly preferable to the grand boasts of progress. But innovation can't be our goal as a species. We actually do face grand problems including climate change, widespread abuse of people, threats to political liberty, and communicable diseases. It's not unhealthy or even intellectually invalid to agree that we can and should make progress (with a very small "p") against Ebola, HIV, rape, racism, and the melting of the polar ice caps. Somewhere between the tiny vision of innovation and the arrogance of grand progress lies a vision of collective destiny and confidence that with the right investments, a strong consensus, and patience we can generate a more just and stable world. We passed right by that point in the rush from the twentieth century to the twenty-first. We must reclaim it.

"THE INTERNET" AND ITS DISCONTENTS

With this new medium, we were told, things would only get better. Innovation would save us. Transactions would be fairer. Decisions would be more rational. Markets and firms would be more competitive. States would be more humane. Societies would be more free. This was a myth, of course. Even in its earliest, foggiest, most theoretical manifestations the myth was easily dispersed and discounted.

But the myth retained its explanatory power ("This is how things are"), its predictive power ("This is how things will be"), and its aspirational power ("This is how things should be"). The most rational among us, the myth explained, had built a communicative system that could not be centralized or corrupted. It could not be regulated or censored. It would engage us all on equal terms. It would allow people to connect with thoughts and facts that would be new to them, thus challenging superstitions and prejudices. Its openness, its configurability, and its extensibility would invite bold, creative people to build magnificent structures on it and maintain enriching communities within it. Dozens of books and hundreds of essays proclaimed the myth. If you were anything like me in the 1990s, you devoured these tales and subscribed to the movement. If you were like me, of course, you were an educated, cosmopolitan man living in a wealthy country with too heady a belief in its rectitude. People very much like me, not coincidentally, would transform this myth into millions—ultimately billions—of users and dollars. I failed to see that the systems we were building on this myth would primarily benefit people like me.[14]

The myth was a fulfillment of Enlightenment assumptions. Conversation, deliberation, argumentation, information, mutual recognition, and communication would generate an ideal setting for making good decisions. The eighteenth-century coffeehouse had nothing on this new medium. It would not be constrained by a scarcity of channels, the way radio and television were. It would not have high barriers to entry, as newspaper, magazine, and book publishing had. Markers of identity could be masked or soon would be rendered irrelevant, so that ancient prejudices would evaporate over time and only the value of one's ideas and arguments would matter. The myth and the system itself emerged from an academic and scientific culture. So it would likely carry on the best attributes of that culture. Everything would be subject to peer review. Everything would be contingent. Everything would be, in computer science terms, "beta." The radical freedom that seemed built into "the internet" determined many of the engineering, policy, and investment decisions of the last decade of the twentieth century and the first decade of the twenty-first century. The world was being introduced to embodied, technological anarchism. And it promised to be glorious.[15]

"The internet" was never a discrete object one could draw or even point to. The term describes a relationship among discrete digital networks—a network of networks. But the invocation of it as a proper noun was important to support the power of the myth. The interconnectedness of "the internet" did amplify the power of networks and those who used them. So it was not without its effects. Still, "the internet" is a metaphor that has taken shape in our minds such that we now speak of it as if it's a discrete thing, place, or force in the world. Had we never used this heuristic, then the rise of networked digital media might have happened with more care and criticism. Instead, one had to be for or against "the internet," and thus "innovation," and thus "the future." There was no way to explain any other position.

Media theorist Pierre Lévy described the myth best in his 1995 book *Collective Intelligence*. "What then will our new communication tools be used for?" Levy asked at the moment Americans and Europeans were being invited to taste the pleasures of online media through dial-up modems connected to large desktop computers with monochrome monitors. "The most socially useful goal will no doubt be to supply ourselves with the instruments for sharing our mental abilities in the construction of collective intellect or imagination. Internetworked data would then provide the technical infrastructure for the collective brain or hypercortex of living communities." Lévy promised a utopia of creative brilliance once we are liberated from relying on heavy documents as foundations for knowledge. Knowledge would be navigated, not collated or collected. Knowledge would be purely social. In this, Lévy predicted, three years before the birth of Google and nine years before Facebook, the justification for both.[16]

Much of that myth could have remained and blossomed but for those pesky humans, with their histories, identities, alliances, presumptions, prejudices, and power discrepancies. Once millions and then billions of people who had not subscribed to the core ethics of the myth got their hands on "the internet," they shaped the medium toward their own desires and habits. "The internet" became as good and as bad as the people who used it. It certainly changed daily life and assumptions for people. But people changed "the internet" more. That happened almost immediately upon its public debut, around 1995 or 1996 in North America and Western Europe and across the rest of the world by 2002 or 2004. By that time the commercialization of digital communication channels had become a priority for both policy makers and technology companies. Strong encryption, which empowered dissidents, terrorists, and secure bank and credit-card transactions, had proliferated widely by 2000. Google rose out of a Stanford University computer science lab to bring order to the World Wide Web, allowing us to outsource decisions to the wisdom of other web users under the coercion of Google's coders. Attention became one form of currency. Data became another. Either could be transformed into specie rather easily, once advertising and commerce became joined by the simple click.

Then things got concentrated. By 2004 Google had mastered two concepts that served as models for the development of other digital platforms. It instituted an auction system for advertisements and it targeted those advertisements to reflect the patterns the company detected among its users. Google also introduced an advertisement market that other web pages could use to generate revenue. Money poured into Mountain View, California (although appropriate tax revenue has not flowed out), and the torrent has not abated since. By 2010 Google had dominated every aspect of the World Wide Web and email. Libraries, schools, universities, governments, newspapers, publishers, entertainment companies, and retail stores all looked to Google as a model for success. A few fought Google on matters of copyright and privacy. But many of these same institutions explicitly joined with Google to restructure their enterprises.[17]

In 2007 Apple introduced the iPhone. It was not the first mobile device that would host email and web-based communication. But it was the most interesting and best designed to date. The iPhone and its smartphone clones that mostly run on Google software have become our assistants and the source of constant connection with flows of data around us. They have tethered us to great databases and tracked our thoughts and movements. They are leashes that talk to us. Most significant, our mobile devices record images and sound. And they have enlisted us in a massive, global, surveillance effort run for the benefit of both commercial powers and states. They have tethered us to flows of data and the companies that own that data.

We get to crush candy. And we get to put dog ear and deer antler filters on our selfies. And we get to manage our increasingly difficult and precarious lives through our phones, juggling child care, jobs, romantic relationships, finances, transportation, and social lives through these tiny, expensive blocks of plastic and glass that chirp and buzz at us throughout the day and night.

The one thing Google never could master was social networking. The concept of tracking and facilitating connections among friends, friends of friends, and complete strangers did not occur to the leaders at Google until it was far too late for the company to corner the market on that ultimate aspect of digital culture. Once Sheryl Sandberg left Google and joined Facebook as chief operating officer in 2007 the then rudderless and profitless company began leveraging its popularity and rich data collections to deliver responsive advertisements and steady investment in the quality and features of the product. Facebook focused on its mobile platforms and quickly matched Google in cultural importance, if not the generation of wealth.

Since 2004 we have seen a steady movement of activity and communication from everyday, face-to-face, real-life transactions to Facebook. Facebook is the medium through which more than two billion people now conduct their political lives, connect with those who share their interests and passions (and hatreds), and proclaim their identities and affiliations. Increasingly, Facebook is the source of entertainment, distraction, information, and comfort for people around the world. And, as we have seen in this book, Facebook has amplified some of our best and worst collective habits. But one thing has surely suffered: our ability to think through problems together.

TECHNOPOLY

Between Google and Facebook we have witnessed a global concentration of wealth and power not seen since the British and Dutch East India Companies ruled vast territories, millions of people, and the most valuable trade routes. Remarkably, and unlike the East India Companies, Google and Facebook have achieved this feat nonviolently and with only tangential state support. Like the East India Companies, they excuse their zeal and umbrage around the world by appealing to the missionary spirit: they are, after all, making the world better, right? They did all this by inviting us in, tricking us into allowing them to make us their means to wealth and power, distilling our activities and identities into data, and launching a major ideological movement—what Neil Postman described yet only predicted in 1992: technopoly.

"Technopoly is a state of culture," Postman wrote. "It is also a state of mind. It consists of the deification of technology, which means that the culture seeks its authorization in technology, finds its satisfactions in technology, and takes its orders from technology." This ideological domination demands a sacrifice of all previously stable belief systems. So trust in institutions, ancient or modern, erodes. Any order, system, or tradition is deemed suspicious or ripe for "disruption" simply because of its date of origin, as if durability were a sign of weakness instead of strength. Local identities and traditions are rendered valueless except as raw material for remixes, parody, tourism, tapestries, and games rather than expressions of deep human narratives and connections.

Learning becomes a matter of searching, copying, and pasting rather than immersing, considering, and deliberating. Meditation becomes a hobby, a holiday for those privileged enough to purchase the time, rather than a practice that connects one with a spirit or purpose. Religion grows coarse, brittle, simplified, portable, and too certain of its righteousness as an angry, insecure response to the new global technocultural vertigo. Everyone is quantified. Everyone is exposed. Everyone is on guard. Everyone is exhausted. The apparent winners in this ideological shift are those who predicted and prescribed it: the already privileged and sophisticated, but only a subset of those. "Those who feel most comfortable in Technopoly are those who are convinced that technical progress is humanity's supreme achievement and the instrument by which our most profound dilemmas may be solved," Postman wrote. "They also believe that information is an unmixed blessing, which through its continued and uncontrolled production and dissemination offers increased freedom, creativity, and peace of mind." Postman did not live long enough to see the sign that adorned a church in my neighborhood in 2010: "God has an app for that." That would have made him smile and lean back in his seat, acknowledging with a wink that he had named the force that had triumphed in the world.[18]

"Technopoly eliminates alternatives to itself in precisely the way Aldous Huxley outlined in *Brave New World*," Postman wrote. "It does not make them illegal. It does not make them immoral. It does not even make them unpopular. It makes them invisible and therefore irrelevant." So while we still read books, attend lectures, argue from adjacent bar stools and barber chairs, all of those exercises—"thought worlds," Postman called them— disappear from what matters. If it didn't happen on Facebook (or, less often and less important, on WeChat, Twitter, YouTube, Weibo, Snapchat, or Instagram), it didn't happen. Technopoly did not happen suddenly, Postman explained. It crept in from the dawn of the twentieth century. Postman thought technopoly hit its apex with the domination of television over our minds and lives. The same year that Postman published his book by that name, Bruce Springsteen described technopoly without naming it: "Fifty-seven channels and nothin' on."[19]

Now we have lost count of all the channels. The problem is that there is too much on. The few institutions we depended on to filter for quality information or credible sources are being starved and distorted by the cultural and market power of Facebook and Google. We are left with too much that is shady, shallow, manipulative, or hyperbolic. Facebook rewards hyperbole. Hyperbole rewards Facebook.

Of course, it's no longer about "the internet," if it ever was. It was about the power and influence of a suite of technologies that work synergistically to increase the efficiency of human activities. The elements of that suite include powerful computers that can process massive amounts of data through complex and malleable algorithms, inexpensive data storage, fast data connections, tiny computers that can fit in devices and appliances or on bodies. Now it's about the operating system of our lives.

RESISTANCE AND RESIGNATION

In 2013 noted internet culture writer Douglas Rushkoff declared in a column for CNN.com that he was quitting Facebook. He had had enough. The ways Facebook works, the things Facebook enhances, and the things Facebook obscures did not comport with Rushkoff's values. Long one of the most interesting cultural analysts of the digital realm, Rushkoff had been able to clearly mark out his guiding ethic for digital platforms and tools: use only what enhances human agency, and dispense with technologies that limit us. "Facebook is just such a technology," Rushkoff wrote. "It does things on our behalf when we're not even there. It actively misrepresents us to our friends, and worse, misrepresents those who have befriended us to still others." Rushkoff sees Facebook as particularly pernicious and dishonest. It uses terms like "Friends" yet treats every relationship as a flat transactional connection. And it exploits our labor. "The efforts of a few thousand employees at Facebook's Menlo Park campus pale in comparison to those of the hundreds of millions of users meticulously tweaking their pages," Rushkoff wrote.

Fundamentally, Rushkoff saw more ways that Facebook repurposed the content we created and the data we generated for its own purposes. This process contradicted his core argument and advice. Rushkoff closed his essay with a reminder that "Facebook is not the Internet." The problem is, Facebook in 2013 already was so dominant that for many people absence from Facebook meant invisibility. By 2018, that is certainly the case in much of the world. Rushkoff received significant attention for his principled move. He did not, however, change Facebook in any measurable way. Nor did he stem the flow of new Facebook users who quickly replaced the handful who might have followed him after reading his argument. I respect Rushkoff immensely. I find him persuasive about many things. Yet I'm still a Facebook user. And I have no plans to resign.[20]

What can we do about the outsized influence Facebook has on how we see each other? Not much, unfortunately. If every person who read this sentence canceled her or his Facebook account today, it would not register as a blip on Facebook's revenue or metrics. Resistance is futile. But resistance seems necessary. If every person who read this sentence wrote a kind letter to Facebook to urge it to change some of its features or consider more deeply its effects on the world, it's likely no one at Facebook would react or respond. Facebook's membership is too vast and is growing too fast for the company to care about a few thousand English-speaking readers. If we pressured advertisers to protest Facebook, we should not expect them to stand with us. Soon Facebook and Google will be the major advertising platforms around the world. Opting out of the Facebook-generated revenue stream would be corporate malpractice.

But the unlikeliness of immediate response should not dissuade us from accounting for problems and calling for interventions. This will be a long process. Those concerned about the degradation of public discourse and the erosion of trust in experts and institutions will have to mount a campaign to challenge the dominant techno-fundamentalist myth. The long, slow process of changing minds, cultures, and ideologies never yields results in the short term. It sometimes yields results over decades or centuries. I'm confident that soon more powerful books than this one will follow. Those books would update these arguments and generate even better conversations in those few quarters remaining for deep debate. The scholarship that informs this book should keep coming and improving as long as enough people still believe in the value of scholarship. And as the deleterious effects of excessive dependence on Facebook become clearer and warnings more urgent, capable activists could rise bearing clear and achievable agendas. None of this is certain. All of it requires a strong commitment by enough concerned and powerful people and institutions. But it's not over yet. The community of scholars, critics, writers, activists, and policy makers currently concerned about these issues is likely to grow. The most fruitful response to the problems that Facebook creates, reveals, or amplifies would be to reinvest and strengthen institutions that generate deep, meaningful knowledge. We must support scientific communities, universities, libraries, and museums around the world. We must also foster deliberation through publicly funding better journalism, forums for debate, and commissions that could harness expertise to address our most pressing challenges. Foolishly, we have let investment flow from institutions such as these to projects that promise "innovation" without considering what we have lost. This must not continue.

REGULATION AND REFORM

There are some policy interventions that could slightly improve the prospects for working our way through these problems. They lie in the areas of privacy, data protection rights, and antitrust and competition. In all of these areas the European Union serves its citizens better than the United States does. United States policymaking has long put the interests of companies and, significantly, innovation above concerns about potential harms. And harms in the United States have been limited to demonstrable monetary damage. That thousands suffer from harassment every day has not motivated U.S. policymakers to address that problem systematically. And antitrust law (what the Europeans call competition policy) has also stagnated in recent decades. The least we should do is embrace European-style data protection laws worldwide. Individuals should have a right to be informed how data about them—data they generated—will be used by private companies. People should have the power to remove data from the dossiers that companies like Facebook and Google keep on every user. The foundations for these rights and powers exist in the latest versions of European privacy and data protection law. Facebook might change some of its practices across the world to conform to European Union standards. Or it might not. Other major states such as Brazil, India, Australia, Canada, Mexico, Japan, and the United States should follow and model data protection laws after the European Union's.[21]

Strong antitrust intervention would be the best way to address the concentration of power that is Facebook. The United States should break up Facebook. It should sever WhatsApp, Instagram, Oculus Rift, and even Facebook Messenger from the core Facebook application and company. Each of these parts should exist separately, competing against each other for labor, capital, users, data, and advertisers. Future mergers and acquisitions should raise serious questions about the potential power of Facebook (or Instagram or Oculus Rift) with even more user data to exploit. Such a breakup is impossible under current theories of American antitrust law. Currently, consumer prices matter more than factors such as political power or the social consequences of concentration. Since Facebook users pay nothing to use the service and advertisers have many market players from which to choose, there is no clear cause for antitrust intervention in the short term. The rise of Facebook and Google should spark a deep examination of the spirit and purpose of antitrust and competition law around the world.[22]

On the other hand, maybe we don't have to execute anything. We are a resilient species. We have endured—and continue to endure—greater humiliations and depredations than Facebook generates or amplifies. Perhaps we should recognize that when it comes to the operating system of our lives, we are all just babies. We might figure out modes of resistance, plans for reform, and modest regulation and we can let cultural, market, and political forces work it all out. That's what we have been doing for forty years, after all, as computer technology has enhanced our lives and connected our minds. Maybe that's not so bad.

But it *is* bad. And even Mark Zuckerberg seems to know that something is deeply, deeply wrong. He even seems to admit that Facebook might have contributed to the growing threats. Alas, Zuckerberg has done everything wrong. He has proposed responses that are either inadequate or counterproductive. And he has mistaken listening and experimenting with actual learning. Just after the U.S. election in November 2016 Zuckerberg dismissed concerns about the role that Facebook played in distributing misinformation and propaganda. Then, when he could no longer ignore the facts, he launched a plan in the United States to enroll the services of news organizations to help mark suspicious content. Other similar experiments followed, in hopes that Facebook users would trust the markers of quality that they had already rejected. Facebook did nothing to change the fact that Facebook users like to feel good about themselves. Facebook did nothing to confront and correct for confirmation bias and self-gratification. It merely hoped against all evidence and experience that more and better information would push back and minimize the effects of propaganda. Worse, Zuckerberg pushed forward on Facebook groups as the solution for the malevolent spirit that was choking the world. Groups allow people of like mind to converse and organize efficiently and effectively. They do not facilitate encounters or immersion across interests or across ideological distance. If anything, the emphasis on Facebook groups will only further fracture societies and nations. The existence of hundreds of Facebook groups devoted to convincing others that the earth is flat should have raised some doubt among Facebook's leaders that empowering groups might not enhance the information ecosystem of Facebook. Groups are as likely to divide us and make us dumber as any other aspect of Facebook. There is no reason to believe, as Zuckerberg clearly does, that Facebook groups will help us treat each other kindly and understand each other better.

What about the larger technology industry? Can Silicon Valley reform itself? Can peer pressure influence Facebook? Tristan Harris believes it can. The former product manager at Google left to found a not-for-profit organization to convince technology leaders that they should refrain from deploying casino-like design techniques and should reform their advertising practices to rely less on massive data collection. Harris wants to influence how the community of interface designers think about their roles and duties. Frustratingly, Harris offers no response to the incentives that have pushed Facebook and Google to gather and deploy vast troves of data to rise as the most powerful and profitable advertising firms in the history of the world. And Harris offers no incentive to those who design the devices, platforms, and applications to curb their addictive features. Why would a company be the first to move on a more humane or ethical design scheme? It would get crushed as investment and usage would rush to competitors. Why would a company be the first to abandon personalized advertising that exploits the attention economy? Again, the competition would pounce. And even if every Silicon Valley–based firm adopted some sort of code of conduct that Harris and his group pushed, nothing would stop firms from Manila, Moscow, or Mumbai from moving in on those markets.[23]

This is where Harris and most Silicon Valley reformers fall down. Apolitical responses to complex problems can't possibly work. We need to build a political movement to raise awareness, rally support, define an agenda, and build alliances. This movement must be global, or at least multinational. The movement must put pressure on Facebook and other companies through markets and competition, through legislatures, and through multilateral standard-setting organizations. The idea of corporations behaving responsibly, as we have seen, invites the hubris of self-righteousness. There is a fine line between declaring that one won't "be evil" and believing that one can do no wrong. Only the threat and force of stern state regulation can push companies to straighten up. That's both how it is and how it should be.

Here is where my plan stumbles, too. As I write this, the very concept of "policy" in the United States is a cruel joke. Washington and every state capitol are full of people committed to serious policy work. Some work for legislatures. Others work in agencies or for councils. Many work for nongovernmental organizations and think tanks. This policy tribe, made up of people of all political persuasions, traditionally conforms to clear norms. They make proposals and arguments forged to convince those in power that their positions are disinterested, are based on empirically sound studies, would benefit more people than they would harm, and would serve the greater good over the long term. Even if a policy worker makes such an argument disingenuously, she or he conforms to these cultural expectations. But all of that has changed since the inauguration of Donald Trump as president of the United States. Trump has installed into every federal agency a crew of people who do not take seriously the norms and traditions of policy. They merely execute the interests of whatever agenda Trump and his supporters have put forth. So federal agencies in the United States almost immediately rolled back data privacy protections and set about dismantling network neutrality. All of this was done without study, without public comment, and without any consideration for objective analysis or the public interest. Washington under Trump is beyond cynical. American businesses and consumers will never enjoy stability and security until Washington rediscovers respect for policymakers and policy processes. Serious people should study these issues, construct proposals that take all stakeholders into account, introduce them carefully, assess their effects, and argue honestly about the best ways forward. Such habits remind us that we live in a country that takes the fate of its citizens seriously. I know, it seems an impossible dream. But it's something we benefited from until just recently.[24]

Europe, Canada, Japan, South Korea, Australia, Brazil, Mexico, New Zealand, and even India still offer some hope that reasonable policies can emerge. But as anti-rational, authoritarian, nationalist movements gain strength, enabled by Facebook, the prospects for the necessary movements and deliberation get more remote every year. If we are going to take a global stand to resist the rising illiberal oligopoly and reform our information ecosystem, we must do it soon. It's getting dark—quickly.

ACKNOWLEDGMENTS

Working in Neil Postman's department at NYU offered me an opportunity to work with people who have influenced just about everything I have thought or written about technology and society ever since. First was Helen Nissenbaum, already known among the leaders of the subfield of applied philosophy known as computer ethics. Helen became a trusted colleague and mentor when she joined the faculty the year after I did. Her work on the ethics of search engines served as the foundational idea for my book *The Googlization of Everything*. And her idea of privacy as "contextual integrity" influenced both that book and this one.

Helen's presence on the faculty allowed my department to deserve two brilliant people who have taught me much more than I ever taught them. Michael Zimmer combined a moral commitment with a keen analytic mind and an unsurpassed work ethic. He blends the influences of Neil Postman and Helen Nissenbaum with his own brilliant insights. His work has informed every page of this book. Specifically, Michael's archival project that collects the public speeches and writings of Mark Zuckerberg, the Zuckerberg Files, was essential to my research. I pity anyone who tries to write a book about Facebook without that resource. Through the Zuckerberg Files, hosted by the University of Wisconsin at Milwaukee, I have been able to spend hundreds of hours reading Mark Zuckerberg's interviews, watching his television appearances, and listening to his public addresses.[1]

Alice Marwick arrived in her Ph.D. program with a master's thesis from the University of Washington. It was the first scholarly treatment I had ever seen about this new phenomenon called social media. During our time together Alice served as my teaching assistant and research assistant. But in both cases she guided me through unfamiliar subjects and fields of knowledge. Alice is one of the most disciplined and imaginative scholars I have ever met. When in 2005 I received a call from a producer at *The Daily Show with Jon Stewart* asking if I would like to serve as an "expert" on social media for a spoof segment done by the show's "senior youth correspondent," comedian Demetri Martin, I quickly accepted. Then I realized I knew almost nothing about social media. So I called Alice. She talked me through a few ideas. And I reread her thesis. So I was able to play the role of grumpy, cynical old professor and received much undeserved credit for seeming articulate about social media. In the past dozen years Alice has continued to pour out brilliant work that continues to inspire and surprise the entire field of digital media studies.

The greatest intellectual influence on this book was not affiliated with NYU until years later, after she finished her Ph.D. at Berkeley and moved to New York to start Data and Society, a think tank devoted to examining the social ramifications of networks, data, privacy, and just about everything else that matters. That would be danah boyd. Like Michael and Alice, danah started her scholarly career while I was already well into mine. From her early days as a blogger, danah impressed me and almost everyone else who was trying to make sense of digital media with her wit, her conscience, and her erudition. I am sure our intellectual relationship has been far from reciprocal. So I am grateful that danah has allowed me to hang out with Data and Society and has indulged my questions and requests over the years. As with Neil, Helen, Alice, and Michael, danah's ideas echo through every page of this book.

This book would not have been possible if Nancy Baym had not invited me to spend three inspiring months of 2014 at Microsoft Research in Cambridge, Massachusetts. Spending time and sharing ideas with Tarleton Gillespie, Mary Gray, Lana Swartz, Kevin Driscoll, Tressie McMillan Cottom, Jessa Lingel, Kate Miltner, Jennifer Chayes, and Christian Borgs was crucial to reigniting my sense of wonder and curiosity after three years as department chair.

My time in Cambridge also afforded me the opportunity to check in with my friends at the Berkman Klein Center for Internet and Society at

Harvard University. I must thank Urs Gasser and Jonathan Zittrain for welcoming me to Harvard. And as he has for many years, Harry Lewis made himself available for consultation and commiseration during my stay in his fair city.

In the service of full disclosure I attest that I have never received research funding or direct payments from any company that offers social media platforms, including Facebook and its major competitors. In 2014 I received payments from Microsoft Research for work I did in residence in Cambridge, Massachusetts, that helped me write an earlier book called *Intellectual Property: A Very Short Introduction*. But that was two years before I decided to write about Facebook. Microsoft invested $240 million in Facebook in 2007 for what was then a 1.6 percent stake. It has since sold many shares and its current level of investment is not clear. In addition, I have never sold any stocks "short" and thus used my criticism of companies to gain an advantage. Much of my retirement savings is invested in broad index funds managed by TIAA-CREF, which has invested almost $2.5 million in Facebook stock as of the summer of 2017. I have no stock or bond investments outside of 403(b) retirement accounts.

Others who have educated me about these matters include Eszter Hargittai, Ian Bogost, David Karpf, Philip Howard, Charlton McIlwain, Gina Neff, Evgeny Morozov, John Naughton, Zizi Papacharissi, Frank Pasquale, Ben Peters, Trebor Scholz, Zeynep Tufekci, Sherry Turkle, Joseph Turow, Kate Crawford, Nick Carr, Gabriella Coleman, Lisa Gitelman, James Grimmelmann, Christian Sandvig, Tim Highfield, Henry Jenkins, Sonia Livingstone, Viktor Mayer-Schönberger, Lisa Nakamura, Jay Rosen, Joseph Reagle, Molly Sauter, Yochai Benkler, Tim Wu, Ethan Zuckerman, Clay Shirky, Eli Pariser, James Fishkin, Chad Wellmon, Marwan Kraidy, Anna Lauren Hoffman, Phil Napoli, Whitney Phillips, Ryan Milner, Robyn Caplan, David Carroll, Caroline Jack, David Parisi, Anna Jobin, Judith Donath, Nicholas John, and Paul Dourish.

Julia Ticona and Francesca Tripodi both gave me the honor of serving on their dissertation committees, through which they taught me much about the social influences of mobile and social media. Francesca was my teaching partner for about seven years while she pursued her doctorate from the University of Virginia. I will always be grateful for her help and patience. She is a joy to work with and I will miss her as she launches her professional academic career. This book benefited from two outstanding research assistants, Jesse Spear and Patricia O'Donnell. Jessica Hatch read and commented on the entire manuscript. She helped me avoid many embarrassing errors.

I owe special thanks to Eric Klinenberg, Caitlin Zaloom, Rebecca Solnit, Joel Dinerstein, Garnette Cadogan, Chris Sprigman, and Dahlia Lithwick for inspiration, advice, hugs, and high-fives.

I hope my work builds on a rich tradition of unheeded social and cultural criticism. This book has a genealogy that runs through Thorstein Veblen, C. Wright Mills, James Baldwin, Jane Jacobs, Hannah Arendt, Richard Sennett, Susan Sontag, Christopher Lasch, Tony Judt, Susan Douglas, Todd Gitlin, and Pankaj Mishra. Rereading their work helped me frame the argument and set both pace and pitch for the prose. Still, Neil Postman's voice was the loudest one in my head as I composed this book. And my memories of our conversations, especially that first one, remain strong.

Much of Chapter 3 previously appeared in an article I wrote for the *Hedgehog Review*. Editor Jay Tolson was kind enough to grant permission to use it in this work. Jay deftly edited the original piece and helped me clarify much of what I was trying to argue.[2]

My first effort to come to terms with Facebook and social media came from an assignment to write a chapter for the *Sage Handbook of Social Media*, edited by Alice Marwick, Jean Burgess, and Thomas Poell. Many of the ideas I generated for that article ended up in this book. The section of the conclusion comparing the concepts of innovation and progress first appeared in *Aeon*.[3]

In early 2017 I was able to present elements of this work before helpful scholars at the Centre for Research in the Arts, Social Sciences, and Humanities at the University of Cambridge and some days later at the Oxford Internet Institute. John Naughton, Gina Neff, and Philip Howard were perfect hosts and gave me crucial feedback. I also presented a lecture based on the book at the Chicago Humanities Festival in the fall of 2017 and introduced elements of its argument at the inaugural Obama

Foundation Summit in 2017. I will always be grateful for the opportunity to present my ideas to the president and First Lady at that event.

The research for this book was made possible by the generosity of Lisa and Tim Robertson, who endowed the professorship at the University of Virginia that it is my great honor to hold. This book also benefited from the support and encouragement of Leonard Schoppa, associate dean for the social sciences, and Ian Baucom, dean of the College and Graduate School of Arts and Sciences at the University of Virginia. President Teresa Sullivan cheered me on through the composition of this book, as she has my entire career. My colleagues in the Department of Media Studies and at the Center for Media and Citizenship have put up with my travel, my obsessions, and my distractions for years. I could not ask for a more collegial and accomplished set of friends with whom to work. Barbara Gibbons deserves special praise for being a patient and supportive friend as well as one of the best university administrators I have ever worked with.

My greatest motivation and deepest rewards come from my students. They make every day a pleasure.

This book was not my idea. Mark Warren, a longtime magazine editor and old friend from my Texas days, drove down to Charlottesville from New York to visit me a few weeks after the worst election of our lifetimes. He was seeking camaraderie, vision, and a sense of mission. He wanted to know how we should respond to the disgrace that had visited our great nation in 2016. We wondered about the degree to which Facebook had contributed to the degradation of our ability to think and communicate clearly and calmly, to discriminate between truth and lies, and we considered the role Facebook had played in allowing Donald Trump's campaign to leverage data to target voters with precision never before seen. "You should write a book about what Facebook has done to us," Mark told me. *Virginia Quarterly Review* executive editor Allison Wright, who had joined us for dinner, quickly agreed. I looked to my wife, Melissa Henriksen, and she nodded. That was all I needed. The next morning I drafted a proposal and chapter outline. Mark, Melissa, and Allison helped me polish it. My wonderful agent, Sam Stoloff, expressed strong enthusiasm and gave the proposal a solid edit. He sent it out a few days later.

The confidence my old friends David McBride and Niko Pfund at Oxford University Press have shown in me is gratifying. The support they have given this project has enabled me to be bolder and more ambitious than I might otherwise have been. Niko acquired my first book, *Copyrights and Copywrongs*, back in 1999 when he ran New York University Press, and we've often pondered how we could work together again. This project seemed right. I've trusted David's judgment on just about everything for more than thirty-five years. One day in 1983 in Mrs. Parisi's AP American History class at Williamsville East High School David slipped me a cassette with Elvis Costello's *Armed Forces* on it. "I think you'll like this," David said. He was right, as usual. He was right about all the changes he asked me to make to this manuscript as well. At Williamsville East High School, Ellen Parisi, as much as anyone, taught me how to research and write. Ellen first suggested I read Richard Hofstadter's *Anti-Intellectualism in American Life*. So that class has served me well over the years.

The morning after Mark Warren gave me the idea for this book, I told Melissa that I would have to apologize to her mother, Ann Henriksen. Ann had for years been telling me that Facebook was not so good for us, that its social cost exceeded its personal value. I often argued back or told her that it was too early to tell what the overall effects of Facebook were. It's no longer too early. Ann was right. I should always listen to my mother-in-law. She spent her life as an elementary school teacher inspiring and training young minds. Like most teachers, she knows what she's talking about when it comes to learning and behavior.

While I now pose as a critic of social media, I am, in fact, indebted to it. I met my wife, Melissa, through an online dating service—an early model for so many social network sites that would rise in the early years of the twenty-first century. We would never have met if not for that site's uncanny ability to connect two disparate profiles. Melissa and I had no common friends—even at six degrees of separation. We had no common hobbies or activities that would have brought us together under any other circumstances. We worked at different universities in completely different fields in different parts of Manhattan. We rode different subways. This wonderful life that I share with Melissa was made possible by an internet-based social networking site.

My daughter, Jaya, has put up with our social media habits over the years. It was Jaya's idea, when she was seven, to ban all electronic devices from meals. And she is the first to complain when one of us is too immersed in our phone to pay full attention to the moment. Jaya has disciplined herself to use Instagram and Snapchat for only a few minutes per day. I'm not sure that fortitude will survive her pending adolescence, as group texting and FaceTime chats have commenced already. But she is stronger than Melissa is or I am when it comes to the lure of social media. I am most proud of Jaya's will to express herself among adults and her thoughtfulness about important matters. She challenges and questions me often. I hope her spirit infused my work, as it has the rest of my life.

Like my first book, this book is dedicated to my parents. One day in Little Rock, Arkansas, in 1965, two years before the U.S. Supreme Court ruled that a person with brown skin could marry a person with white skin, an immigrant scientist and a child of a U.S. Navy officer took a chance. They would not let xenophobia, racism, and stupidity stand in their way. They built a life and dared the rest of the country to catch up to them. At this perilous moment for American citizenship and identity, their union represents all the best this country can be. They are true patriots.

NOTES

Introduction: The Problem with Facebook Is Facebook

1. Mark Zuckerberg, "As of This Morning, the Facebook Community Is Now Officially 2 Billion People!," Facebook, June 27, 2017, https://www.facebook.com/zuck/posts/10103831654565331.

2. Mark Zuckerberg, "Building Global Community," Facebook, February 16, 2017, https://www.facebook.com/notes/mark-zuckerberg/building-global-community/10154544292806634; Mark Zuckerberg, "Building Jarvis," Zuckerberg Transcripts 269, December 19, 2016, http://dc.uwm.edu/zuckerberg_files_transcripts/269; Mark Zuckerberg, "F8 2017 Keynote," Zuckerberg Transcripts 271, April 18, 2017, http://dc.uwm.edu/zuckerberg_files_transcripts/271; Mark Zuckerberg, "Facebook Post on 'Bringing the World Together,'" Zuckerberg Transcripts 281, June 22, 2017, http://dc.uwm.edu/zuckerberg_files_transcripts/281; Mark Zuckerberg, "Facebook's Mark Zuckerberg's Townhall in Delhi," Zuckerberg Transcripts 168, October 28, 2015, http://dc.uwm.edu/zuckerberg_files_transcripts/168; Mark Zuckerberg, "Free Basics Protects Net Neutrality," *Times of India*, December 28, 2015, http://blogs.timesofindia.indiatimes.com/toi-edit-page/free-basics-protects-net-neutrality; Mark Zuckerberg, "From Facebook, Answering Privacy Concerns with New Settings," *Washington Post*, May 24, 2010, http://www.washingtonpost.com/wp-dyn/content/article/2010/05/23/AR2010052303828.html; Mark Zuckerberg, "I Want to Respond to President Trump's Tweet This Morning Claiming Facebook Has Always Been Against Him," Facebook, September 27, 2017, https://www.facebook.com/zuck/posts/10104067130714241; Mark Zuckerberg, "Live from the Facebook Communities Summit in Chicago," Zuckerberg Transcripts 280, June 22, 2017, http://dc.uwm.edu/zuckerberg_files_transcripts/280; Kathleen Chaykowski, "Mark Zuckerberg: 2 Billion Users Means Facebook's 'Responsibility Is Expanding,'" *Forbes*, June 27, 2017, https://www.forbes.com/sites/kathleen-chaykowski/2017/06/27/facebook-officially-hits-2-billion-users; Mark Zuckerberg, "Mark Zuckerberg on Connecting the World with Internet.org," Zuckerberg Transcripts 175, February 19, 2015, http://dc.uwm.edu/zuckerberg_files_transcripts/175; Mark Zuckerberg, "Mark Zuckerberg on Facebook's Social Good Forum," Zuckerberg Transcripts 251, November 17, 2016, http://dc.uwm.edu/

zuckerberg_files_transcripts/251; Mark Zuckerberg, "Mark Zuckerberg's Letter to Investors: 'The Hacker Way,'" *Wired*, February 1, 2012, http://www.wired.com/2012/02/zuck-letter; Mark Zuckerberg, "Video on Expansion of Internet.org," Zuckerberg Transcripts 258, May 4, 2015, http://dc.uwm.edu/zuckerberg_files_transcripts/258; Richard Feloni, "Why Mark Zuckerberg Wants Everyone to Read a Book That Claims Human Potential Is Infinite," *Business Insider*, December 28, 2015, http://www.businessinsider.com/why-mark-zuckerberg-is-reading-the-beginning-of-infinity-2015-12; Nitasha Tiku, "Why People Can't Stop Talking About Zuckerberg 2020," *Wired*, August 6, 2017, https://www.wired.com/story/mark-zuckerberg-america-travels; Steven Levy, "Zuckerberg Explains Facebook's Plan to Get Entire Planet Online," *Wired*, August 26, 2013, in Zuckerberg Transcripts 101, http://dc.uwm.edu/zuckerberg_files_transcripts/101; CNBC, "Zuckerberg One-on-One (September 2011)," Zuckerberg Transcripts 68, September 22, 2011, http://dc.uwm.edu/zuckerberg_files_transcripts/68.

3. Zuckerberg, "Building Global Community."
4. Zuckerberg, "Building Global Community."
5. William Easterly, "Democracy Is Dying as Technocrats Watch," *Foreign Policy*, December 23, 2016, https://foreignpolicy.com/2016/12/23/democracy-is-dying-as-technocrats-watch; Siva Vaidhyanathan, "Facebook Wins, Democracy Loses," *New York Times*, September 8, 2017, https://www.nytimes.com/2017/09/08/opinion/facebook-wins-democracy-loses.html; Alex Hern, "Thirty Countries Use 'Armies of Opinion Shapers' to Manipulate Democracy—Report," *Guardian*, November 14, 2017, http://www.theguardian.com/technology/2017/nov/14/social-media-influence-election-countries-armies-of-opinion-shapers-manipulate-democracy-fake-news; Sanja Kelly et al., "Freedom on the Net 2017: Manipulating Social Media to Undermine Democracy," October 27, 2017, https://freedom-house.org/report/freedom-net/freedom-net-2017; Derek Willis, "Narendra Modi, the Social Media Politician," *New York Times*, September 25, 2014, https://www.nytimes.com/2014/09/26/upshot/narendra-modi-the-social-media-politician.html; Katy E. Pearce and Sarah Kendzior, "Networked Authoritarianism and Social Media in Azerbaijan," *Journal of Communication* 62, no. 2 (April 1, 2012): 283–98, https://doi.org/10.1111/j.1460-2466.2012.01633.x; Bilge Yesil, *Media in New Turkey: The Origins of an Authoritarian Neoliberal State* (Urbana: University of Illinois Press, 2016).
6. Zuckerberg, "Building Global Community."
7. Zuckerberg, "Mark Zuckerberg's Letter to Investors."
8. Kerry Jones, Kelsey Libert, and Kristin Tynski, "The Emotional Combinations That Make Stories Go Viral," *Harvard Business Review*, May 23, 2016, https://hbr.org/2016/05/research-the-link-between-feeling-in-control-and-viral-content.
9. Eli Pariser, *The Filter Bubble: What the Internet Is Hiding from You* (New York: Penguin, 2011).
10. Zuckerberg, "Building Global Community."
11. Sandy Parakilas, "We Can't Trust Facebook to Regulate Itself," *New York Times*, November 19, 2017, https://www.nytimes.com/2017/11/19/opinion/facebook-regulation-incentive.html.

12. Lynn Neary, "Classic Novel '1984' Sales Are Up in the Era of 'Alternative Facts,'" NPR, January 25, 2017, http://www.npr.org/sections/thetwo-way/2017/01/25/511671118/classic-novel-1984-sales-are-up-in-the-era-of-alternative-facts; Travis M. Andrews, "Sales of Orwell's '1984' Spike After Kellyanne Conway's 'Alternative Facts,'" *Washington Post*, January 25, 2017, https://www.washingtonpost.com/news/morning-mix/wp/2017/01/25/sales-of-orwells-1984-spike-after-kellyanne-conways-alternative-facts.

13. Masha Gessen, "Arguing the Truth with Trump and Putin," *New York Times*, December 17, 2016, https://www.nytimes.com/2016/12/17/opinion/sunday/arguing-the-truth-with-trump-and-putin.html.

14. Masha Gessen, "The Autocrat's Language," *New York Review of Books*, May 13, 2007, http://www.nybooks.com/daily/2017/05/13/the-autocrats-language. "Using words to lie destroys language," Gessen wrote. "Using words to cover up lies, however subtly, destroys language. Validating incomprehensible drivel with polite reaction also destroys language. This isn't merely a question of the prestige of the writing art or the credibility of the journalistic trade: it is about the basic survival of the public sphere."

15. Thomas M. Nichols, *The Death of Expertise: The Campaign Against Established Knowledge and Why It Matters* (New York: Oxford University Press, 2017).

16. Gallup Inc., "Americans' Confidence in Institutions Stays Low," June 13, 2016, http://www.gallup.com/poll/192581/americans-confidence-institutions-stays-low.aspx; Gallup Inc., "Confidence in Institutions," June 13, 2016, http://www.gallup.com/poll/1597/Confidence-Institutions.aspx.

17. Jessica Taylor, "Americans Say Civility Has Worsened Under Trump; Trust in Institutions Down," NPR, June 3, 2017, http://www.npr.org/2017/07/03/535044005/americans-say-civility-has-worsened-under-trump-trust-in-institutions-down.

18. Adam Epstein, "People Trust Google for Their News More than the Actual News," *Quartz*, January 18, 2017, https://qz.com/596956/people-trust-google-for-their-news-more-than-the-actual-news; Kimberlee Morrison, "Nearly Half of Social Media Users Trust Friends for Financial Advice (Infographic)," *Ad Week*, February 22, 2016, http://www.adweek.com/digital/nearly-half-of-social-media-users-trust-facebook-friends-for-financial-advice-infographic; Jesse Singal, "People Spread Fake News Because They Believe Anything Their Friends Post," Select All, March 21, 2017, http://nymag.com/selectall/2017/03/fake-news-spreads-because-people-trust-their-friends-too-much.html; "'Who Shared It?' How Americans Decide What News to Trust on Social Media," American Press Institute, March 20, 2017, https://www.americanpressinstitute.org/publications/reports/survey-research/trust-social-media; Michela Del Vicario, Alessandro Bessi, Fabiana Zollo, Fabio Petroni, Antonio Scala, Guido Caldarelli, H. Eugene Stanley, and Walter Quattrociocchi, "The Spreading of Misinformation Online," *Proceedings of the National Academy of Sciences* 113, no. 3 (January 19, 2016): 554–59, doi:10.1073/pnas.1517441113.

19. Siva Vaidhyanathan, *The Googlization of Everything (And Why We Should Worry)* (Berkeley: University of California Press, 2012).

20. Naomi Oreskes and Erik M. Conway, *Merchants of Doubt: How a Handful of Scientists Obscured the Truth on Issues from Tobacco Smoke to Global Warming* (New York: Bloomsbury, 2010).

21. In 2011 I delivered my account of how Google had changed our lives for both better and worse. Since I wrote *The Googlization of Everything (And Why We Should Worry)* the company has Googlized even more areas of life than I had predicted and given us many more reasons to worry. Now it's time that I take an account of Facebook.

22. Andrew Postman, "My Dad Predicted Trump in 1985—It's Not Orwell, He Warned, It's Brave New World," *Guardian*, February 2, 2017, https://www.theguardian.com/media/2017/feb/02/amusing-ourselves-to-death-neil-postman-trump-orwell-huxley.

23. Neil Postman, *Amusing Ourselves to Death: Public Discourse in the Age of Show Business* (New York: Penguin, 2006), 78–79.

24. Postman, *Amusing Ourselves to Death*, 79.

25. Walter J. Ong, *Orality and Literacy: The Technologizing of the Word* (London: Routledge, 1990); Neil Postman, *Technopoly: The Surrender of Culture to Technology* (New York: Knopf, 1992); Marshall McLuhan and Eric McLuhan, *Laws of Media: The New Science* (Toronto: University of Toronto Press, 1988); Marshall McLuhan, *The Gutenberg Galaxy: The Making of Typographic Man* (New York: New American Library, 1969); Marshall McLuhan and Lewis H. Lapham, *Understanding Media: The Extensions of Man*, 1994; Nicholas G. Carr, *The Shallows: What the Internet Is Doing to Our Brains* (New York: W. W. Norton, 2010); Postman, *Amusing Ourselves to Death*, 27.

26. Clay Shirky, *Here Comes Everybody: The Power of Organizing Without Organizations* (New York: Penguin, 2008); Carr, *The Shallows*; Nicholas G. Carr, *The Glass Cage: Automation and Us* (New York: W. W. Norton, 2014); Elizabeth L. Eisenstein, *The Printing Press as an Agent of Change: Communications and Cultural Transformations in Early Modern Europe* (Cambridge, UK: Cambridge University Press, 1979); Elizabeth L. Eisenstein, "[How to Acknowledge a Revolution]: Reply," *American Historical Review* 107, no. 1 (2002): 126–28, doi:10.1086/532100; Elizabeth L. Eisenstein, "An Unacknowledged Revolution Revisited," *American Historical Review* 107, no. 1 (2002): 87–105, doi:10.1086/532098; Anthony Grafton, "How Revolutionary Was the Printing Revolution: Introduction," *American Historical Review* 107 (2002): 84–128; Adrian Johns, "How to Acknowledge a Revolution," *American Historical Review* 107, no. 1 (2002): 106–25, doi:10.1086/532099. Historian Elizabeth Eisenstein committed the error of rough and simple technological determinism in her influential tome, *The Printing Press as an Agent of Change*. Many writers on digital media have continued to compound Eisenstein's errors by citing her work uncritically, as if it had not been challenged severely and convincingly by more subtle historians of the book.

27. Andrew Feenberg and Alastair Hannay, *Technology and the Politics of Knowledge* (Bloomington: Indiana University Press, 1995); Andrew Feenberg, *Questioning Technology* (London: Routledge, 1999); Andrew Feenberg, *Transforming Technology: A Critical Theory Revisited* (New York: Oxford University Press, 2002); Wiebe E. Bijker et al., *The Social Construction of Technological Systems: New Directions in the Sociology and History of Technology* (Cambridge, MA: MIT Press, 2012); Donald

A. MacKenzie and Judy Wajcman, *The Social Shaping of Technology* (Buckingham, UK: Open University Press, 1999); Sheila Jasanoff, *Handbook of Science and Technology Studies* (Thousand Oaks, CA: Sage Publications, 1995); Edward J. Hackett, *The Handbook of Science and Technology Studies* (Cambridge, MA: MIT Press, 2008); Eric Higgs, Andrew Light, and David Strong, *Technology and the Good Life?* (Chicago: University of Chicago Press, 2000); Pablo J. Boczkowski, "The Mutual Shaping of Technology and Society in Videotex Newspapers: Beyond the Diffusion and Social Shaping Perspectives," *Information Society* 20, no. 4 (2004): 255–67.

28. Andrew Postman, "Eulogy for Neil Postman," October 10, 2003, http://www. faculty.rsu.edu/users/f/felwell/www/Theorists/Postman/Articles/Neil%20 Postman,%201931-2003%20Andrew%20Postman.htm. At Neil's funeral in October 2003, his son, Andrew, gave a moving eulogy. He told this story, which not only offered a glimpse of Neil's character but his habits of mind: "It wasn't simply that our father was unsurpassed for his generosity, a man unconcerned with money in those ways that really shouldn't concern us. It was that, in the bygone era before EZ Pass, when my family went on vacations and passed through a tollbooth, my father would frequently pay for the car behind us—total strangers. When the lucky car was waved through by the tollbooth operator and finally pulled up alongside us, and everyone in their car would squint, trying to figure out where they must know their mystery benefactors from, my sister Madeline and my brother Marc and my mother and father and I would be smiling and waving at them like fools until the other car finally waved back, realizing that— what do you know?—they'd just had a very unique experience, and saved fifty cents in the process. By the way: I can hear my father asking, 'What question is EZ Pass the answer to?' Sure, he'd say, it decreases the time you wait in line at the tollbooth. But, like all new technologies, there's a Faustian bargain to it. Use an EZ Pass and you'll never again know the pleasure of turning a mundane tollbooth trip into an occasion to connect with your fellow humans."

29. Bari M. Schwartz, "Hot or Not? Website Briefly Judges Looks," *Harvard Crimson*, November 4, 2003, http://www.thecrimson.com/article/2003/11/4/hot-or-not-website-briefly-judges/?page=single.

30. Alan J. Tabak, "Hundreds Register for New Facebook," *Harvard Crimson*, February 9, 2004, http://www.thecrimson.com/article/2004/2/9/hundreds-register-for-new-facebook-website/?page=single.

31. David Fincher, *The Social Network*, DVD (Culver City, CA: Sony Pictures Home Entertainment, 2011).

Chapter 1: The Pleasure Machine

1. David Ginsberg and Moira Burke, "Hard Questions: Is Spending Time on Social Media Bad for Us?," Facebook Newsroom, December 15, 2017, https://newsroom. fb.com/news/2017/12/hard-questions-is-spending-time-on-social-media-bad-for-us; Mark Zuckerberg, "Continuing Our Focus for 2018 to Make Sure the Time We All Spend on Facebook Is Time Well Spent," Facebook, January 19, 2018, https://

www.facebook.com/zuck/posts/10104445245963251?pnref=story; Royal Society for Public Health, "Social Media and Young People's Mental Health and Wellbeing," May 2017, http://www.rsph.org.uk/our-work/policy/social-media-and-young-people-s-mental-health-and-wellbeing.html; Moira Burke and Robert E. Kraut, "The Relationship Between Facebook Use and Well-Being Depends on Communication Type and Tie Strength," *Journal of Computer-Mediated Communication* 21, no. 4 (July 1, 2016): 265–81, https://doi.org/10.1111/jcc4.12162; Holly B. Shakya and Nicholas A. Christakis, "Association of Facebook Use with Compromised Well-Being: A Longitudinal Study," *American Journal of Epidemiology* 185, no. 3 (February 1, 2017): 203–11, https://doi.org/10.1093/aje/kww189.

2. Donna Freitas, *The Happiness Effect: How Social Media Is Driving a Generation to Appear Perfect at Any Cost* (Oxford: Oxford University Press, 2016); Deirdre N. McCloskey, "Happyism," *New Republic*, June 8, 2012, https://newrepublic.com/article/103952/happyism-deirdre-mccloskey-economics-happiness; Deirdre N. McCloskey, "Not by P Alone: A Virtuous Economy," *Review of Political Economy* 20, no. 2 (April 1, 2008): 181–97, https://doi.org/10.1080/09538250701819636; Adam D. I. Kramer, Jamie E. Guillory, and Jeffrey T. Hancock, "Experimental Evidence of Massive-Scale Emotional Contagion Through Social Networks," *Proceedings of the National Academy of Sciences* 111, no. 24 (June 17, 2014): 8788–90, https://doi.org/10.1073/pnas.1320040111.

3. Michael Moss, "The Extraordinary Science of Addictive Junk Food," *New York Times*, February 20, 2013, https://www.nytimes.com/2013/02/24/magazine/the-extraordinary-science-of-junk-food.html.

4. TEDxObserver—Cory Doctorow, March 22, 2011, https://www.youtube.com/watch?v=RAGjNe1YhMA.

5. B. F. Skinner, *The Behavior of Organisms: An Experimental Analysis* (New York: D. Appleton-Century, 1938).

6. Bill Davidow, "Skinner Marketing: We're the Rats, and Facebook Likes Are the Reward," *Atlantic*, June 10, 2013, https://www.theatlantic.com/technology/archive/2013/06/skinner-marketing-were-the-rats-and-facebook-likes-are-the-reward/276613.

7. Natasha Dow Schüll, *Addiction by Design: Machine Gambling in Las Vegas* (Princeton, NJ: Princeton University Press, 2012), 92.

8. Schüll, *Addiction by Design*, 2.

9. Bill Allison and John McCormick, "Casino Billionaires, NFL Owners Fueled Trump's Record Inaugural Fundraising," Bloomberg, April 19, 2017, https://www.bloomberg.com/news/articles/2017-04-19/billionaires-and-corporations-push-trump-to-record-inaugural.

10. Schüll, *Addiction by Design*, 5.

11. Evelyn M. Rusli, "Facebook Buys Instagram for $1 Billion," *Dealbook* (blog), *New York Times*, April 9, 2012, https://dealbook.nytimes.com/2012/04/09/facebook-buys-instagram-for-1-billion.

12. Adam L. Alter, *Irresistible: The Rise of Addictive Technology and the Business of Keeping Us Hooked* (New York: Penguin, 2017), 214–20.

13. "Hot or Not," Wikipedia, May 29, 2017, https://en.wikipedia.org/w/index. php?title=Hot_or_Not&oldid=782779787.

14. Bari M. Schwartz, "Hot or Not? Website Briefly Judges Looks," *Harvard Crimson*, November 4, 2003, http://www.thecrimson.com/article/2003/11/4/hot-or-not-website-briefly-judges/?page=single.

15. Alter, *Irresistible*, 214–26.

16. Sarah Smarsh, "Working-Class Women Are Too Busy for Gender Theory—but They're Still Feminists," *Guardian*, June 25, 2017, https://www.theguardian.com/world/2017/jun/25/feminism-working-class-women-gender-theory-dolly-parton.

17. Neil Postman, *Amusing Ourselves to Death: Public Discourse in the Age of Show Business* (New York: Penguin, 2006), 70.

18. Susan Sontag, *On Photography* (New York: Picador, 2001); Nicholas Mirzoeff, *How to See the World: An Introduction to Images, from Self-Portraits to Selfies, Maps to Movies, and More* (New York: Basic Books, 2016); Roland Barthes, *Camera Lucida: Reflections on Photography* (New York: Hill and Wang, 2010); Susie Linfield, *The Cruel Radiance: Photography and Political Violence* (Chicago: University of Chicago Press, 2012); John Berger, *Ways of Seeing* (London: Penguin, 1977).

19. Sam Levin, Julia Carrie Wong, and Luke Harding, "Facebook Backs Down from 'Napalm Girl' Censorship and Reinstates Photo," *Guardian*, September 9, 2016, https://www.theguardian.com/technology/2016/sep/09/facebook-reinstates-napalm-girl-photo; "Facebook's Sheryl Sandberg on 'Napalm Girl' Photo: 'We Don't Always Get It Right,'" *Guardian*, September 12, 2016, https://www.theguardian.com/technology/2016/sep/12/facebook-mistake-napalm-girl-photo-sheryl-sandberg-apologizes; Tarleton Gillespie, "Platforms Intervene," *Social Media + Society* 1, no. 1 (April 29, 2015): 2056305115580479, https://doi.org/10.1177/2056305115580479; Tarleton Gillespie, *Custodians of the Internet: Platforms, Content Moderation, and the Hidden Decisions That Shape Social Media* (New Haven, CT: Yale University Press, 2018); Tarleton Gillespie, "Facebook Can't Moderate in Secret Any More," Data and Society: Points, May 24, 2017, https://points.datasociety.net/facebook-cant-moderate-in-secret-any-more-ca2dbcd9d2.

20. Sontag, *On Photography*, 8–10; Rose Eveleth, "How Many Photographs of You Are Out There in the World?," *Atlantic*, November 2, 2015, https://www.theatlantic.com/technology/archive/2015/11/how-many-photographs-of-you-are-out-there-in-the-world/413389.

21. Sontag, *On Photography*, 14.

22. David Kirkpatrick, *The Facebook Effect: The Inside Story of the Company That Is Connecting the World* (New York: Simon & Schuster, 2010), 20–31.

23. Aristotle, *The Basic Works of Aristotle*, ed. Richard McKeon (New York: Random House, 1941), 1060–61.

24. Aristotle, *Basic Works*, 1058.

25. Jonathan Barnes, *Aristotle: A Very Short Introduction* (Oxford: Oxford University Press, 2000); Aristotle, *Basic Works*; Aristotle, *The Politics*, ed. Carnes Lord (Chicago: University of Chicago Press, 1985); Aristotle, *The Politics of Aristotle*, ed. Ernest Barker (Oxford: Clarendon Press, 1952); Anthony Grafton, Glenn W. Most, and Salvatore

Settis, eds., *The Classical Tradition* (Cambridge, MA: Harvard University Press, 2010); Alan Ryan, *On Politics: A History of Political Thought from Herodotus to the Present* (New York: Liveright, 2012).

26. Ryan, *On Politics*, 76–77.

27. Judith Donath, "Why Fake News Stories Thrive Online," CNN, November 20, 2016, http://www.cnn.com/2016/11/20/opinions/fake-news-stories-thrive-donath/index.html.

Chapter 2: The Surveillance Machine

1. Elliot Ackerman, "Screen Shot," *Esquire*, August 2017, http://classic.esquire.com/screen-shot.

2. Amanda Lenhart, Michele Ybarra, and Myeshia Price-Feeney, "Nonconsensual Image Sharing," Data and Society, December 13, 2016, https://datasociety.net/pubs/oh/Nonconsensual_Image_Sharing_2016.pdf.

3. Andy Kroll, "Cloak and Data: The Real Story Behind Cambridge Analytica's Rise and Fall," *Mother Jones*, March 23, 2018, https://www.motherjones.com/politics/2018/03/cloak-and-data-cambridge-analytica-robert-mercer; Ryan Mac, "Cambridge Analytica Whistleblower Said He Wanted to Create NSA's 'Wet Dream,'" BuzzFeed, March 22, 2018, https://www.buzzfeed.com/ryanmac/christopher-wylie-cambridge-analytica-scandal; Siva Vaidhyanathan, "Facebook Was Letting Down Users Years Before Cambridge Analytica," *Slate*, March 20, 2018, https://slate.com/technology/2018/03/facebooks-data-practices-were-letting-down-users-years-before-cambridge-analytica.html; Siva Vaidhyanathan, "Don't Delete Facebook. Do Something About It," *New York Times*, March 24, 2018, https://www.nytimes.com/2018/03/24/opinion/sunday/delete-facebook-does-not-fix-problem.html.

4. Julia Angwin, *Stealing MySpace: The Battle to Control the Most Popular Website in America* (New York: Random House, 2009); danah boyd, *It's Complicated: The Social Lives of Networked Teens* (New Haven, CT: Yale University Press, 2014); https://doi.org/10.1177/2056305115580148, danah boyd, "Social Media: A Phenomenon to Be Analyzed," *Social Media + Society* 1, no. 1 (April 29, 2015): 2056305115580148, https://doi.org/10.1177/2056305115580148; danah boyd and Alice E. Marwick, "Social Privacy in Networked Publics: Teens' Attitudes, Practices, and Strategies," September 22, 2011, available at Social Science Research Network, http://papers.ssrn.com/abstract=1925128.

5. David Kirkpatrick, *The Facebook Effect: The Inside Story of the Company That Is Connecting the World* (New York: Simon & Schuster, 2010); Computer History Museum, "The Facebook Effect (Interview with Zuckerberg and Kirkpatrick)," Zuckerberg Transcripts 30, July 25, 2010, http://dc.uwm.edu/zuckerberg_files_transcripts/30; Antonio García Martínez, *Chaos Monkeys: Obscene Fortune and Random Failure in Silicon Valley* (New York: Harper, 2016).

6. García Martínez, *Chaos Monkeys*; Joseph Turow, *The Aisles Have Eyes: How Retailers Track Your Shopping, Strip Your Privacy, and Define Your Power* (New Haven, CT: Yale University Press, 2017); Joseph Turow, *The Daily You: How the New Advertising Industry Is Defining Your Identity and Your World* (New Haven, CT: Yale University Press, 2011);

Joseph Turow, *Niche Envy: Marketing Discrimination in the Digital Age* (Cambridge, MA: MIT Press, 2006); Tim Peterson, "How Facebook's Custom Audiences Won Over Adland," *Ad Age*, March 23, 2015, http://adage.com/article/digital/facebook-s-custom-audiences-won-adland/297700; Tim Wu, *The Attention Merchants: The Epic Scramble to Get Inside Our Heads* (New York: Knopf, 2016); Casandra Campbell, "The Beginner's Guide to Facebook Custom Audiences," *Shopify's Ecommerce Blog—Ecommerce News, Online Store Tips and More*, October 6, 2015, https://www.shopify.com/blog/56441413-the-beginners-guide-to-facebook-custom-audiences.

7. "Using the Graph API—Documentation," Facebook for Developers, accessed July 6, 2017, https://developers.facebook.com/docs/graph-api/using-graph-api; "Graph API—Documentation," Facebook for Developers, accessed November 12, 2017, https://developers.facebook.com/docs/graph-api; Josh Constine, "Facebook Is Done Giving Its Precious Social Graph to Competitors," TechCrunch, accessed November 12, 2017, http://social.techcrunch.com/2013/01/24/my-precious-social-graph; Angela M. Cirucci, "Facebook's Affordances, Visible Culture, and Anti-Anonymity," in *Proceedings of the 2015 International Conference on Social Media and Society* (New York: ACM, 2015), 11:1–11:5, https://doi.org/10.1145/2789187.2789202; Anne Shields, "ID Graph Is a New Feature for Oracle's Marketing Cloud This Spring," Market Realist, April 14, 2015, http://market-realist.com/2015/04/id-graph-new-feature-oracles-marketing-cloud-spring; Boonsri Dickinson, "So What the Heck Is the 'Social Graph' Facebook Keeps Talking About?," Business Insider, accessed November 12, 2017, http://www.businessinsider.com/explainer-what-exactly-is-the-social-graph-2012-3.

8. Julia Angwin, Terry Parris, and Surya Mattu, "Facebook Doesn't Tell Users Everything It Really Knows About Them," ProPublica, December 27, 2016, https://www.propublica.org/article/facebook-doesnt-tell-users-everything-it-really-knows-about-them; "How Does Facebook Work with Data Providers?," Facebook Help Center, accessed November 12, 2017, https://www.facebook.com/help/494750870625830?helpref=uf_permalink.

9. Daniel J. Solove, *The Future of Reputation: Gossip, Rumor, and Privacy on the Internet* (New Haven, CT: Yale University Press, 2007); Queenie Wong, "Twitter, Facebook Users Name and Shame White Nationalists in Charlottesville Rally," *Mercury News*, August 15, 2017, http://www.mercurynews.com/2017/08/14/twitter-facebook-users-name-and-shame-white-nationalists-in-charlottesville-rally; Sarah Jeong, *The Internet of Garbage* (Forbes Media, 2015), Kindle ed.

10. Kashmir Hill, "Facebook Figured Out My Family Secrets, and It Won't Tell Me How," Gizmodo, August 25, 2017, http://gizmodo.com/facebook-figured-out-my-family-secrets-and-it-wont-tel-1797696163; Kashmir Hill, "How Facebook Figures Out Everyone You've Ever Met," Gizmodo, November 7, 2017, https://gizmodo.com/how-facebook-figures-out-everyone-youve-ever-met-1819822691.

11. Katy E. Pearce, "Democratizing Kompromat: The Affordances of Social Media for State-Sponsored Harassment," *Information, Communication and Society* 18, no. 10 (October 3, 2015): 1158–74, https://doi.org/10.1080/1369118X.2015.1021705; Katy E. Pearce and Sarah Kendzior, "Networked Authoritarianism and Social Media in

Azerbaijan," *Journal of Communication* 62, no. 2 (April 1, 2012): 283–98, https://doi.org/10.1111/j.1460-2466.2012.01633.x; Julia Angwin, *Dragnet Nation: A Quest for Privacy, Security, and Freedom in a World of Relentless Surveillance* (New York: Times Books, 2015); Christian Fuchs, *Internet and Surveillance: The Challenges of Web 2.0 and Social Media* (New York: Routledge, 2012); Ewen MacAskill et al., "NSA Files Decoded: Edward Snowden's Surveillance Revelations Explained," *Guardian*, November 1, 2013, http://www.theguardian.com/world/interactive/2013/nov/01/snowden-nsa-files-surveillance-revelations-decoded; James Risen and Laura Poitras, "N.S.A. Gathers Data on Social Connections of U.S. Citizens," *New York Times*, September 28, 2013, http://www.nytimes.com/2013/09/29/us/nsa-examines-social-networks-of-us-citizens.html; Shane Harris, *The Watchers: The Rise of America's Surveillance State* (New York: Penguin, 2010); Randolph Lewis, *Under Surveillance: Being Watched in Modern America* (Austin: University of Texas Press, 2017); Scott Nover and Nikki Usher, "Why Haven't Reporters Mass-Adopted Secure Tools for Communicating with Sources?," *Slate*, July 12, 2017, http://www.slate.com/articles/technology/future_tense/2017/07/women_young_people_experience_the_chilling_effects_of_surveillance_at_higher.html.

12. Francis Ford Coppola et al., *The Conversation* (Hollywood, CA: Paramount Pictures, 2000); Tony Scott et al., *Enemy of the State* (Burbank, CA: Touchstone Home Entertainment, 1999).

13. Julie E. Cohen, *Configuring the Networked Self: Law, Code, and the Play of Everyday Practice* (New Haven, CT: Yale University Press, 2012).

14. Samuel D. Warren and Louis D. Brandeis, "The Right to Privacy," *Harvard Law Review* 4, no. 5 (December 15, 1890): 193–220, doi:10.2307/1321160. Also see Robert Post, "Rereading Warren and Brandeis: Privacy, Property, and Appropriation," Faculty Scholarship Series, Yale University Law School, January 1, 1991, http://digitalcommons.law.yale.edu/fss_papers/206.

15. Jim Miller, *The Passion of Michel Foucault* (New York: Simon & Schuster, 1993), 222–23; Michel Foucault, *Discipline and Punish: The Birth of the Prison* (New York: Vintage Books, 1995).

16. Timothy Garton Ash, *The File: A Personal History* (New York: Random House, 1997).

17. In my first effort to describe this phenomenon, I dubbed it the "Nonopticon." See Siva Vaidhyanathan, "Naked in the 'Nonopticon': Surveillance and Marketing Combine to Strip Away Our Privacy," *Chronicle of Higher Education*, February 15, 2008, http://chronicle.com/free/v54/i23/23b00701.htm. That was clumsy and inaccurate. Later my friend Bill Pugsley suggested that "Cryptopticon" accurately captures my intended meaning. I am grateful to him for the suggestions. I later employed "Cryptopticon" in Siva Vaidhyanathan, *The Googlization of Everything (And Why We Should Worry)* (Berkeley: University of California Press, 2011).

18. Vaidhyanathan, *The Googlization of Everything*.

19. Joseph Turow, *Niche Envy: Marketing Discrimination in the Digital Age* (Cambridge, MA: MIT Press, 2006); Chris Anderson, *The Long Tail: Why the Future of Business Is Selling Less of More* (New York: Hyperion, 2006).

20. Quirin Berg et al., *The Lives of Others* (Culver City, CA: Sony Pictures Home Entertainment, 2007).

21. Vaidhyanathan, *The Googlization of Everything*; Fred Vogelstein, "Great Wall of Facebook: The Social Network's Plan to Dominate the Internet," *Wired*, July 2009, http://www.wired.com/techbiz/it/magazine/17-07/ff_facebookwall? currentPage=all; Michael Agger, "Google and Facebook Battle for Your Friends," *Slate*, January 14, 2009, http://www.slate.com/id/2208676/pagenum/all/#p2.

22. Jack M. Balkin, "The Constitution in the National Surveillance State," *Minnesota Law Review* 93, no. 1 (2008), http://ssrn.com/paper=1141524; James X. Dempsey and Lara M. Flint, "Commercial Data and National Security," *George Washington Law Review* 72 (2003–4): 1459; Chris Jay Hoofnagle, "Big Brother's Little Helpers: How ChoicePoint and Other Commercial Data Brokers Collect and Package Your Data for Law Enforcement," *North Carolina Journal of International Law and Commercial Regulation* 29 (2003–4): 595.

23. James Rule, *Privacy in Peril* (Oxford: Oxford University Press, 2007).

24. Dahlia Lithwick, "Alito vs. Scalia," *Slate*, January 23, 2012, http://www.slate.com/ articles/news_and_politics/jurisprudence/2012/01/u_s_v_jones_supreme_ court_justices_alito_and_scalia_brawl_over_technology_and_privacy_.html.

25. Charles Arthur, "Google Glass: Is It a Threat to Our Privacy?," *Guardian*, March 6, 2013, http://www.guardian.co.uk/technology/2013/mar/06/google-glass-threat-to-our-privacy.

26. Solove, *The Future of Reputation*.

27. Helen Nissenbaum, "Protecting Privacy in an Information Age: The Problem of Privacy in Public," *Law and Philosophy* 17, nos. 5/6 (1998): 559–96, http://www.jstor.org/stable/3505189.

28. boyd, *It's Complicated*.

29. James B. Rule, *Private Lives and Public Surveillance: Social Control in the Computer Age* (New York: Schocken Books, 1974); Rule, *Privacy in Peril*; Fred Turner, *From Counterculture to Cyberculture: Stewart Brand, the Whole Earth Network, and the Rise of Digital Utopianism* (Chicago: University of Chicago Press, 2006).

30. Mark Zuckerberg, "From Facebook, Answering Privacy Concerns with New Settings," *Washington Post*, May 24, 2010, http://www.washingtonpost.com/wp-dyn/ content/article/2010/05/23/AR2010052303828.html.

31. Michael Zimmer, "Mark Zuckerberg's Theory of Privacy," *Washington Post*, February 3, 2014, https://www.washingtonpost.com/lifestyle/style/mark-zucker-bergs-theory-of-privacy/2014/02/03/2c1d780a-8cea-11e3-95dd-36ff657a4dae_ story.html; Michael Zimmer and Anna Lauren Hoffmann, "Privacy and Control in Mark Zuckerberg's Discourse on Facebook," *AoIR Selected Papers of Internet Research* 4, no. 0 (2014), http://spir.aoir.org/index.php/spir/article/view/1004; Michael Zimmer, "The Zuckerberg Files: A Digital Archive of All Public Utterances of Facebook's Founder and CEO, Mark Zuckerberg," accessed July 4, 2017, https:// www.zuckerbergfiles.org.

32. Vaidhyanathan, *The Googlization of Everything*; Helen Nissenbaum, *Privacy in Context Technology, Policy, and the Integrity of Social Life* (Stanford, CA: Stanford

University Press, 2010); Nancy K. Baym, *Personal Connections in the Digital Age* (Cambridge, UK: Polity, 2010).

33. Alice E. Marwick and danah boyd, "I Tweet Honestly, I Tweet Passionately: Twitter Users, Context Collapse, and the Imagined Audience," *New Media and Society* 13, no. 1 (February 1, 2011): 114–33, https://doi.org/10.1177/1461444810365313; boyd, *It's Complicated*; danah boyd, "Privacy and Publicity in the Context of Big Data," talk presented April 29, 2010, http://www.danah.org/papers/talks/2010/WWW2010.html; boyd and Marwick, "Social Privacy in Networked Publics"; author interview with Alice Marwick, New York, 2017; Alice Emily Marwick, *Status Update: Celebrity, Publicity, and Branding in the Social Media Age* (New Haven, CT: Yale University Press, 2013); Zimmer and Hoffmann, "Privacy and Control in Mark Zuckerberg's Discourse on Facebook."

34. Olivia Solon, "Facebook Asks Users for Nude Photos in Project to Combat Revenge Porn," *Guardian*, November 7, 2017, http://www.theguardian.com/technology/2017/nov/07/facebook-revenge-porn-nude-photos; Nick Statt, "Facebook's Unorthodox New Revenge Porn Defense Is to Upload Nudes to Facebook," The Verge, November 7, 2017, https://www.theverge.com/2017/11/7/16619690/facebook-revenge-porn-defense-strategy-test-australia; Danielle Keats Citron, *Hate Crimes in Cyberspace* (Cambridge, MA: Harvard University Press, 2014).

35. Tarleton Gillespie, *Custodians of the Internet: Platforms, Content Moderation, and the Hidden Decisions That Shape Social Media* (New Haven, CT: Yale University Press, 2018); Tarleton Gillespie, "Facebook Can't Moderate in Secret Any More," Data & Society: Points, May 24, 2017, https://points.datasociety.net/facebook-cant-moderate-in-secret-any-more-ca2dbcd9d2; Sarah T. Roberts, "Content Moderation," February 5, 2017, http://escholarship.org/uc/item/7371c1hf; Sarah T. Roberts, "Social Media's Silent Filter," *Atlantic*, March 8, 2017, https://www.theatlantic.com/technology/archive/2017/03/commercial-content-moderation/518796/?utm_source=atltw; Adrian Chen, "The Laborers Who Keep Dick Pics and Beheadings out of Your Facebook Feed," *Wired*, October 23, 2014, http://www.wired.com/2014/10/content-moderation.

36. April Glaser, "Facebook's Tone-Deaf Plan to Tackle Revenge Porn by Having Victims Upload Nude Photos," *Slate*, November 8, 2017, http://www.slate.com/blogs/future_tense/2017/11/08/facebook_wants_victims_of_revenge_porn_to_upload_a_nude_photo_to_prevent.html.

Chapter 3: The Attention Machine

1. Sumathi Reddy, "How the Ice-Bucket Challenge Got Its Start," *Wall Street Journal*, August 14, 2014, http://www.wsj.com/articles/how-the-ice-bucket-challenge-got-its-start-1408049557; Josh Levin, "Who Invented the Ice Bucket Challenge?," *Slate*, August 22, 2014, http://www.slate.com/articles/technology/technology/2014/08/who_invented_the_ice_bucket_challenge_a_slate_investigation.single.html.

2. Lucy Townsend, "How Much Has the Ice Bucket Challenge Achieved?," BBC News, September 2, 2014, http://www.bbc.com/news/magazine-29013707; Ian Sample and Nicky Woolf, "How the Ice Bucket Challenge Led to an ALS Research Breakthrough," *Guardian*, July 27, 2016, http://www.theguardian.com/science/2016/

jul/27/how-the-ice-bucket-challenge-led-to-an-als-research-breakthrough; Emily Steel, "'Ice Bucket Challenge' Has Raised Millions for ALS Association," *New York Times*, August 17, 2014, https://www.nytimes.com/2014/08/18/business/ice-bucket-challenge-has-raised-millions-for-als-association.html; "New Ice Bucket Challenge? Gazans Launch 'Rubble Bucket Challenge,'" NBC News, August 25, 2014, https://www.nbcnews.com/storyline/middle-east-unrest/new-ice-bucket-challenge-gazans-launch-rubble-bucket-challenge-n188191; Diksha Madhok, "The Story Behind India's Rice Bucket Challenge," *Quartz*, August 25, 2014, https://qz.com/254910/india-adapts-the-ice-bucket-challenge-to-suit-local-conditions-meet-the-rice-bucket-challenge; Julia Belluz, "The Truth About the Ice Bucket Challenge," Vox, August 20, 2014, https://www.vox.com/2014/8/20/6040435/als-ice-bucket-challenge-and-why-we-give-to-charity-donate; Rick Cohen, "Throwing Cold Water on Ice Bucket Philanthropy," *Nonprofit Quarterly*, August 19, 2014, https://nonprofitquarterly.org/2014/08/19/throwing-cold-water-on-ice-bucket-philanthropy.

3. Townsend, "How Much Has the Ice Bucket Challenge Achieved?"; Sample and Woolf, "How the Ice Bucket Challenge Led to an ALS Research Breakthrough."

4. Sander van der Linden, "The Nature of Viral Altruism and How to Make It Stick," *Nature Human Behaviour* 1, no. 3 (February 13, 2017): s41562-016-0041-016, https://doi.org/10.1038/s41562-016-0041.

5. Nausicaa Renner, "Empathy vs. Rationality: The Ice Bucket Challenge," *Boston Review*, September 4, 2014, http://bostonreview.net/blog/andrew-mayersohn-als-ice-bucket-challenge-empathy-viral-activism; Belluz, "The Truth About the Ice Bucket Challenge"; Cohen, "Throwing Cold Water on Ice Bucket Philanthropy."

6. Tim Wu, "Blind Spot: The Attention Economy and the Law," March 26, 2017, available at Social Science Research Network, https://papers.ssrn.com/abstract=2941094.

7. Wu, "Blind Spot."

8. Alice Emily Marwick, *Status Update: Celebrity, Publicity, and Branding in the Social Media Age* (New Haven, CT: Yale University Press, 2013).

9. Judith Donath, "Why Fake News Stories Thrive Online," CNN, November 20, 2016, http://www.cnn.com/2016/11/20/opinions/fake-news-stories-thrive-donath/index.html; Ben Agger, *Oversharing: Presentations of Self in the Internet Age* (New York: Routledge, 2015); Amy L. Gonzales and Jeffrey T. Hancock, "Mirror, Mirror on My Facebook Wall: Effects of Exposure to Facebook on Self-Esteem," *Cyberpsychology, Behavior, and Social Networking* 14, nos. 1–2 (June 24, 2010): 79–83, https://doi.org/10.1089/cyber.2009.0411; Stuart Hall, *Representation: Cultural Representations and Signifying Practices* (London: Sage, 1997); Ashwini Nadkarni and Stefan G. Hofmann, "Why Do People Use Facebook?," *Personality and Individual Differences* 52, no. 3 (2012): 243–49, http://dx.doi.org/10.1016/j.paid.2011.11.007; Zizi Papacharissi, *A Networked Self: Identity, Community and Culture on Social Network Sites* (New York: Routledge, 2011); Erving Goffman, *The Presentation of Self in Everyday Life* (London: Penguin, 1990); D. E. Wittkower, "Facebook and Dramauthentic Identity: A Post-Goffmanian Theory of Identity Performance on SNS," *First Monday* 19, no. 4 (April 2, 2014), http://journals.uic.edu/ojs/index.php/fm/article/view/4858.

10. Mara Einstein, *Advertising: What Everyone Needs to Know* (New York: Oxford University Press, 2017); Mara Einstein, *Black Ops Advertising: Native Ads, Content Marketing, and the Covert World of the Digital Sell* (New York: OR Books, 2016); C. Edwin Baker, *Advertising and a Democratic Press* (Princeton, NJ: Princeton University Press, 1993); Winston Fletcher, *Advertising: A Very Short Introduction* (Oxford: Oxford University Press, 2010); Michael Schudson, *Advertising, the Uneasy Persuasion: Its Dubious Impact on American Society* (New York: Basic Books, 1986); Nir Eyal, *Hooked: How to Build Habit-Forming Products* (New York: Portfolio/Penguin, 2014); Joseph Turow, *Niche Envy: Marketing Discrimination in the Digital Age* (Cambridge, MA: MIT Press, 2006); Thomas Frank, *The Conquest of Cool: Business Culture, Counterculture, and the Rise of Hip Consumerism* (Chicago: University of Chicago Press, 1997); Joseph Turow, *The Daily You: How the New Advertising Industry Is Defining Your Identity and Your World* (New Haven, CT: Yale University Press, 2011); Joe McGinniss, *The Selling of the President, 1968* (New York: Trident Press, 1969); Susan J. Douglas, *Where the Girls Are: Growing Up Female with the Mass Media* (New York: Times Books, 1994); Matthew P. McAllister and Emily West, *The Routledge Companion to Advertising and Promotional Culture* (New York: Routledge, 2015); Tim Wu, *The Attention Merchants: The Epic Scramble to Get Inside Our Heads* (New York: Knopf, 2016).
11. Wu, *The Attention Merchants*, 3–5.
12. Wu, *The Attention Merchants*.
13. Wu, *The Attention Merchants*, 170–76.
14. Einstein, *Advertising*.
15. Siva Vaidhyanathan, *The Googlization of Everything (And Why We Should Worry)* (Berkeley: University of California Press, 2011); Wu, *The Attention Merchants*; Fred Turner, *From Counterculture to Cyberculture: Stewart Brand, the Whole Earth Network, and the Rise of Digital Utopianism* (Chicago: University of Chicago Press, 2006); Fred Turner, *The Democratic Surround: Multimedia and American Liberalism from World War II to the Psychedelic Sixties* (Chicago: University of Chicago Press, 2013).
16. Mike Isaac and Scott Shane, "Facebook's Russia-Linked Ads Came in Many Disguises," *New York Times*, October 2, 2017, https://www.nytimes.com/2017/10/02/technology/facebook-russia-ads-.html; Scott Shane, "On Facebook and Twitter, a Hunt for Russia's Meddling Hand," *New York Times*, September 7, 2017, https://www.nytimes.com/2017/09/07/us/politics/russia-facebook-twitter-election.html; Scott Shane, "Purged Facebook Page Tied to the Kremlin Spread Anti-Immigrant Bile," *New York Times*, September 12, 2017, https://www.nytimes.com/2017/09/12/us/politics/russia-facebook-election.html; Mike Isaac and Daisuke Wakabayashi, "Russian Influence Reached 126 Million Through Facebook Alone," *New York Times*, October 30, 2017, https://www.nytimes.com/2017/10/30/technology/facebook-google-russia.html; Colin Stretch, "Letter from Colin Stretch, General Counsel for Facebook, to Senator Richard Burr," January 8, 2018, https://www.intelligence.senate.gov/sites/default/files/documents/Facebook%20Response%20to%20Committee%20QFRs.pdf; Craig Timberg, "Russians Got Tens of Thousands of Americans to RSVP for Their Phony Political Events on

Facebook," *Washington Post*, January 25, 2018, https://www.washingtonpost.com/news/the-switch/wp/2018/01/25/russians-got-tens-of-thousands-of-americans-to-rsvp-for-their-phony-political-events-on-facebook.

17. Julia Angwin, Noam Scheiber, and Ariana Tobin, "Facebook Job Ads Raise Concerns About Age Discrimination," *New York Times*, December 20, 2017, https://www.nytimes.com/2017/12/20/business/facebook-job-ads.html; Julia Angwin, Ariana Tobin, and Madeleine Varner, "Facebook (Still) Letting Housing Advertisers Exclude Users by Race," ProPublica, November 21, 2017, https://www.propublica.org/article/facebook-advertising-discrimination-housing-race-sex-national-origin; Madeleine Varner and Julia Angwin, "Facebook Enabled Advertisers to Reach 'Jew Haters,'" ProPublica, September 14, 2017, https://www.propublica.org/article/facebook-enabled-advertisers-to-reach-jew-haters.

18. Eli Pariser, *The Filter Bubble: What the Internet Is Hiding from You* (New York: Penguin, 2011); Brian Feldman, "What Happens When Facebook Controls the News," Select All, October 25, 2017, http://nymag.com/selectall/2017/10/what-happens-when-facebook-controls-the-news.html; Tom Chivers, "How Online Filter Bubbles Are Making Parents of Autistic Children Targets for Fake 'Cures,'" BuzzFeed, August 28, 2017, https://www.buzzfeed.com/tomchivers/how-online-filter-bubbles-are-making-parents-of-autistic; Drake Baer, "The 'Filter Bubble' Explains Why Trump Won and You Didn't See It Coming," Science of Us, November 9, 2016, http://nymag.com/scienceofus/2016/11/how-facebook-and-the-filter-bubble-pushed-trump-to-victory.html; Vaidhyanathan, *The Googlization of Everything*; Miranda Neubauer, "Worth Watching: Pariser, Vaidhyanathan, Morozov and Weisberg on Whether the Internet Is Closing Our Minds," TechPresident, April 18, 2012, http://techpresident.com/news/22074/pariser-convinces-debate-audience-internet-narrowing-points-view; Katy Waldman and Katy Waldman, "The Web Is Turning Us into Narrow-Minded Drones," *Slate*, April 18, 2012, http://www.slate.com/articles/news_and_politics/intelligence_squared/2012/04/yes_the_internet_is_closing_our_minds_who_won_the_slate_intelligence_squared_debate_on_april_17_and_how_.html; Bas Hofstra et al., "Sources of Segregation in Social Networks: A Novel Approach Using Facebook," *American Sociological Review* 82, no. 3 (June 1, 2017): 625–56, https://doi.org/10.1177/0003122417705656; Motahhare Eslami et al., "'I Always Assumed That I Wasn't Really That Close to [Her]': Reasoning About Invisible Algorithms in News Feeds," in *Proceedings of the 33rd Annual ACM Conference on Human Factors in Computing Systems* (New York: ACM, 2015), 153–62, https://doi.org/10.1145/2702123.2702556; Levi Boxell, Matthew Gentzkow, and Jesse M. Shapiro, "Is the Internet Causing Political Polarization? Evidence from Demographics," working paper, National Bureau of Economic Research, March 2017, https://doi.org/10.3386/w23258; Richard Fletcher and Rasmus Kleis Nielsen, "Using Social Media Appears to Diversify Your News Diet, Not Narrow It," Nieman Lab, June 21, 2017, http://www.niemanlab.org/2017/06/using-social-media-appears-to-diversify-your-news-diet-not-narrow-it; Rasmus Kleis Nielsen, "Social Media and Bullshit," *Social Media + Society* 1, no. 1 (April 29, 2015): 2056305115580335, https://doi.org/10.1177/2056305115580335; Boxell, Gentzkow, and Shapiro, "Is the Internet Causing Political

Polarization?"; R. Kelly Garrett, "Facebook's Problem Is More Complicated than Fake News," *Scientific American*, November 17, 2016, https://www.scientificameri-can.com/article/facebook-s-problem-is-more-complicated-than-fake-news; Dimitar Nikolov et al., "Measuring Online Social Bubbles," *PeerJ Computer Science* 1 (December 2, 2015): e38, https://doi.org/10.7717/peerj-cs.38. Researching phenomena on Twitter is much easier. The data can be "scrapped" without many limitations because most accounts are set to distribute posts publicly. So many of the studies casting doubt on the effect of filter bubbles rely on Twitter or general survey opinion data—but not Facebook data. Some studies examine general use of "social media," as if all services work the same way. Twitter is much less algorithmi-cally edited than Facebook is. Twitter has less data on each user. And it has fewer vectors of engagement to measure. So it can't massage the flow of posts each person sees as powerfully as Facebook can. On Twitter, we mostly choose whose posts we see by actively choosing to follow particular people. Twitter has a much smaller user base. Although easier to study, Twitter is less significant in every way than Facebook is.

19. Eytan Bakshy et al., "Social Influence in Social Advertising: Evidence from Field Experiments," in *Proceedings of the 13th ACM Conference on Electronic Commerce* (New York: ACM, 2012), 146–61, https://doi.org/10.1145/2229012.2229027; Eytan Bakshy, Solomon Messing, and Lada Adamic, "Exposure to Ideologically Diverse News and Opinion on Facebook," *Science*, May 7, 2015, aaa1160, https://doi.org/10.1126/science.aaa1160; Eli Pariser, "Did Facebook's Big Study Kill My Filter Bubble Thesis?," *Wired*, May 7, 2015, https://www.wired.com/2015/05/did-facebooks-big-study-kill-my-filter-bubble-thesis.

20. Thomas Hanitzsch, Arjen Van Dalen, and Nina Steindl, "Caught in the Nexus: A Comparative and Longitudinal Analysis of Public Trust in the Press," *International Journal of Press/Politics*, November 15, 2017, 1940161217740695, https://doi.org/10.1177/1940161217740695; Gallup Inc., "Confidence in Institutions," June 13, 2016, http://www.gallup.com/poll/1597/Confidence-Institutions.aspx; Gallup Inc., "Americans' Confidence in Institutions Stays Low," June 13, 2016, http://www.gallup.com/poll/192581/americans-confidence-institutions-stays-low.aspx.

21. Cass R. Sunstein, *Republic.com* (Princeton, NJ: Princeton University Press, 2001).

22. Sunstein, *Republic.com*; Cass R. Sunstein, *Republic.com 2.0* (Princeton, NJ: Princeton University Press, 2007); Cass R. Sunstein, *Infotopia: How Many Minds Produce Knowledge* (Oxford: Oxford University Press, 2006); Cass R. Sunstein, *Going to Extremes: How Like Minds Unite and Divide* (Oxford: Oxford University Press, 2009); Cass R. Sunstein, *#Republic: Divided Democracy in the Age of Social Media* (Princeton, NJ: Princeton University Press, 2017).

23. Eszter Hargittai, Jason Gallo, and Matthew Kane, "Cross-Ideological Discussions Among Conservative and Liberal Bloggers," *Public Choice* 134, nos. 1–2 (2008): 67–86.

24. Daniel Drezner and Henry Farrell, "Web of Influence," *Foreign Policy*, October 26, 2009, https://foreignpolicy.com/2009/10/26/web-of-influence; Henry Farrell, Eric Lawrence, and John Sides, "Self-Segregation or Deliberation? Blog Readership, Participation and Polarization in American Politics," July 1, 2008, available on Social Science Research Network, https://papers.ssrn.com/abstract=1151490.

25. Vaidhyanathan, *The Googlization of Everything*.
26. Eric Alterman, "Out of Print," *New Yorker*, March 24, 2008, https://www.newyorker.com/magazine/2008/03/31/out-of-print.
27. Jonah Peretti, "How Andrew Breitbart Helped Launch Huffington Post," BuzzFeed, March 1, 2012, https://www.buzzfeed.com/buzzfeedpolitics/how-andrew-breitbart-helped-launch-huffington-post.
28. David Rowan, "How BuzzFeed Mastered Social Sharing to Become a Media Giant for a New Era," *Wired*, January 2, 2014, http://www.wired.co.uk/article/buzzfeed; Amol Sharma and Lukas I. Alpert, "BuzzFeed Set to Miss Revenue Target, Signaling Turbulence in Media," *Wall Street Journal*, November 16, 2017, https://www.wsj.com/articles/buzzfeed-set-to-miss-revenue-target-signaling-turbulence-in-media-1510861771.
29. Elisa Shearer and Jeffrey Gottfried, "News Use Across Social Media Platforms 2017," Pew Research Center: Journalism and Media, September 7, 2017, http://www.journalism.org/2017/09/07/news-use-across-social-media-platforms-2017; Michael Barthel et al., "The Evolving Role of News on Twitter and Facebook," Pew Research Center: Journalism and Media, July 14, 2015, http://www.journalism.org/2015/07/14/the-evolving-role-of-news-on-twitter-and-facebook; Jeffrey Gottfried and Elisa Shearer, "News Use Across Social Media Platforms 2016," Pew Research Center: Journalism and Media, May 26, 2016, http://www.journalism.org/2016/05/26/news-use-across-social-media-platforms-2016; Shannon Greenwood, Andrew Perrin, and Maeve Duggan, "Social Media Update 2016," Pew Research Center: Internet and Technology, November 11, 2016, http://www.pewinternet.org/2016/11/11/social-media-update-2016; Emily Bell, "Facebook Is Eating the World," *Columbia Journalism Review*, March 7, 2016, http://www.cjr.org/analysis/facebook_and_media.php; Fidji Simo, "Introducing: The Facebook Journalism Project," Facebook Media, January 11, 2017, https://media.fb.com/2017/01/11/facebook-journalism-project; Benjamin Mullin, "Seeking to Deepen Ties with Publishers, Facebook Rolls Out Journalism Program," Poynter, January 11, 2017, https://www.poynter.org/2017/seeking-to-deepen-ties-with-publishers-facebook-rolls-out-journalism-program/445020; Peter Kafka, "Facebook Says It's Going to Try to Help Journalism 'Thrive,'" Recode, January 11, 2017, https://www.recode.net/2017/1/11/14237118/facebook-journalism-project; Shan Wang, "Who's Really Driving Traffic to Articles? Depends on the Subject: Facebook (Lifestyle, Entertainment) or Google (Tech, Business, Sports)," Nieman Lab, May 23, 2017, http://www.niemanlab.org/2017/05/whos-really-driving-traffic-to-articles-depends-on-the-subject-facebook-lifestyle-entertainment-or-google-tech-business-sports; Efrat Nechushtai, "Could Digital Platforms Capture the Media Through Infrastructure?," *Journalism*, August 15, 2017, 1464884917725163, https://doi.org/10.1177/1464884917725163; Pablo J. Boczkowski and Eugenia Mitchelstein, *The News Gap: When the Information Preferences of the Media and the Public Diverge* (Cambridge, MA: MIT Press, 2013).
30. Areas of crossover competition, such as Bing with Google or Google+ with Facebook, have not amounted to much beyond token efforts. Microsoft and Google offer servers and accompanying services to businesses and organizations, and thus compete with Amazon's most profitable line of work. But for neither Google nor

Microsoft is the server business a significant source of revenue. I have excluded Weibo, Ali Baba, Yandex, VK, Tencent, and other powerful and important social media and web search companies in places such as China and Russia, where Google and Facebook have struggled to establish markets. The effort to leverage data flows to become the operating system of our lives includes small companies as well. I would suggest watching the activities of SoftBank, Uber, and Palantir as well.

31. Philip N. Howard, *Pax Technica: How the Internet of Things May Set Us Free or Lock Us Up* (New Haven, CT: Yale University Press, 2015); Ian Bogost, "The Internet of Things You Don't Really Need," *Atlantic*, June 23, 2015, https://www.theatlantic.com/technology/archive/2015/06/the-internet-of-things-you-dont-really-need/396485.

32. Frank Pasquale, *The Black Box Society: The Secret Algorithms That Control Money and Information* (Cambridge, MA: Harvard University Press, 2015).

33. Facebook Messenger is Facebook's strongest response to WeChat. Messenger's user base is smaller than WeChat's but is growing steadily. The company regularly adds features to Messenger. Users can make free video calls, send and share videos and text messages among groups of friends, share location, transfer money, share files when connected to file management systems such as Dropbox, request a ride from Uber or Lyft, scan QR codes, and engage with some companies' customer support. Facebook plans to use Messenger to introduce its own virtual assistant that would respond to voice commands and leverage Facebook's data and its formidable artificial intelligence initiatives. Facebook calls its version of Apple's Siri "M." While WeChat is growing in popularity in the Chinese diaspora, and thus is gaining influence across the globe, Facebook sees WeChat as its model and a threat. It's one of the reasons that Mark Zuckerberg has been plotting ways to get Facebook back into service in the People's Republic of China. However, swaying people who have used one application for so many important life and lifestyle features would be difficult, even for Facebook. Connie Chan, "When One App Rules Them All: The Case of WeChat and Mobile in China," Andreessen Horowitz, August 6, 2015, http://a16z.com/2015/08/06/wechat-china-mobile-first; "WeChat's World: China's WeChat Shows the Way to Social Media's Future," *Economist*, August 6, 2018, https://www.economist.com/news/business/21703428-chinas-wechat-shows-way-social-medias-future-wechats-world; "From Weibo to WeChat," *Economist*, January 18, 2014, http://www.economist.com/news/china/21594296-after-crackdown-microblogs-sensitive-online-discussion-has-shifted-weibo-wechat; Che Hui Lien and Yang Cao, "Examining WeChat Users' Motivations, Trust, Attitudes, and Positive Word-of-Mouth: Evidence from China," *Computers in Human Behavior* 41 (December 1, 2014): 104–11, https://doi.org/10.1016/j.chb.2014.08.013; Xiaobo Wang and Baotong Gu, "The Communication Design of WeChat: Ideological as Well as Technical Aspects of Social Media," *Communication Design Quarterly Review* 4, no. 1 (November 2016): 23–35, https://doi.org/10.1145/2875501.2875503; Yang Wang, Yao Li, and Jian Tang, "Dwelling and Fleeting Encounters: Exploring Why People Use WeChat—A Mobile Instant Messenger," in *Proceedings of the 33rd Annual ACM Conference Extended Abstracts on Human Factors in Computing Systems* (New York: ACM, 2015), 1543–48, https://doi.org/10.1145/2702613.2732762; Qunyi Wei and

Yang Yang, "WeChat Library: A New Mode of Mobile Library Service," *Electronic Library* 35, no. 1 (January 2017): 198–208, https://doi.org/10.1108/EL-12-2015-0248; Xingting Zhang et al., "How the Public Uses Social Media WeChat to Obtain Health Information in China: A Survey Study," *BMC Medical Informatics and Decision Making* 17 (July 5, 2017): 71–79, https://doi.org/10.1186/s12911-017-0470-0; Shuai Yang, Sixing Chen, and Bin Li, "The Role of Business and Friendships on WeChat Business: An Emerging Business Model in China," *Journal of Global Marketing* 29, no. 4 (September 2016): 174–87, https://doi.org/10.1080/08911762.2016.1184363; Xiaoming Yang, Sunny Li Sun, and Ruby P. Lee, "Micro-Innovation Strategy: The Case of WeChat," *Asian Case Research Journal* 20, no. 2 (December 1, 2016): 401–27, https://doi.org/10.1142/S0218927516500152; Yuan Pingfang and Wang Rong, "On the Spreading of 'Rumors' in WeChat and It's [*sic*] Regulating Model Building: Taking the 'Rumors' Preventing in WeChat Official Account as an Example," *China Media Report Overseas* 11, no. 1 (January 2015): 17–23

34. Henry Jenkins, *Convergence Culture: Where Old and New Media Collide* (New York: New York University Press, 2008); Henry Jenkins, Sam Ford, and Joshua Green, *Spreadable Media: Creating Value and Meaning in a Networked Culture* (New York: New York University Press, 2013).

35. Olivia Solon, "Facebook's Oculus Reveals Stand-Alone Virtual Reality Headset," *Guardian*, October 11, 2017, http://www.theguardian.com/technology/2017/oct/11/oculus-go-virtual-reality-facebook; "How Virtual Reality Facilitates Social Connection," Facebook IQ, January 9, 2017, https://www.facebook.com/iq/articles/how-virtual-reality-facilitates-social-connection; Mark Zuckerberg, "Zuckerberg Facebook Post About Virtual Reality Demo at Oculus Connect—2016-10-6," Zuckerberg Transcripts 207, October 6, 2016, http://dc.uwm.edu/zuckerberg_files_transcripts/207.

36. Mark Zuckerberg, "Here's the Crazy Virtual Reality Demo I Did Live on Stage at Oculus Connect Today," Facebook, October 6, 2016, https://www.facebook.com/zuck/videos/10103154531425531; Zuckerberg, "Zuckerberg Facebook Post About Virtual Reality Demo at Oculus Connect—2016-10-6"; Mark Zuckerberg, "Oculus Connect 3 Opening Keynote: Mark Zuckerberg," Zuckerberg Transcripts 213, October 10, 2016, http://dc.uwm.edu/zuckerberg_files_transcripts/213.

Chapter 4: The Benevolence Machine

1. Mark Zuckerberg, "Mark Zuckerberg on Facebook's Social Good Forum," Zuckerberg Transcripts 251, November 17, 2016, http://dc.uwm.edu/zuckerberg_files_transcripts/251.

2. Siva Vaidhyanathan, *The Googlization of Everything (And Why We Should Worry)* (Berkeley: University of California Press, 2011).

3. Mark Zuckerberg, "Mark Zuckerberg's Letter to Investors: 'The Hacker Way,'" *Wired*, February 1, 2012, http://www.wired.com/2012/02/zuck-letter.

4. Zuckerberg, "Mark Zuckerberg's Letter to Investors"; Ben Agger, *Oversharing: Presentations of Self in the Internet Age* (New York: Routledge, 2015); Nicholas A. John, *The Age of Sharing* (London: Polity Press, 2017).

5. Zuckerberg, "Mark Zuckerberg's Letter to Investors."
6. David Vogel, *The Market for Virtue: The Potential and Limits of Corporate Social Responsibility* (Washington, DC: Brookings Institution Press, 2005).
7. Peter Nowak, "Zero Rating: How ISPs Give Some Customers Preferential Treatment," CBC News, April 7, 2015, http://www.cbc.ca/news/business/why-zero-rating-is-the-new-battleground-in-net-neutrality-debate-1.3015070; "Zero Rating: What It Is and Why You Should Care," Electronic Frontier Foundation, February 18, 2016, https://www.eff.org/deeplinks/2016/02/zero-rating-what-it-is-why-you-should-care.
8. Rahul Bhatia, "The Inside Story of Facebook's Biggest Setback," *Guardian*, May 12, 2016, https://www.theguardian.com/technology/2016/may/12/facebook-free-basics-india-zuckerberg. The sixty countries in which Facebook has launched Free Basics as of October 2017 include (in Africa and the Mideast) Angola, Benin, Cape Verde, Chad, Democratic Republic of the Congo, Gabon, Ghana, Guinea, Guinea-Bissau, Iraq, Jordan, Kenya, Liberia, Madagascar, Malawi, Mauritania, Mozambique, Niger, Nigeria, Republic of Congo, Rwanda, Senegal, Seychelles, South Africa, Tanzania, and Zambia; (in Asia and Oceania) Bangladesh, Cambodia, Indonesia, Maldives, Mongolia, Pakistan, Philippines, Thailand, Timor-Leste, Vanuatu, and Vietnam; and (in the Americas) Anguilla, Antigua and Barbuda, Aruba, Barbados, British Virgin Islands, Bonaire, Colombia, Curaçao, Dominica, El Salvador, Grenada, Guatemala, Honduras, Jamaica, Mexico, Montserrat, Panama, Peru, St. Kitts and Nevis, St. Lucia, St. Vincent and the Grenadines, Suriname, and Turks and Caicos.
9. Mark Zuckerberg, "Mark Zuckerberg on Connecting the World with Internet.org," Zuckerberg Transcripts 175, February 19, 2015, http://dc.uwm.edu/zuckerberg_files_transcripts/175; Mark Zuckerberg, "Video on Expansion of Internet.org," Zuckerberg Transcripts 258, May 4, 2015, http://dc.uwm.edu/zuckerberg_files_transcripts/258; Mark Zuckerberg, "Facebook's Mark Zuckerberg's Townhall in Delhi," Zuckerberg Transcripts 168, October 28, 2015, http://dc.uwm.edu/zuckerberg_files_transcripts/168; Mark Zuckerberg, "Free Basics Protects Net Neutrality," *Times of India*, December 28, 2015, http://blogs.timesofindia.indiatimes.com/toi-edit-page/free-basics-protects-net-neutrality; "India Blocks Zuckerberg's Free Net App," BBC News, February 8, 2016, http://www.bbc.com/news/technology-35522899; "Facebook Campaigns to Defend 'Free Basics,'" *Hindu*, December 23, 2015, http://www.thehindu.com/business/Industry/facebook-campaigns-to-defend-free-basics/article8022408.ece; "India Puts Brakes on Facebook's Free Basics Scheme," BBC News, December 23, 2015, http://www.bbc.com/news/technology-35169226; "TRAI Supports Net Neutrality, Effectively Bans Free Basics: All That Happened in This Debate," *Indian Express*, February 9, 2016, http://indianexpress.com/article/technology/tech-news-technology/facebook-free-basics-ban-net-neutrality-all-you-need-to-know.
10. Bhatia, "The Inside Story of Facebook's Biggest Setback."
11. Bhatia, "The Inside Story of Facebook's Biggest Setback."
12. Bhatia, "The Inside Story of Facebook's Biggest Setback."
13. Sheryl Sandberg, "Sheryl Sandberg Writes: Empowering Women Economically Is Good for Everyone," *Indian Express*, December 8, 2015, http://indianexpress.com/

article/opinion/columns/the-internet-gender-gap-widening-the-global-development-gap-needs-to-be-bridged.

14. Adi Narayan, "Andreessen Regrets India Tweets; Zuckerberg Laments Comments," Bloomberg, February 10, 2016, http://www.bloomberg.com/news/articles/2016-02-10/marc-andreessen-pro-colonialism-tweet-riles-up-india-tech-world.

15. A. A. Berle, "Corporate Powers as Powers in Trust," *Harvard Law Review* 44, no. 7 (1931): 1049–74, https://doi.org/10.2307/1331341; Adolf A. Berle et al., *The Modern Corporation and Private Property* (New York: Macmillan, 1933).

16. E. Merrick Dodd, "For Whom Are Corporate Managers Trustees?," *Harvard Law Review* 45, no. 7 (1932): 1153; Adolf A. Berle, *The 20th Century Capitalist Revolution* (New York: Harcourt, Brace, 1954).

17. Thomas Frank, *The Conquest of Cool: Business Culture, Counterculture, and the Rise of Hip Consumerism* (Chicago: University of Chicago Press, 1997); Gavin Wright, *Sharing the Prize: The Economics of the Civil Rights Revolution in the American South* (Cambridge, MA: Belknap Press of Harvard University Press, 2013); Frederick Allen, *Secret Formula: How Brilliant Marketing and Relentless Salesmanship Made Coca-Cola the Best-Known Product in the World* (New York: HarperBusiness, 1994).

18. Milton Friedman, "The Social Responsibility of Business Is to Increase Its Profits," *New York Times*, September 13, 1970, https://www.nytimes.com/1970/09/13/archives/article-15-no-title.html; Milton Friedman and Rose D. Friedman, *Capitalism and Freedom* (Chicago: University of Chicago Press, 2002).

19. Lynn A. Stout, *The Shareholder Value Myth: How Putting Shareholders First Harms Investors, Corporations, and the Public* (San Francisco: Berrett-Koehler, 2012).

20. R. Edward Freeman and John McVea, "A Stakeholder Approach to Strategic Management," 2001, available at Social Science Research Network, http://papers.ssrn.com/sol3/papers.cfm?abstract_id=263511; R. Edward Freeman, *Environmentalism and the New Logic of Business: How Firms Can Be Profitable and Leave Our Children a Living Planet* (New York: Oxford University Press, 2000); R. Edward Freeman, *Managing for Stakeholders: Survival, Reputation, and Success* (New Haven, CT: Yale University Press, 2007); John Mackey and Rajendra Sisodia, *Conscious Capitalism: Liberating the Heroic Spirit of Business* (Boston, MA: Harvard Business Review Press, 2013); Herman Aguinis and Ante Glavas, "What We Know and Don't Know About Corporate Social Responsibility: A Review and Research Agenda," *Journal of Management*, March 1, 2012, https://doi.org/10.1177/0149206311436079; "The Inside Story of Starbucks's Race Together Campaign, No Foam," *Fast Company*, June 15, 2015, https://www.fastcompany.com/3046890/the-inside-story-of-starbuckss-race-together-campaign-no-foam; Howard Schultz and Rajiv Chandrasekaran, *For Love of Country: What Our Veterans Can Teach Us About Citizenship, Heroism, and Sacrifice* (New York: Knopf, 2014); Howard Schultz and Dori Jones Yang, *Pour Your Heart into It: How Starbucks Built a Company One Cup at a Time* (New York: Hyperion, 1997); Howard Schultz and Joanne Gordon, *Onward: How Starbucks Fought for Its Life Without Losing Its Soul* (New York: Rodale, 2011); David Bollier, Aiming Higher: *25 Stories of How Companies Prosper by Combining Sound Management and Social*

Vision (New York: Amacom, 1996); Siva Vaidhyanathan, "Starbucks's Race to the Center of Civic Life," *Baffler*, March 18, 2015, https://thebaffler.com/latest/starbucks-race-together; John Seabrook, "Snacks for a Fat Planet," *New Yorker*, May 9, 2011, https://www.newyorker.com/magazine/2011/05/16/snacks-for-a-fat-planet; Econostats, "Unilever and the Failure of Corporate Social Responsibility," *Forbes*, March 15, 2017, https://www.forbes.com/sites/econostats/2017/03/15/unilever-and-the-failure-of-corporate-social-responsibility; Vivienne Walt, "Unilever's Paul Polman Shares His Plans to Save the World," *Fortune*, February 17, 2017, http://fortune.com/2017/02/17/unilever-paul-polman-responsibility-growth.

21. Milton Friedman, John Mackey, and T. J. Rodgers, "Rethinking the Social Responsibility of Business," *Reason*, October 2005, http://reason.com/archives/2005/10/01/rethinking-the-social-responsi.

22. "Largest Companies by Market Cap Today," Dogs of the Dow, October 23, 2017, http://dogsofthedow.com/largest-companies-by-market-cap.htm.

23. Christine A. Hemingway, *Corporate Social Entrepreneurship: Integrity Within* (Cambridge, UK: Cambridge University Press, 2013); Christine A. Hemingway, "Personal Values as a Catalyst for Corporate Social Entrepreneurship," *Journal of Business Ethics* 60, no. 3 (September 2005): 233–49, https://doi.org/10.1007/s10551-005-0132-5; Jeremy Moon, *Corporate Social Responsibility: A Very Short Introduction* (Oxford: Oxford University Press, 2014); Barry Smart, "Good for Business, Good Without Reservation? Veblen's Critique of Business Enterprise and Pecuniary Culture," *Journal of Classical Sociology* 15, no. 3 (August 1, 2015): 253–69, https://doi.org/10.1177/1468795X14558767; Subhabrata Bobby Banerjee, *Corporate Social Responsibility: The Good, the Bad and the Ugly* (Cheltenham, UK: Edward Elgar, 2009); Nicholas Thompson, "Instagram's CEO Wants to Clean Up the Internet—But Is That a Good @&#ing Idea?," *Wired*, September 2017, https://www.wired.com/2017/08/instagram-kevin-systrom-wants-to-clean-up-the-internet; Zuckerberg, "Mark Zuckerberg on Facebook's Social Good Forum"; Andrew Palmer, *Smart Money: How High-Stakes Financial Innovation Is Reshaping Our World—for the Better* (New York: Basic Books, 2015); Stephanie Strom, "To Be Good Citizens, Report Says, Companies Should Just Focus on Bottom Line," *New York Times*, June 14, 2011, http://www.nytimes.com/2011/06/15/business/15charity.html; Robert H. Frank, *What Price the Moral High Ground? Ethical Dilemmas in Competitive Environments* (Princeton, NJ: Princeton University Press, 2004); Vogel, *The Market for Virtue*; Andrew Crane, *The Oxford Handbook of Corporate Social Responsibility* (Oxford: Oxford University Press, 2008); Brad Stone and Mark Bergen, "Everyone's Mad at Google and Sundar Pichai Has to Fix It," *Bloomberg*, October 19, 2017, https://www.bloomberg.com/news/features/2017-10-19/everyone-s-mad-at-google-and-sundar-pichai-has-to-fix-it.

24. James Buchanan, "Politics Without Romance: A Sketch of Positive Public Choice Theory and Its Normative Implications," in *The Logical Foundation of Constitutional Liberty*, vol. 1 of *The Collected Works of James M. Buchanan* (Indianapolis, IN: Liberty Fund, 1999); James M. Buchanan and Gordon Tullock, *The Calculus of Consent: Logical Foundations of Constitutional Democracy* (Ann Arbor:

University of Michigan Press, 1965); James M. Buchanan and Robert D. Tollison, *Theory of Public Choice; Political Applications of Economics* (Ann Arbor: University of Michigan Press, 1972); Hugh Stretton and Lionel Orchard, *Public Goods, Public Enterprise, Public Choice: Theoretical Foundations of the Contemporary Attack on Government* (New York: St. Martin's Press, 1994); Lars Udehn, *The Limits of Public Choice: A Sociological Critique of the Economic Theory of Politics* (London; Routledge, 1996); Anthony Downs, *An Economic Theory of Democracy* (New York: Harper, 1957); Mancur Olson, *The Logic of Collective Action; Public Goods and the Theory of Groups* (Cambridge, MA: Harvard University Press, 1971).

25. Udehn, *The Limits of Public Choice*; Vaidhyanathan, *The Googlization of Everything*.

26. Aguinis and Glavas, "What We Know and Don't Know About Corporate Social Responsibility"; Banerjee, *Corporate Social Responsibility*; Bidyut Chakrabarty, *Corporate Social Responsibility in India* (Abingdon, Oxon: Routledge, 2011); Crane, *The Oxford Handbook of Corporate Social Responsibility*; Econostats, "Unilever and the Failure of Corporate Social Responsibility"; Jean-Pascal Gond and Jeremy Moon, eds., *Corporate Social Responsibility*, 4 vols. (London: Routledge, 2012); André Habisch, *Corporate Social Responsibility Across Europe* (Berlin: Springer, 2005); Hemingway, *Corporate Social Entrepreneurship*; Hemingway, "Personal Values as a Catalyst for Corporate Social Entrepreneurship"; David Henderson, *Misguided Virtue: False Notions of Corporate Social Responsibility* (London: Institute of Economic Affairs, 2001); Steve May, George Cheney, and Juliet Roper, *The Debate over Corporate Social Responsibility* (Oxford: Oxford University Press, 2007); Abagail McWilliams and Donald Siegel, "Corporate Social Responsibility: A Theory of the Firm Perspective," *Academy of Management Review* 26, no. 1 (January 1, 2001): 117–27, https://doi.org/10.5465/AMR.2001.4011987; Moon, *Corporate Social Responsibility*; Vogel, *The Market for Virtue*.

27. Clay Shirky, *Here Comes Everybody: The Power of Organizing Without Organizations* (New York: Penguin, 2008); Clay Shirky, "The Political Power of Social Media: Technology, the Public Sphere, and Political Change," *Foreign Affairs* 90, no. 1 (2011): 28–41, http://www.jstor.org/stable/25800379.

28. Zuckerberg, "Mark Zuckerberg's Letter to Investors."

Chapter 5: The Protest Machine

1. "We Are All Khaled Said," accessed December 3, 2017, https://www.facebook.com/elshaheeed.co.uk; Jennifer Preston, "Facebook and YouTube Fuel the Egyptian Protests," *New York Times*, February 5, 2011, https://www.nytimes.com/2011/02/06/world/middleeast/06face.html.

2. Wael Ghonim, "Inside the Egyptian Revolution," TED Talk, March 2011, https://www.ted.com/talks/wael_ghonim_inside_the_egyptian_revolution.

3. Michael Slackman and Mona El-Naggar, "Egyptian Forces Beat Back Demonstration for Judges," *New York Times*, May 11, 2006, https://www.nytimes.com/2006/05/11/world/middleeast/11cnd-egypt.html; Preston, "Facebook and YouTube Fuel the

Egyptian Protests"; Adham Hamed, *Revolution as a Process: The Case of the Egyptian Uprising*, Contemporary Studies on the MENA Region (Vienna: Wiener Verlag für Sozialforschung, 2014); Jeroen Gunning and Ilan Zvi Baron, *Why Occupy a Square? People, Protests, and Movements in the Egyptian Revolution* (Oxford: Oxford University Press, 2014); Wael Ghonim, *Revolution 2.0: The Power of the People Is Greater than the People in Power: A Memoir* (Boston: Houghton Mifflin Harcourt, 2012); Ghonim, "Inside the Egyptian Revolution."

4. Sam Gustin, "Social Media Sparked, Accelerated Egypt's Revolutionary Fire," *Wired*, February 11, 2011, https://www.wired.com/2011/02/egypts-revolutionary-fire.

5. Zeynep Tufekci, *Twitter and Tear Gas: The Power and Fragility of Networked Protest* (New Haven, CT: Yale University Press, 2017).

6. Ghonim, "Inside the Egyptian Revolution."

7. "We Are All Khaled Said."

8. Tufekci, *Twitter and Tear Gas*.

9. Siva Vaidhyanathan, *The Googlization of Everything (And Why We Should Worry)* (Berkeley: University of California Press, 2011), 121–24.

10. Andrew Shapiro, *The Control Revolution: How the Internet Is Putting Individuals in Charge and Changing the World We Know* (New York: PublicAffairs, 1999), 6–7. Also see Gladys Ganley, *Unglued Empire: The Soviet Experience with Communications Technologies* (Norwood, NJ: Ablex, 1996).

11. Marshall McLuhan, *The Gutenberg Galaxy: The Making of Typographic Man* (Toronto: University of Toronto Press, 1962); Marshall McLuhan, *Understanding Media: The Extensions of Man* (New York: Routledge, 2008); Elizabeth Eisenstein, *The Printing Press as an Agent of Change: Communications and Cultural Transformations in Early Modern Europe* (Cambridge, UK: Cambridge University Press, 1979); Elizabeth L. Eisenstein, "An Unacknowledged Revolution Revisited," *American Historical Review* 107, no. 1 (February 2002): 87–105, http://www.jstor.org/stable/2692544; Bernard Bailyn, *The Ideological Origins of the American Revolution*, enlarged ed. (Cambridge, MA: Belknap Press of Harvard University Press, 1992).

12. Gordon Wood, *The Radicalism of the American Revolution* (New York: Knopf, 1992); Adrian Johns, "How to Acknowledge a Revolution," *American Historical Review* 107, no. 1 (February 2002): 106–25, http://www.jstor.org/stable/2692545; Adrian Johns, *The Nature of the Book: Print and Knowledge in the Making* (Chicago: University of Chicago Press, 1998).

13. Tony Judt, *Postwar: A History of Europe Since 1945* (New York: Penguin, 2005), 628–29. Also see Brian Hanrahan, "How Tiananmen Shook Europe," BBC, June 5, 2009, http://news.bbc.co.uk/2/hi/asia-pacific/8077883.stm.

14. Judt, *Postwar*, 585–605.

15. Rebecca MacKinnon, *Consent of the Networked: The World-Wide Struggle for Internet Freedom* (New York: Basic Books, 2012); Evgeny Morozov, *The Net Delusion: The Dark Side of Internet Freedom* (New York: PublicAffairs, 2011); Marc Lynch, "The Internet Freedom Agenda," *Foreign Policy*, January 22, 2010, https://foreignpolicy.com/2010/01/22/the-internet-freedom-agenda.

16. "Twitter Revolution in Iran," CNN, June 18, 2009, https://youtu.be/OpQC-DJL_ Ho; "Lessons from the 'Twitter Revolution,'" CNN, February 15, 2011, https:// youtu.be/OktVofgzoOo.

17. Tufekci, *Twitter and Tear Gas*.

18. Clay Shirky, *Here Comes Everybody: The Power of Organizing Without Organizations* (New York: Penguin, 2008); Clay Shirky, "The Political Power of Social Media: Technology, the Public Sphere, and Political Change," *Foreign Affairs* 90, no. 1 (2011): 28–41, http://www.jstor.org/stable/25800379; Tufekci, *Twitter and Tear Gas*; Siva Vaidhyanathan, *The Anarchist in the Library: How the Clash Between Freedom and Control Is Hacking the Real World and Crashing the System* (New York: Basic Books, 2004); Mary Jordan, "Going Mobile: Text Messages Guide Filipino Protesters," *Washington Post*, August 25, 2006, http://www.washingtonpost.com/ wp-dyn/content/article/2006/08/24/AR2006082401379.html; Daniel Trottier and Christian Fuchs, *Social Media, Politics and the State: Protests, Revolutions, Riots, Crime and Policing in the Age of Facebook, Twitter and YouTube* (New York: Routledge, 2015); Gunning and Baron, *Why Occupy a Square?*

19. Malcolm Gladwell, "Small Change," *New Yorker*, September 27, 2010, https://www. newyorker.com/magazine/2010/10/04/small-change-malcolm-gladwell.

20. Robert Mackey, "Video That Set Off Tunisia's Uprising," *The Lede* (blog), *New York Times*, January 22, 2011, https://thelede.blogs.nytimes.com/2011/01/22/video- that-triggered-tunisias-uprising; Mohamed Zayani, *Networked Publics and Digital Contention: The Politics of Everyday Life in Tunisia* (New York: Oxford University Press, 2015); Marwan M. Kraidy, *The Naked Blogger of Cairo: Creative Insurgency in the Arab World* (Cambridge, MA: Harvard University Press, 2016).

21. Shirky, *Here Comes Everybody*; Shirky, "The Political Power of Social Media"; Bill Wasik, "Gladwell vs. Shirky: A Year Later, Scoring the Debate over Social-Media Revolutions," *Wired*, December 27, 2011, https://www.wired.com/2011/12/gladwell-vs-shirky.

22. Shirky, "The Political Power of Social Media," 38.

23. Shirky, "The Political Power of Social Media," 31.

24. Shirky, "The Political Power of Social Media," 32–35.

25. Katy E. Pearce, "Democratizing Kompromat: The Affordances of Social Media for State-Sponsored Harassment," *Information, Communication and Society* 18, no. 10 (October 3, 2015): 1158–74, https://doi.org/10.1080/1369118X.2015.1021705; Katy E. Pearce and Sarah Kendzior, "Networked Authoritarianism and Social Media in Azerbaijan," *Journal of Communication* 62, no. 2 (April 1, 2012): 283–98, https:// doi.org/10.1111/j.1460-2466.2012.01633.x; Katy E. Pearce and Jessica Vitak, "Performing Honor Online: The Affordances of Social Media for Surveillance and Impression Management in an Honor Culture," *New Media and Society* 18, no. 11 (December 1, 2016): 2595–612, https://doi.org/10.1177/1461444815600279; Pearce, "Two Can Play at That Game," https://www.questia.com/library/ journal/1G1-358056868/two-can-play-at-that-game-social-media-opportunities.

26. Wael Ghonim, "Let's Design Social Media That Drives Real Change," TED Talk, December 2015, https://www.ted.com/talks/wael_ghonim_let_s_design_social_ media_that_drives_real_change.

27. Ghonim, "Let's Design Social Media."

Chapter 6: The Political Machine

1. Alex Hunt and Brian Wheeler, "Brexit: All You Need to Know About the UK Leaving the EU," BBC News, August 15, 2017, http://www.bbc.com/news/uk-politics-32810887; Nate Cohn, "Why the Surprise over 'Brexit'? Don't Blame the Polls," *New York Times*, June 24, 2016, https://www.nytimes.com/2016/06/25/upshot/why-the-surprise-over-brexit-dont-blame-the-polls.html.

2. Hunt and Wheeler, "Brexit"; Michael Bosetta, "#25: The 2017 British Elections on Social Media, with Dr. Anamaria Dutceac Segesten," Social Media and Politics, June 15, 2017, https://socialmediaandpolitics.simplecast.fm//25.

3. "2016 Election Results: State Maps, Live Updates," accessed August 19, 2017, http://www.cnn.com/election/results; "Presidential Election Results: Donald J. Trump Wins," *New York Times*, accessed August 19, 2017, http://www.nytimes.com/elections/results/president.

4. "2016 Election Results"; "Presidential Election Results."

5. "The Power of Big Data and Psychographics," Concordia Summit, 2016, https://www.youtube.com/watch?v=n8Dd5aVXLCc.

6. *Secrets of Silicon Valley*, series 1, episode 2, "The Persuasion Machine," BBC, accessed August 15, 2017, http://www.bbc.co.uk/iplayer/episode/b091zhtk/secrets-of-silicon-valley-series-1-2-the-persuasion-machine; Jamie Bartlett, "Tonight— 8pm on BBC2. I Get Inside Trump Digital HQ to Understand How He Won. #SecretsOfSiliconValley https://T.co/xnIdT7kod6," August 13, 2017, https://twitter.com/JamieJBartlett/status/896794978072092672; Sasha Issenberg, "Cruz-Connected Data Miner Aims to Get Inside U.S. Voters' Heads," Bloomberg, November 12, 2015, https://www.bloomberg.com/news/features/2015-11-12/is-the-republican-party-s-killer-data-app-for-real-; Jamie Doward and Alice Gibbs, "Did Cambridge Analytica Influence the Brexit Vote and the US Election?," *Observer*, March 4, 2017, http://www.theguardian.com/politics/2017/mar/04/nigel-oakes-cambridge-analytica-what-role-brexit-trump; Michael Bosetta, "#24: Donald Trump and Scott Walker's Digital Strategy on Social Media, with Matthew Oczkowski," Social Media and Politics, May 29, 2017, https://socialmediaandpolitics.simplecast.fm//24.

7. "The Power of Big Data and Psychographics."

8. "The Power of Big Data and Psychographics."

9. "Cambridge Analytica Congratulates President-Elect Donald Trump and Vice President-Elect Mike Pence," November 9, 2016, http://www.prnewswire.com/news-releases/cambridge-analytica-congratulates-president-elect-donald-trump-and-vice-president-elect-mike-pence-300359987.html.

10. Hannes Grassegger and Mikael Krogerus, "Ich Habe Nur Gezeigt, Dass Es die Bombe Gibt," *Das Magazin*, December 3, 2016, https://www.dasmagazin.ch/2016/12/03/ich-habe-nur-gezeigt-dass-es-die-bombe-gibt; Hannes Grassegger and Mikael Krogerus, "The Data That Turned the World Upside Down," *Motherboard*, January 28, 2017, https://motherboard.vice.com/en_us/article/mg9vvn/how-our-likes-helped-trump-win.

11. Grassegger and Krogerus, "The Data That Turned the World Upside Down."

12. Joseph Stromberg, "Watch: Why the Myers-Briggs Test Is Totally Meaningless," *Vox*, July 15, 2014, https://www.vox.com/2014/7/15/5881947/myers-briggs-personality-test-meaningless.

13. Michal Kosinski, David Stillwell, and Thore Graepel, "Private Traits and Attributes Are Predictable from Digital Records of Human Behavior," *Proceedings of the National Academy of Sciences* 110, no. 15 (April 9, 2013): 5802–5, doi:10.1073/pnas.1218772110.

14. Grassegger and Krogerus, "The Data That Turned the World Upside Down."

15. Matthew Rosenberg, Nicholas Confessore, and Carole Cadwalladr, "How Trump Consultants Exploited the Facebook Data of Millions," *New York Times*, March 17, 2018, https://www.nytimes.com/2018/03/17/us/politics/cambridge-analytica-trump-campaign.html; Ryan Mac, "Cambridge Analytica Whistleblower Said He Wanted to Create 'NSA's Wet Dream,'" BuzzFeed, accessed March 22, 2018, https://www.buzzfeed.com/ryanmac/christopher-wylie-cambridge-analytica-scandal; Shivam Vij, "The Inside Story of What Cambridge Analytica Actually Did in India," ThePrint, March 22, 2018, https://theprint.in/politics/exclusive-inside-story-cambridge-analytica-actually-india/44012; Andy Kroll, "Cloak and Data: The Real Story Behind Cambridge Analytica's Rise and Fall," *Mother Jones*, March 23, 2018, https://www.motherjones.com/politics/2018/03/cloak-and-data-cambridge-analytica-robert-mercer; Siva Vaidhyanathan, "Don't Delete Facebook. Do Something About It," *New York Times*, March 24, 2018, https://www.nytimes.com/2018/03/24/opinion/sunday/delete-facebook-does-not-fix-problem.html.

16. Nicholas Confessore and Danny Hakim, "Data Firm Says 'Secret Sauce' Aided Trump; Many Scoff," *New York Times*, March 6, 2017, https://www.nytimes.com/2017/03/06/us/politics/cambridge-analytica.html.

17. David Karpf, "Will the Real Psychometric Targeters Please Stand Up?," Civic Hall, February 1, 2017, https://civichall.org/civicist/will-the-real-psychometric-targeters-please-stand-up.

18. Jane Mayer, "The Reclusive Hedge-Fund Tycoon Behind the Trump Presidency," *New Yorker*, March 17, 2017, http://www.newyorker.com/magazine/2017/03/27/the-reclusive-hedge-fund-tycoon-behind-the-trump-presidency.

19. Alexis C. Madrigal, "Hillary Clinton Was the First Casualty in the New Information Wars," *Atlantic*, May 31, 2017, https://www.theatlantic.com/technology/archive/2017/05/hillary-clinton-information-wars/528765.

20. Alexander Nix, "How Big Data Got the Better of Donald Trump," Campaign, February 10, 2016, http://www.campaignlive.co.uk/article/big-data-better-donald-trump/1383025; Doward and Gibbs, "Did Cambridge Analytica Influence the Brexit Vote and the US Election?"

21. Carole Cadwalladr, "The Great British Brexit Robbery: How Our Democracy Was Hijacked," *Observer*, May 7, 2017, http://www.theguardian.com/technology/2017/may/07/the-great-british-brexit-robbery-hijacked-democracy; Carole Cadwalladr, "Robert Mercer: The Big Data Billionaire Waging War on Mainstream Media," *Observer*, February 26, 2017, http://www.theguardian.com/politics/2017/feb/26/robert-mercer-breitbart-war-on-media-steve-bannon-donald-trump-nigel-farage; *Secrets of Silicon Valley*, series 1, episode 2, "The Persuasion Machine"; "Did Cambridge

Analytica Play a Role in the EU Referendum?," BBC, June 27, 2017, http://www.bbc.com/news/av/uk-40423629/did-cambridge-analytica-play-a-role-in-the-eu-referendum; Robert Booth, "Inquiry Launched into Targeting of UK Voters Through Social Media," *Guardian*, May 17, 2017, http://www.theguardian.com/technology/2017/may/17/inquiry-launched-into-how-uk-parties-target-voters-through-social-media.

22. Siva Vaidhyanathan, "Facebook Was Letting Down Users Years Before Cambridge Analytica," *Slate*, March 20, 2018, https://slate.com/technology/2018/03/facebooks-data-practices-were-letting-down-users-years-before-cambridge-analytica.html.

23. Lauren Etter, Vernon Silver, and Sarah Frier, "The Facebook Team Helping Regimes That Fight Their Opposition," Bloomberg, December 21, 2017, https://www.bloomberg.com/news/features/2017-12-21/inside-the-facebook-team-helping-regimes-that-reach-out-and-crack-down.

24. Zeynep Tufekci, "Engineering the Public: Big Data, Surveillance and Computational Politics," *First Monday* 19, no. 7 (July 2, 2014), http://firstmonday.org/ojs/index.php/fm/article/view/4901; Joe McGinniss, *The Selling of the President, 1968* (New York: Trident Press, 1969); danah boyd and Kate Crawford, "Critical Questions for Big Data," *Information, Communication and Society* 15, no. 5 (June 1, 2012): 662–79, doi:10.1080/1369118X.2012.678878; Daniel Kreiss, *Prototype Politics: Technology-Intensive Campaigning and the Data of Democracy* (Oxford: Oxford University Press, 2016).

25. Philip N. Howard, *New Media Campaigns and the Managed Citizen*, Communication, Society, and Politics (Cambridge, UK: Cambridge University Press, 2006), 172–79.

26. Howard, *New Media Campaigns*, 185–86.

27. Michael X. Delli Carpini, "Gen.com: Youth, Civic Engagement, and the New Information Environment," *Political Communication* 17, no. 4 (2000): 341–49; Michael X. Delli Carpini and Scott Keeter, *What Americans Know About Politics and Why It Matters* (New Haven, CT: Yale University Press, 1996).

28. Zizi Papacharissi, *Affective Publics: Sentiment, Technology, and Politics* (New York: Oxford University Press, 2014); Zizi Papacharissi, *A Private Sphere: Democracy in a Digital Age* (Cambridge, UK: Polity, 2010).

29. Karpf, "Will the Real Psychometric Targeters Please Stand Up?"; David Karpf, *The MoveOn Effect: The Unexpected Transformation of American Political Advocacy* (New York: Oxford University Press, 2012); Sasha Issenberg, *The Victory Lab: The Secret Science of Winning Campaigns* (New York: Crown, 2012); Kreiss, *Prototype Politics*; Eitan D. Hersh, *Hacking the Electorate: How Campaigns Perceive Voters* (New York: Cambridge University Press, 2015).

30. Jonathan Zittrain, "Facebook Could Decide an Election—Without You Ever Finding Out," *New Republic*, June 1, 2014, https://newrepublic.com/article/117878/information-fiduciary-solution-facebook-digital-gerrymandering.

31. Philip Bump, "How Facebook Plans to Become One of the Most Powerful Tools in Politics," *Washington Post*, November 26, 2014, https://www.washingtonpost.com/news/the-fix/wp/2014/11/26/how-facebook-plans-to-become-one-of-the-most-powerful-tools-in-politics.

32. Hersh, *Hacking the Electorate*; Grassegger and Krogerus, "The Data That Turned the World Upside Down."

33. Steven Bertoni, "Exclusive Interview: How Jared Kushner Won Trump the White House," *Forbes*, November 22, 2016, http://www.forbes.com/sites/stevenbertoni/2016/11/22/exclusive-interview-how-jared-kushner-won-trump-the-white-house.

34. Charlie Warzel, "Trump Fundraiser: Facebook Employee Was Our 'MVP,'" BuzzFeed, November 12, 2016, https://www.buzzfeed.com/charliewarzel/trump-fundraiser-facebook-employee-was-our-mvp; Bosetta, "Donald Trump and Scott Walker's Digital Strategy on Social Media"; Issie Lapowsky, "The Man Behind Trump's Bid to Finally Take Digital Seriously," *Wired*, August 19, 2016, https://www.wired.com/2016/08/man-behind-trumps-bid-finally-take-digital-seriously; Issie Lapowsky, "This Is How Facebook Actually Won Trump the Presidency," *Wired*, November 15, 2016, https://www.wired.com/2016/11/facebook-won-trump-election-not-just-fake-news; Sue Halpern, "How He Used Facebook to Win," *New York Review of Books*, June 8, 2017, http://www.nybooks.com/articles/2017/06/08/how-trump-used-facebook-to-win.

35. Author interview with David Carroll, New York, 2017; Joshua Green and Sasha Issenberg, "Inside the Trump Bunker, with Days to Go," Bloomberg, October 27, 2016, https://www.bloomberg.com/news/articles/2016-10-27/inside-the-trump-bunker-with-12-days-to-go.

36. Author interview with David Carroll, New York, 2017.

37. Daniel Kreiss and Shannon McGregor, "Technology Firms Shape Political Communication: The Work of Microsoft, Facebook, Twitter, and Google with Campaigns During the 2016 U.S. Presidential Cycle," *Political Communication*, published online October 26, 2017, https://doi.org/10.1080/10584609.2017.1364814.

Chapter 7: The Disinformation Machine

1. Alex Stamos, "An Update on Information Operations on Facebook," Facebook Newsroom, September 6, 2017, https://newsroom.fb.com/news/2017/09/information-operations-update; Carol D. Leonnig, Tom Hamburger, and Rosalind S. Helderman, "Facebook Says It Sold Political Ads to Russian Company During 2016 Election," *Washington Post*, September 6, 2017, https://www.washingtonpost.com/politics/facebook-says-it-sold-political-ads-to-russian-company-during-2016-election/2017/09/06/32f01fd2-931e-11e7-89fa-bb822a46da5b_story.html; Craig Silverman, "Facebook's Russian Ads Disclosure Opens a New Front That Could Lead to Regulation," BuzzFeed, accessed September 7, 2017, https://www.buzzfeed.com/craigsilverman/facebooks-russian-ads-disclosure-opens-a-new-front-that.

2. Jen Weedon, William Nuland, and Alex Stamos, "Information Operations and Facebook," April 27, 2017, 3, https://fbnewsroomus.files.wordpress.com/2017/04/facebook-and-information-operations-v1.pdf.

3. "Facebook Unpublished Page Post Ads," Facebook for Business, accessed September 7, 2017, https://www.facebook.com/business/a/online-sales/unpublished-page-posts.

4. Spencer Ackerman, Ben Collins, and Kevin Poulsen, "Exclusive: Russia Used Facebook Events to Organize Anti-Immigrant Rallies on U.S. Soil," *Daily Beast*, September 11, 2017, http://www.thedailybeast.com/exclusive-russia-used-facebook-events-to-organize-anti-immigrant-rallies-on-us-soil; Ned Parker, Jonathan Landay, and John Walcott, "Putin-Linked Think Tank Drew Up Plan to Sway 2016 US

Election—Documents," Reuters, April 21, 2017, https://www.reuters.com/article/us-usa-russia-election-exclusive/exclusive-putin-linked-think-tank-drew-up-plan-to-sway-2016-u-s-election-documents-idUSKBN17L2N3; Craig Timberg, "Russian Propaganda Effort Helped Spread 'Fake News' During Election, Experts Say," *Washington Post*, November 24, 2016, https://www.washingtonpost.com/business/economy/russian-propaganda-effort-helped-spread-fake-news-during-election-experts-say/2016/11/24/793903b6-8a40-4ca9-b712-716af66098fe_story.html; Casey Michel, "How Russia Created the Most Popular Texas Secession Page on Facebook," Medium, September 7, 2017, https://medium.com/@cjcmichel/how-russia-created-the-most-popular-texas-secession-page-on-facebook-fd4dfd05ee5c.

5. David Ingram, "Facebook to Keep Wraps on Political Ads Data Despite Researchers' Demands," Reuters, June 22, 2017, http://www.reuters.com/article/us-usa-politics-facebook-idUSKBN19D1CN.

6. Josh Constine, "Facebook Beats in Q4 with $8.81B Revenue, Slower Growth to 1.86B Users," TechCrunch, accessed September 8, 2017, http://social.techcrunch.com/2017/02/01/facebook-q4-2016-earnings.

7. Ingram, "Facebook to Keep Wraps on Political Ads Data Despite Researchers' Demands."

8. "Germany Approves Plans to Fine Social Media Firms up to €50m," *Guardian*, June 30, 2017, https://www.theguardian.com/media/2017/jun/30/germany-approves-plans-to-fine-social-media-firms-up-to-50m; "Hate Speech and Anti-Migrant Posts: Facebook's Rules," *Guardian*, May 24, 2017, http://www.theguardian.com/news/gallery/2017/may/24/hate-speech-and-anti-migrant-posts-facebooks-rules; Robert Booth, "Inquiry Launched into Targeting of UK Voters Through Social Media," *Guardian*, May 17, 2017, http://www.theguardian.com/technology/2017/may/17/inquiry-launched-into-how-uk-parties-target-voters-through-social-media.

9. Sam Woolley and Philip N. Howard, "Computational Propaganda Worldwide: Executive Summary," Computational Propaganda Research Project, Oxford Internet Institute, June 19, 2017, http://comprop.oii.ox.ac.uk/2017/06/19/computational-propaganda-worldwide-executive-summary; author interview with Philip Howard, Oxford, UK, 2017; Samantha Bradshaw and Philip N. Howard, "Troops, Trolls and Troublemakers: A Global Inventory of Organized Social Media Manipulation," working paper, Oxford Internet Institute, 2017, http://comprop.oii.ox.ac.uk/2017/07/17/troops-trolls-and-trouble-makers-a-global-inventory-of-organized-social-media-manipulation.

10. Caroline Jack, "What's Propaganda Got to Do with It?," Data and Society, January 5, 2017, https://points.datasociety.net/whats-propaganda-got-to-do-with-it-5b88d78c3282#.4iz7eltzy; Caroline Jack, "Lexicon of Lies: Terms for Problematic Information," Data and Society, August 9, 2017, https://datasociety.net/output/lexicon-of-lies; Whitney Phillips and Ryan M. Milner, *The Ambivalent Internet: Mischief, Oddity, and Antagonism Online* (Cambridge, UK: Polity, 2017); Whitney Phillips, *This Is Why We Can't Have Nice Things: Mapping the Relationship Between Online Trolling and Mainstream Culture* (Cambridge, MA: MIT Press, 2016); Whitney Phillips, Jessica Beyer, and Gabriella Coleman, "Trolling Scholars Debunk the Idea That the Alt-Right's Shitposters Have Magic Powers," Motherboard,

March 22, 2017, https://motherboard.vice.com/en_us/article/z4k549/trolling-scholars-debunk-the-idea-that-the-alt-rights-trolls-have-magic-powers; danah boyd, "Hacking the Attention Economy," Data and Society, January 5, 2017, https://points.datasociety.net/hacking-the-attention-economy-9fa1daca7a37#.bnbbhk723; danah boyd, "The Information War Has Begun," January 27, 2017, *Apophenia* (blog), http://www.zephoria.org/thoughts/archives/2017/01/27/the-information-war-has-begun.html.

11. Alice E. Marwick and Rebecca Lewis, "Media Manipulation and Disinformation Online," Data and Society, May 15, 2017, https://datasociety.net/output/media-manipulation-and-disinfo-online; author interview with Alice Marwick, New York, 2017; Samanth Subramanian, "Meet the Macedonian Teens Who Mastered Fake News and Corrupted the US Election," *Wired*, February 15, 2017, https://www.wired.com/2017/02/veles-macedonia-fake-news; Ryan Holiday, *Trust Me, I'm Lying: The Tactics and Confessions of a Media Manipulator* (New York: Portfolio, 2012); boyd, "Hacking the Attention Economy."

12. boyd, "Hacking the Attention Economy"; danah boyd, "Google and Facebook Can't Just Make Fake News Disappear," *Wired*, March 27, 2017, https://www.wired.com/2017/03/google-and-facebook-cant-just-make-fake-news-disappear.

13. Judith Donath, "Why Fake News Stories Thrive Online," CNN, November 20, 2016, http://www.cnn.com/2016/11/20/opinions/fake-news-stories-thrive-donath/index.html.

14. David Rowan, "How BuzzFeed Mastered Social Sharing to Become a Media Giant for a New Era," *Wired*, January 2, 2014, http://www.wired.co.uk/article/buzzfeed.

15. Timothy P. Carney, "Study Showing 'Fake News' Beating 'Real News' Looks like Garbage," *Washington Examiner*, November 16, 2016, http://www.washington-examiner.com/study-showing-fake-news-beating-real-news-looks-like-garbage/article/2607626; Paul Crookston, "Report on Scourge of Fake News Turns Out to Be Faked," *National Review*, November 17, 2016, http://www.nationalreview.com/article/442291/buzzfeed-facebook-fake-news-study-methodology-questioned; Jerome Hudson, "How BuzzFeed Editor Craig Silverman Helped Generate the 'Fake News' Crisis," Breitbart, December 20, 2016, http://www.breitbart.com/big-journalism/2016/12/20/how-buzzfeed-editor-craig-silverman-helped-generate-the-fake-news-crisis.

16. Margaret Sullivan, "It's Time to Retire the Tainted Term 'Fake News,'" *Washington Post*, January 6, 2017, https://www.washingtonpost.com/lifestyle/style/its-time-to-retire-the-tainted-term-fake-news/2017/01/06/a5a7516c-d375-11e6-945a-76f69a399dd5_story.html.

17. Marc Fisher, John Woodrow Cox, and Peter Hermann, "Pizzagate: From Rumor, to Hashtag, to Gunfire in D.C.," *Washington Post*, December 6, 2016, https://www.washingtonpost.com/local/pizzagate-from-rumor-to-hashtag-to-gunfire-in-dc/2016/12/06/4c7def50-bbd4-11e6-94ac-3d324840106c_story.html.

18. Jack, "Lexicon of Lies."

19. Peter Pomerantsev, *Nothing Is True and Everything Is Possible: The Surreal Heart of the New Russia* (New York: PublicAffairs, 2015); Ezra Klein, "Danah Boyd on Why Fake News Is So Easy to Believe," *The Ezra Klein Show*, June 27, 2017, https://

soundcloud.com/ezra-klein-show/danah-boyd-on-why-fake-news-is-so-easy-to-believe; danah boyd, "Did Media Literacy Backfire?," Data and Society, January 5, 2017, https://points.datasociety.net/did-media-literacy-backfire-7418c084d88d#.td2jdvf4n; boyd, "The Information War Has Begun."

20. Katy E. Pearce, "Democratizing Kompromat: The Affordances of Social Media for State-Sponsored Harassment," *Information, Communication and Society* 18, no. 10 (October 3, 2015): 1158–74, https://doi.org/10.1080/1369118X.2015.1021705; Katy E. Pearce and Sarah Kendzior, "Networked Authoritarianism and Social Media in Azerbaijan," *Journal of Communication* 62, no. 2 (April 1, 2012): 283–98, https://doi.org/10.1111/j.1460-2466.2012.01633.x; Katy E. Pearce and Jessica Vitak, "Performing Honor Online: The Affordances of Social Media for Surveillance and Impression Management in an Honor Culture," *New Media and Society* 18, no. 11 (December 1, 2016): 2595–612, https://doi.org/10.1177/1461444815600279; Katy E. Pearce, "Two Can Play at That Game: Social Media Opportunities in Azerbaijan for Government and Opposition," accessed September 13, 2017, https://www.academia.edu/5833149/Two_Can_Play_at_that_Game_Social_Media_Opportunities_in_Azerbaijan_for_Government_and_Opposition.

21. Seva Gunitsky, "Corrupting the Cyber-Commons: Social Media as a Tool of Autocratic Stability," October 6, 2014, available at Social Science Research Network, https://papers.ssrn.com/abstract=2506038.

22. Pearce, "Democratizing Kompromat"; Gunitsky, "Corrupting the Cyber-Commons."

23. Scott Shane, "Purged Facebook Page Tied to the Kremlin Spread Anti-Immigrant Bile," *New York Times*, September 12, 2017, https://www.nytimes.com/2017/09/12/us/politics/russia-facebook-election.html; Adrian Chen, "The Agency," *New York Times Magazine*, June 2, 2015, https://www.nytimes.com/2015/06/07/magazine/the-agency.html; Jim Rutenberg, "RT, Sputnik and Russia's New Theory of War," *New York Times Magazine*, September 13, 2017, https://www.nytimes.com/2017/09/13/magazine/rt-sputnik-and-russias-new-theory-of-war.html; Julia Carrie Wong, "Facebook Blocks Chechnya Activist Page in Latest Case of Wrongful Censorship," *Guardian*, June 6, 2017, https://www.theguardian.com/technology/2017/jun/06/facebook-chechnya-political-activist-page-deleted; Alexis C. Madrigal, "Hillary Clinton Was the First Casualty in the New Information Wars," *Atlantic*, May 31, 2017, https://www.theatlantic.com/technology/archive/2017/05/hillary-clinton-information-wars/528765; Ben Schreckinger, "How Russia Targets the U.S. Military," *Politico Magazine*, June 12, 2017, http://politi.co/2rhgLNx; Jill Dougherty, "How the Media Became One of Putin's Most Powerful Weapons," *Atlantic*, April 21, 2015, https://www.theatlantic.com/international/archive/2015/04/how-the-media-became-putins-most-powerful-weapon/391062; Masha Gessen, "Arguing the Truth with Trump and Putin," *New York Times*, December 17, 2016, https://www.nytimes.com/2016/12/17/opinion/sunday/arguing-the-truth-with-trump-and-putin.html; Parker, Landay, and Walcott, "Putin-Linked Think Tank Drew Up Plan to Sway 2016 US Election—Documents."

24. Chris Ogden, "A Lasting Legacy: The BJP-Led National Democratic Alliance and India's Politics," *Journal of Contemporary Asia* 42, no. 1 (February 1, 2012): 22–38, https://doi.org/10.1080/00472336.2012.634639; Tania Goklany, "#NarendraModi:

How the BJP Leader's Popularity Soars on Social Media," *Hindustan Times*, March 11, 2014, http://www.hindustantimes.com/india/narendramodi-how-the-bjp-leader-s-popularity-soars-on-social-media/story-ionRqC51BuNZ3CuyOotmTI.html; Derek Willis, "Narendra Modi, the Social Media Politician," *New York Times*, September 25, 2014, https://www.nytimes.com/2014/09/26/upshot/narendra-modi-the-social-media-politician.html; Basharat Peer, *A Question of Order: India, Turkey, and the Return of Strongmen* (New York: Westland, 2017).

25. Prabhat Patnaik, "The Fascism of Our Times," *Social Scientist* 21, nos. 3/4 (1993): 69–77, https://doi.org/10.2307/3517631; Raheel Dhattiwala and Michael Biggs, "The Political Logic of Ethnic Violence: The Anti-Muslim Pogrom in Gujarat, 2002," *Politics and Society* 40, no. 4 (December 1, 2012): 483–516, https://doi.org/10.1177/0032329212461125.

26. Swati Chaturvedi, *I Am a Troll: Inside the Secret World of the BJP's Digital Army* (New Delhi: Juggernaut, 2016), 62–65.

27. Lauren Etter, Vernon Silver, and Sarah Frier, "The Facebook Team Helping Regimes That Fight Their Opposition," Bloomberg, December 21, 2017, https://www.bloomberg.com/news/features/2017-12-21/inside-the-facebook-team-helping-regimes-that-reach-out-and-crack-down; Ankhi Das, "How 'Likes' Bring Votes—Narendra Modi's Campaign on Facebook," *Quartz*, March 21, 2018, https://qz.com/210639/how-likes-bring-votes-narendra-modis-campaign-on-facebook; Goklany, "#NarendraModi"; Derek Willis, "Narendra Modi, the Social Media Politician," *New York Times*, September 25, 2014, https://www.nytimes.com/2014/09/26/upshot/narendra-modi-the-social-media-politician.html; Sushil Aaron, "Can Narendra Modi Win Elections Using Big Data as Trump Did?," *Hindustan Times*, February 6, 2017, http://www.hindustantimes.com/analysis/can-narendra-modi-win-elections-using-big-data-as-trump-did/story-enX2d675sYlGWBEurdmBpJ.html.

28. Aaron, "Can Narendra Modi Win Elections"; India Today, "Social Media Gangsters: Trolls Who Ruin People's Reputations for a Price," July 20, 2016, https://www.youtube.com/watch?v=GUZzOxNWqes; Goklany, "#NarendraModi"; Peer, *A Question of Order*.

29. Charmie Desiderio, "Facebook Offers Free Internet Access in Phl," *Philippine Star*, March 20, 2015, http://www.philstar.com/headlines/2015/03/20/1435536/facebook-offers-free-internet-access-phl.

30. Mark Zuckerberg, "We're One Step Closer to Connecting the World as We Launched Internet.org in the Philippines Today," Facebook, March 18, 2015, https://www.facebook.com/photo.php?fbid=10101979373122191&set=a.612287952871.2204760.4&type=1&theater.

31. Sean Williams, "Rodrigo Duterte's Army of Online Trolls," *New Republic*, January 4, 2017, https://newrepublic.com/article/138952/rodrigo-dutertes-army-online-trolls; Desiderio, "Facebook Offers Free Internet Access in Phl"; Pia Ranada, "Duterte Says Online Defenders, Trolls Hired Only During Campaign," Rappler, July 25, 2017, http://www.rappler.com/nation/176615-duterte-online-defenders-trolls-hired-campaign.

32. Jodesz Gavilan, "Duterte's P10M Social Media Campaign: Organic, Volunteer-Driven," Rappler, June 1, 2016, http://www.rappler.com/newsbreak/rich-media/134979-rodrigo-duterte-social-media-campaign-nic-gabunada.

33. Lauren Etter, "Rodrigo Duterte Turned Facebook into a Weapon, with a Little Help from Facebook," Bloomberg, December 7, 2017, https://www.bloomberg.com/news/features/2017-12-07/how-rodrigo-duterte-turned-facebook-into-a-weapon-with-a-little-help-from-facebook.

34. Etter, "Rodrigo Duterte Turned Facebook into a Weapon."

35. Sheila Coronel, "New Media Played a Role in the People's Uprising," Nieman Reports, June 15, 2002, http://niemanreports.org/articles/new-media-played-a-role-in-the-peoples-uprising; Siva Vaidhyanathan, *The Anarchist in the Library: How the Clash Between Freedom and Control Is Hacking the Real World and Crashing the System* (New York: Basic Books, 2004).

36. Etter, "Rodrigo Duterte Turned Facebook into a Weapon"; Katia Moskvitch, "Asia Gets Its Fastest Data Cable," BBC News, August 20, 2012, http://www.bbc.com/news/technology-19275490.

37. Megha Rajagopalan, "This Country's Leader Shut Down Democracy—with a Little Help from Facebook," BuzzFeed, January 21, 2018, https://www.buzzfeed.com/meghara/facebook-cambodia-democracy.

38. Sheera Frenkel, Nicholas Casey, and Paul Mozur, "In Some Countries, Facebook's Fiddling Has Magnified Fake News," *New York Times*, January 14, 2018, https://www.nytimes.com/2018/01/14/technology/facebook-news-feed-changes.html; Rajagopalan, "This Country's Leader Shut Down Democracy"; Stevan Dojcinovic, "Hey, Mark Zuckerberg: My Democracy Isn't Your Laboratory," *New York Times*, November 15, 2017, https://www.nytimes.com/2017/11/15/opinion/serbia-facebook-explore-feed.html.

39. Catherine Trautwein, "Facebook Free Basics Lands in Myanmar," *Myanmar Times*, June 6, 2016, http://www.mmtimes.com/index.php/business/technology/20685-facebook-free-basics-lands-in-myanmar.html; Philip Heijmans, "The Unprecedented Explosion of Smartphones in Myanmar," Bloomberg, July 10, 2017, https://www.bloomberg.com/news/features/2017-07-10/the-unprecedented-explosion-of-smartphones-in-myanmar; Matt Schissler, "New Technologies, Established Practices: Developing Narratives of Muslim Threat in Myanmar," in *Islam and the State in Myanmar: Muslim-Buddhist Relations and the Politics of Belonging*, ed. Melissa Crouch (Oxford: Oxford University Press, 2015), https://www.academia.edu/9587031/New_Technologies_Established_Practices_Developing_Narratives_of_Muslim_Threat_in_Myanmar.

40. Schissler, "New Technologies, Established Practices"; Michael Safi, "Aung San Suu Kyi Defends Her Handling of Myanmar Violence," *Guardian*, September 7, 2017, http://www.theguardian.com/world/2017/sep/07/aung-san-suu-kyi-defends-handling-myanmar-violence-rohingya; Michael Safi, "Aung San Suu Kyi Says 'Terrorists' Are Misinforming World About Myanmar Violence," *Guardian*, September 6, 2017, http://www.theguardian.com/world/2017/sep/06/aung-san-suu-kyi-blames-terrorists-for-misinformation-about-myanmar-violence.

Conclusion: The Nonsense Machine

1. John Edwin Mason, "#Charlottesville," VQR, August 24, 2017, http://www.vqronline.org/2017/08/charlottesville.

2. Ashley Feinberg, "The Alt-Right Can't Disown Charlottesville," *Wired*, August 13, 2017, https://www.wired.com/story/alt-right-charlottesville-reddit-4chan; Taylor Hatmaker, "Tech Is Not Winning the Battle Against White Supremacy," TechCrunch, accessed September 6, 2017, http://social.techcrunch.com/2017/08/16/hatespeech-white-supremacy-nazis-social-networks; Kevin Roose, "This Was the Alt-Right's Favorite Chat App. Then Came Charlottesville," *New York Times*, August 15, 2017, https://www.nytimes.com/2017/08/15/technology/discord-chat-app-alt-right.html; George Joseph, "White Supremacists Joked About Using Cars to Run Over Opponents Before Charlottesville," ProPublica, August 28, 2017, https://www.propublica.org/article/white-supremacists-joked-about-using-cars-to-run-over-opponents-before-charlottesville.

3. Joseph, "White Supremacists Joked About Using Cars to Run Over Opponents Before Charlottesville."

4. Ryan Holiday, *Trust Me, I'm Lying: The Tactics and Confessions of a Media Manipulator* (New York: Portfolio, 2012); Whitney Phillips, *This Is Why We Can't Have Nice Things: Mapping the Relationship Between Online Trolling and Mainstream Culture* (Cambridge, MA: MIT Press, 2016); Whitney Phillips and Ryan M. Milner, *The Ambivalent Internet: Mischief, Oddity, and Antagonism Online* (Cambridge, UK: Polity, 2017).

5. Siva Vaidhyanathan, "Why the Nazis Came to Charlottesville," *New York Times*, August 14, 2017, https://www.nytimes.com/2017/08/14/opinion/why-the-nazis-came-to-charlottesville.html.

6. Tarleton Gillespie, *Custodians of the Internet: Platforms, Content Moderation, and the Hidden Decisions That Shape Social Media* (New Haven, CT: Yale University Press, 2018); Sarah T. Roberts, "Content Moderation," Department of Information Studies, University of California, Los Angeles, February 5, 2017, http://escholarship.org/uc/item/7371c1hf; Sarah Roberts, "Digital Refuse: Canadian Garbage, Commercial Content Moderation and the Global Circulation of Social Media's Waste," 2016, http://ir.lib.uwo.ca/commpub/14.

7. Jeffrey Gettleman, "More than 1,000 Died in South Asia Floods This Summer," *New York Times*, August 29, 2017, https://www.nytimes.com/2017/08/29/world/asia/floods-south-asia-india-bangladesh-nepal-houston.html; Haroon Siddique, "South Asia Floods Kill 1,200 and Shut 1.8 Million Children out of School," *Guardian*, August 31, 2017, http://www.theguardian.com/world/2017/aug/30/mumbai-paralysed-by-floods-as-india-and-region-hit-by-worst-monsoon-rains-in-years; Steve George, "A Third of Bangladesh Under Water as Flood Devastation Widens," CNN, accessed September 6, 2017, http://www.cnn.com/2017/09/01/asia/bangladesh-south-asia-floods/index.html; "Nigeria Floods Displace More than 100,000 People," accessed September 6, 2017, http://www.aljazeera.com/news/2017/08/nigeria-floods-displace-100000-people-170831221301909.html; Stephanie Busari and Osman Mohamed Osman, "Lagos Floods: Heavy Rain, Storms Cause Havoc," CNN, July 10, 2017, http://www.cnn.com/2017/07/09/africa/lagos-flood-storms/index.html.

8. Hannah Arendt and Margaret Canovan, *The Human Condition* (Chicago: University of Chicago Press, 1998); Elisabeth Young-Bruehl, *Why Arendt Matters* (New Haven,

CT: Yale University Press, 2006); Hanna Fenichel Pitkin, *The Attack of the Blob: Hannah Arendt's Concept of the Social* (Chicago: University of Chicago Press, 1998); Craig J. Calhoun and John McGowan, *Hannah Arendt and the Meaning of Politics* (Minneapolis: University of Minnesota Press, 1997); Adah Ushpiz, *Vita Activa: The Spirit of Hannah Arendt* (Zeitgeist Films, 2015).

9. Immanuel Kant and Hans Siegbert Reiss, *Kant: Political Writings* (Cambridge, UK: Cambridge University Press, 1991); Theodor W. Adorno and Max Horkheimer, *Dialectic of Enlightenment* (London: Verso, 2016); Jürgen Habermas, *The Structural Transformation of the Public Sphere: An Inquiry into a Category of Bourgeois Society* (Cambridge, MA: MIT Press, 1991).

10. Ian Bogost, "A Googler's Would-Be Manifesto Reveals Tech's Rotten Core," *Atlantic*, August 6, 2017, https://www.theatlantic.com/technology/archive/2017/08/why-is-tech-so-awful/536052; Jason Tanz, "The Curse of Cow Clicker: How a Cheeky Satire Became a Videogame Hit," *Wired*, December 20, 2011, https://www.wired.com/2011/12/ff_cowclicker.

11. Clayton M. Christensen, *The Innovator's Dilemma: When New Technologies Cause Great Firms to Fail* (Boston, MA: Harvard Business School Press, 1997); Jill Lepore, "What the Gospel of Innovation Gets Wrong," *New Yorker*, June 16, 2014, http://www.newyorker.com/magazine/2014/06/23/the-disruption-machine.

12. "Innovation," UNICEF, accessed August 10, 2017, https://www.unicef.org/innovation.

13. David Brion Davis, *Slavery and Human Progress* (New York: Oxford University Press, 1984).

14. Pierre Lévy, *Collective Intelligence: Mankind's Emerging World in Cyberspace* (Cambridge, MA: Perseus Books, 1999); John Perry Barlow, "Declaring Independence," *Wired*, June 1, 1996, https://www.wired.com/1996/06/independence; Esther Dyson, *Release 2.0: A Design for Living in the Digital Age* (New York: Broadway Books, 1997); Nicholas Negroponte, *Being Digital* (New York: Knopf, 1995).

15. Siva Vaidhyanathan, *The Anarchist in the Library: How the Clash Between Freedom and Control Is Hacking the Real World and Crashing the System* (New York: Basic Books, 2004).

16. Lévy, *Collective Intelligence*, 9–10.

17. Siva Vaidhyanathan, *The Googlization of Everything (And Why We Should Worry)* (Berkeley: University of California Press, 2011).

18. Neil Postman, *Technopoly: The Surrender of Culture to Technology* (New York: Knopf, 1992), 71.

19. Ibid., 48; Bruce Springsteen, "57 Channels (And Nothin' On)," Bruce Springsteen, *Human Touch* (New York: Columbia, 1992), https://www.youtube.com/watch?v=YAlDbP4tdqc.

20. Douglas Rushkoff, "Why I'm Quitting Facebook," CNN, accessed June 8, 2017, http://www.cnn.com/2013/02/25/opinion/rushkoff-why-im-quitting-facebook/index.html.

21. Paul De Hert et al., "The Right to Data Portability in the GDPR: Towards User-Centric Interoperability of Digital Services," *Computer Law and Security Review*, November 20, 2017, https://doi.org/10.1016/j.clsr.2017.10.003; Robert Levine, "Behind the European Privacy Ruling That's Confounding Silicon Valley," *New*

York Times, October 9, 2015, http://www.nytimes.com/2015/10/11/business/international/behind-the-european-privacy-ruling-thats-confounding-silicon-valley.html; Mark Scott, "Europe Is Expected to Approve E.U.-U.S. Data Transfer Pact," *New York Times*, June 29, 2016, http://www.nytimes.com/2016/06/30/technology/europe-is-expected-to-approve-eu-us-data-transfer-pact.html; Mark Scott, "Facebook Gets Slap on the Wrist From 2 European Privacy Regulators," *New York Times*, May 16, 2017, https://www.nytimes.com/2017/05/16/technology/facebook-privacy-france-netherlands.html.

22. Frank A. Pasquale and Siva Vaidhyanathan, "Borking Antitrust: Google Secures Its Monopoly," *Dissent*, January 4, 2013, https://www.dissentmagazine.org/blog/borking-antitrust-google-secures-its-monopoly; Aoife White and Karin Matussek, "Facebook's Small Print Might Be Next Big Antitrust Target," Bloomberg, July 3, 2017, https://www.bloomberg.com/news/articles/2017-07-03/facebook-s-small-print-might-be-antitrust-s-next-big-target; Ariel Ezrachi and Maurice E. Stucke, *Virtual Competition: The Promise and Perils of the Algorithm-Driven Economy* (Cambridge, MA: Harvard University Press, 2016); Peter Thiel, "Competition Is for Losers," *Wall Street Journal*, September 12, 2014, http://www.wsj.com/articles/peter-thiel-competition-is-for-losers-1410535536.

23. Nicholas Thompson, "Social Media Has Hijacked Our Minds. Click Here to Fight It," *Wired*, July 26, 2017, https://www.wired.com/story/our-minds-have-been-hijacked-by-our-phones-tristan-harris-wants-to-rescue-them.

24. Siva Vaidhyanathan, "The Mad Rush to Undo Online Privacy Rules," Bloomberg, March 29, 2017, https://www.bloomberg.com/view/articles/2017-03-29/the-mad-rush-to-undo-online-privacy-rules.

Acknowledgments

1. Michael Zimmer, "The Zuckerberg Files: A Digital Archive of All Public Utterances of Facebook's Founder and CEO, Mark Zuckerberg," accessed July 4, 2017, https://www.zuckerbergfiles.org.

2. Siva Vaidhyanathan, "The Rise of the Cryptopticon," *Hedgehog Review* 17, no. 1 (Spring 2015), http://www.iasc-culture.org/THR/THR_article_2015_Spring_Vaidhyanathan.php.

3. Siva Vaidhyanathan, "Has 'Innovation' Supplanted the Idea of Progress?," *Aeon*, May 13, 2015, https://aeon.co/conversations/why-has-innovation-supplanted-the-idea-of-progress.

INDEX